THE SOCIAL DIMENSIONS OF SECTARIANISM

The Social Dimensions of Sectarianism

Sects and New Religious Movements in Contemporary Society

Bryan R. Wilson

CLARENDON PRESS · OXFORD

Oxford University Press, Walton Street, Oxford OX2 6DP
Oxford New York Toronto
Delhi Bombay Calcutta Madras Karachi
Petaling Jaya Singapore Hong Kong Tokyo
Nairobi Dar es Salaam Cape Town
Melbourne Auckland
and associated companies in
Berlin Ibadan

Published in the United States
by Oxford University Press, New York

Oxford is a trade mark of Oxford University Press

First published 1990
First issued in Clarendon Paperbacks 1992

British Library Cataloguing in Publication Data
Wilson, Bryan R., 1926–
The social dimensions of sectarianism: sects and new
religious movements in contemporary society.
1. Sects – Sociological perspectives
I. Title
306'.6
ISBN 0–19–827883–7

Library of Congress Cataloging in Publication Data
Wilson, Bryan R.
The social dimensions of sectarianism: sects and new religious
movements in contemporary society / Bryan R. Wilson.
p. cm.
Includes bibliographical references.
1. Sects—History—20th century. 2. Cults—History—20th century.
3. Religion and sociological. I. Title.
BP603.W55 1990 89–48343 306'.6919—dc20
ISBN 0–19–827883–7

Printed and bound in
Great Britain by Bookcraft (Bath) Ltd,
Midsomer Norton, Avon

Preface

THE sectarian studies drawn together in these pages were written at various times over the last decade and a half. They constitute research and analysis into various facets of the sectarian phenomenon —a phenomenon growing in importance in contemporary society. The search for meaning, for fulfilling relationships, and for a distinctive mode of living which confers a sense both of belonging and of identity, has become a significant reaction to the encompassing impersonality of the often abrasive rationalization of modern life. The quest for community finds its most vibrant and enduring expression among sects, but even sects that offer little by way of community experience often attract a following among those who seek an alternative value system or new methods by means of which they hope to enhance their life experience.

Sects provide existential and intellectual alternatives to normal social facilities. They present a challenge to quotidian assumptions and values, and this they do despite the diversity of the prospectuses which they canvass—world overturn, communitarian withdrawal, born-again conversion, the enhancement of human potential, or the reform or reconstruction of social institutions. Whatever their programme, they are likely to find themselves at odds with the society in which they arise or spread, and with at least some if not all aspects of its secular (or religious) culture. In these pages, the obvious point of enquiry—why sects appeal to their adherents (examined in Chapters 8 and 9—is augmented by discussion of the nature of the tension that inevitably occurs between the sect and the wider secular world. Conflict may occur formally with the law, but whether an open and explicit divergence of values issues in such public confrontation or not, a sect is necessarily engaged in a process of tension management with the general public in various of the activities that it commissions or the abstentions that it exhorts. This characteristic manifestation of sectarianism is the focus for Chapters 2, 3, 4, and 5, which constitute Part I of this volume.

Tension between sects and society tends to dissipate over time— either as society extends toleration to a wider range of movements, or, in some cases, as sects gradually come to find greater accommodation with the requirements of the secular world. The processes of evolution that sects experience is ultimately related to the specific source of their appeal and to the course of their diffusion. Aspects of these processes are the subject matter of Chapters 6 and 7.

The most conspicuous tensions relative to minority beliefs in recent times have occurred with the emergence of a highly diversified cluster of organizations that have come to be collectively designated as 'new religious movements'. These movements constitute no obvious category: they are lumped together essentially because of their newness rather than in respect of any inherent similarity of teachings, structure, style, or ethos. None the less, in the public mind and in the mass media, many of these movements have become identified as specimens of a single genre. New movements in themselves are not, however, a new phenomenon: old sects were once new movements, and taking this broad perspective certain general propositions can be set forth with respect to them. In Chapters 10 and 11 attention is paid specifically to the circumstances in which new religions arise and survive. Whatever may be said in general terms regarding such movements, it is essential not to disregard the wide diversity among them; Chapters 12 and 13 deal respectively with two such movements, and do so in entirely different ways. One reports on a narrowly focused empirical enquiry into the social composition and activities of the members of a Moonie centre. The other, with a more philosophically oriented perspective, explores the religious status of the teachings of Scientology. Diverse as are these concerns, they serve to exemplify the range of issues which transcend normal theological assumptions in the study of religious bodies, and illustrate the ends of the spectrum of sociological enquiry.

Two of the papers in this collection were written together with Professor K. Dobbelaere of the Katholieke Universiteit Leuven following our rewarding collaboration in research in Belgium at different periods. I am grateful to him for his ready agreement to their republication here. The paper 'Sects and Society in Tension' appears in P. Badham (ed.), *Religion, State and Society in Modern Britain* (New York and Lampeter: Edwin Mellen Press, 1990), and is reprinted here (in slightly amended form) by kind permission of Dr Badham. 'Old Laws and New Religions' was first published in German under the title 'Religious nach Englischem Recht', in J. Neumann and M. W. Fischer (eds.), *Toleranz und Repression: Zur Lage religiöser Minderheiten in modernen Gesellschaft* (Frankfurt am Main: Campus Verlag, 1987), and is reproduced here in English with the publisher's permission. An earlier version of 'A

Sect at Law' appeared in *Encounter* in January 1983, and its publication here, in amended form, is by permission of the editor.

The essay on American sects, now updated, originally appeared in C. W. E. Bigsby (ed.), *Superculture: American Popular Culture and Europe* (London: Paul Elek, 1975). 'Jehovah's Witnesses in a Roman Catholic Country' appeared in *Archives de Sciences Sociales des Religions*, 50/1 (1980), and is reprinted by permission of the editor. The present editor of the Church History series has granted approval for 'Becoming a Sectarian' to appear here: this essay first appeared in D. Baker (ed.), *Religious Motivation: Biographical and Sociological Problems for the Church Historian* (Studies in Church History xv) (Oxford: Blackwell, 1978). The editor of the *Japanese Journal of Religious Studies* has kindly consented to the republication (in amended form) of the paper which constitutes Chapter 10 in these pages, and which appeared in that journal in 1979. 'Factors in the Failure of New Religious Movements' was first published in D. G. Bromley and P. E. Hammond (eds.), *The Future of New Religious Movements* (Macon, Ga.: Mercer University Press, 1987), and is reprinted by courtesy of the publisher. The study on Unificationism, written with K. Dobbelaere, first appeared in 1987 in the *British Journal of Sociology*, the publishers of which have cordially agreed to its reprinting in this volume. The chapter which has been adapted as an introduction to these studies was commissioned in its original form by the editor of the *John Rylands Library Bulletin*, in which it appeared in 1988, and the goodwill of the editor is acknowledged for permission to use it to introduce this volume. The studies which constitute Chapters 2 and 13 are here published for the first time.

Miss Michele Jacottet undertook a considerable amount of the typing of this work, and I should like to record my gratitude to her for her invariably helpful and expeditious work.

Working with sectarians—by no means all of whom readily accept that designation, and for many of whom my detached, but I hope always sympathetic, interest was often something of a puzzle—is not always easy. I should like to put on record my sincere appreciation of the time, assistance, and tolerance of an alien outsider which so many sincere and deeply religious individuals have almost always displayed.

B. R. W.

All Souls College,
Oxford

Note on Copyright

The copyright in the essays in this volume is owned by the author, except as follows:

Contents

List of Tables

1

Sectarian Studies:
Assumptions, Sources,
Scope, and Methods

EVEN though, in many particulars, they differ from one another, the separate and distinctive groups of religious believers that are generally designated as sects or as new religious movements may be said to constitute a field of readily recognizable social phenomena. Initially, they were distinguished from the dominant prevailing form(s) of religion within a society, and this not merely nor even primarily by virtue of their relative minority status (since the dominant denomination in one society may be a minority in another, as are Catholics in England or Episcopalians in Scotland, without thereby being considered as sects) but by their evident divergence in doctrine, practice, social ethos, and form of sociation. Today, they are, by these same criteria and most specifically by their social ethos and the conduct that exemplifies it, also readily distinguished from the generality of the secular society. Almost by definition as a 'deviant' group, a sect is likely to comprise only a very small proportion of a society's total population (always allowing for occasional concentrations such as that of the Mormons in Utah or the Seventh-day Adventists in parts of western Kenya). It is divergence and intensity of commitment, with their implications for relative size, rather than size *per se*, which serve as the indicators of sectarianism.

Religious minorities, particularly among the recently emerged new movements, do not conform to one clearly articulated type, either ideologically or organizationally, but generally it may be said that such a movement is exclusivistic, standing in some degree of protest against the dominant traditions of society and rejecting prevailing patterns of belief and conduct. The sect maintains a degree of tension with the world which is at least an expression of indifference to it, if not of hostility towards it. It is a voluntary organization in the sense that individuals must make an explicit commitment to group standards of conduct and professions of belief. They must, both to be admitted to the group and for the maintenance of their affiliation, satisfy some test of merit, and they must expect discipline and even expulsion if they depart from the movement's norms. For the individual, membership in such a group is his primary source of social identity: the member is a sectarian (of whatever particular persuasion) before he is anything else, and although, in practice, the degree of intensity of commitment inevitably varies from one individual (and sometimes from one generation) to another, the ideal of total allegiance is far more strongly presupposed than is the case with so-called 'main-line' religious bodies.

The term 'sect' is not one that religious groups (at least in Christendom) normally appropriate for themselves: few movements regarded as sects by outsiders see themselves as such, and this because the word was a term of *odium theologicum*, and is one which, in popular usage and that of the mass media, still carries strong pejorative connotations. Most of the theological writing on sects, with rare exceptions, has proceeded from the normative assumptions of that discipline, and has not only tended, but has been explicitly intended, to condemn sectarianism as well as to prove that sects distorted 'true religion'.[1] Nor have historians whose work has involved discussion of sectarianism always demonstrated the objectivity which, with the diffusion of the principles of social science, has been increasingly demanded in studies of social phenomena. As used by sociologists, who have now virtually claimed sectarianism as a field within their discipline, the term 'sect' has become a neutral concept, without evaluative or emotional connotations. Sects are seen as social phenomena, as appropriately the field of sociological study as are other voluntary organizations, social classes, bureaucracy, or the family.

In translation, the concept of the sect has been applied to religious minorities and divisions in diverse cultures and within most, if not all, religious traditions. But the characteristics outlined above, which constitute the specific sociological indicia of the sect, are relevant specifically to movements within Christianity or which

---

[1] The pioneer study of J. H. Blunt, *Dictionary of Sects, Heresies, and Schools of Thought* (London, 1886) exemplifies the point, and even the suave commentary of Mgr. Ronald Knox, *Enthusiasm* (Oxford: Oxford University Press, 1951) oscillates between outright antipathy and alloyed sympathy.

operate in Christian (or post-Christian) social milieux. Exclusivity, voluntarism, tests of merit, expulsion, and protest against dominant cultural traditions are not always, and perhaps not usually, the attributes of the various divisions and schools that are loosely called sects in other religious traditions—for example, in Hinduism, Judaism, or Islam. For a variety of reasons from a variety of sources—having to do with the character of monotheism; the relations of church and temporal power; and the distinctive sacerdotal claims of a non-hereditary class of religious professionals —deviant and separate religiosity has been a particular issue of condemnation within orthodox Christianity. The powerful negative connotations of the word 'sect' are by no means either implicit or intended when, in other countries (for example, Japan), religious groups readily designate each other as sects, or acknowledge their own status by the use of a term which is so translated. Equally, the concept as strictly understood is inappropriately applied outside the context of Christianity, quite apart from its lingering pejorative connotations. It is culturally specific, and it is important not to project on to bodies outside the Christian ambit characteristics that are part of the cultural baggage of Christian religiosity, and that derive from its distinctive organizational character and the competitive claims to a monopoly of truth within an exclusivistic system. There may be possibilities of utilizing some concepts developed in the analysis of Western religious bodies in other cultures and different religious traditions, but discussion here is confined to the Christian and Western context.[2]

Even when the field has been delimited in this way, it remains a large one. In something like their modern form, sects have been a commonplace of Christian history since the Reformation. A wide variety of dissentient movements existed earlier, of course, from the first centuries of the Christian era, but we must suppose that typically they lacked both a fully articulated organizational form and complete doctrinal consistency and rigour. Many of these movements were small and confined to particular localities. The traditional stereotype of the sect as it came to be formulated by early socio-theological studies, drew on just such characteristics.[3]

[2] For some discussion of these issues, see B. R. Wilson, *Magic and the Millennium* (London: Heinemann, 1973) 31–4.
[3] The work of E. Troeltsch, *The Social Teaching of the Christian Churches*, trans. O. Wyon (New York: Macmillan, 1931), although he still laboured under

Those sects were usually also of relatively brief endurance (with very few exceptions) and only one or two of them survived into post-Reformation times. The sects that have emerged since the Reformation display different characteristics. Together these movements have embraced, and still embrace, many millions of people, and some of them have themselves each several million adherents— among them the Mormons, the Seventh-day Adventists, and the congeries of movements generically designated as Pentecostalists.

Such, indeed, is the profusion of sects, and so many are those who are committed to one or another of them, that it may confidently be said that today sects constitute a field of greater significance than that traditionally explored by the discipline of anthropology. There are probably more people leading lives as self-conscious and active sectarians than there are people now living as active tribesmen for whom the tribe is a primary focus of allegiance: and the number of actual operative sects may, indeed, be greater than the number of extant and functioning tribes. These circumstances notwithstanding, the study of tribes is well institutionalized in university departments of anthropology, while sectarian studies have no such institutional presence, nor have those who study sects any distinctive disciplinary designation. Studies of sects have been pursued randomly by sociologists, historians, and, as their own traditional field has dried up, even by some anthropologists who recognize in these relatively well-bounded groups entities in some ways analogous to tribes.[4]

Despite the obvious social importance of movements that not only affect but actually encompass the lives of so many people throughout the world (for today perhaps no societies are sect-less) sectarian studies remain at the fringe of academic disciplines. The study of sects had, of course, no real place in its own right within the (once dominant) schools of theology, except as object-lessons for the faithful, and as objects attracting only anathema and

theological influence, provides the departure point for a more sociological understanding of sects. In contrast to his friend Max Weber, Troeltsch drew on medieval rather than recent or contemporary sectarianism in the construction of the sect as an 'ideal type'.

   [4] For example, M. J. C. Calley, *God's People: West Indian Pentecostal Sects in England* (London: Oxford University Press, 1965); W. La Barre, *They Shall Take Up Serpents: Psychology of the Southern Snake-Handling Cult* (Minneapolis: University of Minnesota Press, 1962); D. J. Davies, *Mormon Spirituality: Latter Day Saints in Wales and Zion* (Nottingham: University of Nottingham, 1987).

derision: there was little attempt to treat them as phenomena worthy of serious, sustained, objective, and disinterested enquiry. The reasons why that was so are obvious. Yet, paradoxically, despised as were sects by the theologians, the marginalization within academic institutions of that discipline, as secularizing societies divested themselves of theological concerns, made religious minorities appear even more inconsequential. If religion was perceived as less relevant to social reality, then sectarian religion was clearly a trivial and perhaps bizarre subject of study. Only the shift from theology to 'religious studies', from normative and confessional approaches to the positivist and *verstehende* perspectives of sociology, offered prospect for the emergence of unprejudiced understanding of sects.

Modern studies of sectarianism stand predominantly in this tradition. Sects are seen as phenomena which, in the best scientific approach, call forth no explicit value-judgements about what they regard to be the truth or what they take as warranty for their practices. Despite this measure of objectivity, sectarian studies— compared, say, to anthropology—have received neither encourage- ment nor endorsement: the subject matter is regarded as academically inconsequential, and the subject area is, within the sociology of religion, something of a pariah, whilst the sociology of religion itself has been called a Cinderella within sociology.

The reputation of the sociology of sects stands in sharp contrast to the esteem in which historical studies of sects are held. For historians, sects have exercised a persistent fascination, from the writings of Josephus and Eusebius to the numerous accounts of Donatists and Bogomils, Cathars and Lollards, Hussites and Fifth Monarchy Men. Such studies have acquired respectability perhaps because the influence of religion, and even of religious dissent, is readily—and perhaps rightly—assumed to have been so much greater in past times. The closer one approaches modern times, however, to the period influenced by the Enlightenment and the gradual diffusion to all disciplines of the methodological principles of rational empirical enquiry, so the less reputable sectarianism appears to be as an object of academic research. An irony lies in the contrast which might be made between historical scholarship and sociological research, and one of its sources is in the gross disparity in the amount of material and the quality of material available for the study of contemporary sects compared to those of more distant

historical times. The sources for the sects studied by the historian
are often both fragmentary and, in large part, derived from the
sect's opponents or persecutors. Augustine, as a source on the
Donatists, was scarcely concerned to present a full, objective, and
detached view of that sect, any more than was Irenaeus of the
Gnostics, or the inquisitors of Montaillou of the local Albigensians.
The sociologist of contemporary sectarianism needs rely neither on
fragments nor on biased witnesses. Indeed, with good reason,
sociologists generally treat the evidence of a sect's theological
opponents, of the aggrieved relatives of sectarians, and of the
disaffected and apostate with some circumspection. The same
principle should, were there any choice in the matter, apply to
evidence about historical sects, but the historian's dilemma, at least
in the case of pre-Reformation sects, is that he often has no choice,
and even for sects in later periods he may face the same problem.
Such is the paucity of material in some cases, that distinguished
scholars have even disagreed about whether a particular sect really
existed or whether, for their own purposes, some commentators did
not 'create' a fact out of what was purely fictional.[5]

While doubts and disagreements exist about some aspects of
contemporary sectarianism in sociological studies, they do not
attain the magnitude of the controversy about the Ranters. Yet,
better sources, more abundant and more reliable evidences do not
appear to reduce, much less reverse, the disparity of esteem
accorded to historical and sociological studies. In part, this
anomaly may be attributable to the fact that the historian's sources
are often not only ancient but may also be intrinsically precious,
manuscripts, old books, scarce tracts—rare items all. In contrast,
the materials available to the sociologist, partly because so
abundant, are often also seen as intrinsically worthless, the bulk-
published ephemera which, in some cases, university libraries
disdain to house. But even this does not wholly explain the
disparity. It has to do also with the fact that it is easier to adopt a
detached attitude to material which is 'dead', which deals with
controversies and disputes long since stilled. It is more difficult to

[5] Thus the case of the Ranters, whose purported history is documented by A. L.
Morton, *The World of the Ranters: Religious Radicalism in the English Revolution*
(London: Lawrence and Wishart, 1970), but whose existence is vigorously
challenged by J. C. Davies, *Fear, Myth and History: The Ranters and the Historians*
(Cambridge: Cambridge University Press, 1987).

appreciate the contemporary expression of opinions that seem incongruous in a secular world, and which are easily branded as outlandish, outmoded, or simply absurd. It is the very fact that, with living material, with material that resonates still in the arena of public life, detachment is so very much more difficult to achieve and maintain, and the fact that every second man (by virtue of the mass media) 'knows about' modern sects and movements, which make sociological studies of sectarianism appear tangential to serious academic enterprise.

The sociologist is not, of course, solely, and perhaps not even mainly dependent on published or written sources, but since modern sects and movements usually (but not invariably) produce a considerable literature, and since some of them make its production a central concern, even taking into account published material alone, the sociologist has copious sources. The value of that literature is highly variable and dependent on the more specific purposes of the research. Much sect literature is directed at outsiders, at potential recruits: if the research is concerned with recruitment, with a movement's appeal, and its projected self-image, this type of literature, even if it is mass-produced, and little as it may tell of the dynamics of sect organization, strategies for coping with change, or financial structure, will be an indispensable resource. If these other issues are the focus of the investigator's interest, then he will need access to other sources and, if access can be obtained, to written material intended for purely internal consumption.

It will be apparent that various aspects of sectarian studies are strongly affected by the methodologies—that is, the techniques and perspectives of enquiry—that the social sciences have made available. The field of investigation is wider, and sociological research into sects and new movements is not devoted, as historical studies often were, merely to the presentation of descriptive accounts. They may take up one specific facet of a sect's operation;[6] they may exploit the advantages of comparative analysis;[7] or they

---

[6] For instance, see the study of the relationship of therapy to conversion in Scientology, H. Whitehead, *Renunciation and Reformulation: A Study of Conversion in an American Sect* (Ithaca: Cornell University Press, 1987).

[7] Comparative studies are not yet so common: see e.g. B. R. Wilson, *Sects and Society: The Sociology of Three Religious Groups in Britain* (London: Heinemann, 1961); and G. Schwartz, *Sect Ideologies and Social Status* (Chicago: University of Chicago Press, 1970).

may utilize general sociological theories (on such matters as sociation, socialization, goal displacement, structures of authority, to name a few). Just how wide the field of enquiry will be will depend, in large measure, on the extent to which leader and/or members of a movement are willing to facilitate research and to co-operate with the researcher. The lack or limitation of co-operation does not entirely prevent research, but it influences what can be discovered, and how what is discovered is understood. None the less, important work has been produced without, or with only very limited, co-operation from the sectarians themselves.[8] When a movement accords co-operation, the armoury of enquiry may extend to perhaps the full range of sociological techniques. Recorded life-histories; specifically focused interviews with leaders or officials; the administration of questionnaires; the use of informants, all become possibilities.[9] A sect may even open up its own records.[10] A standard technique is participant observation: the sociologist participates in the activities of the sect as a revealed outsider, seeking by observation and association to understand its members, who accept him in their midst and submit to being observed. Perhaps the furthest reach of co-operation is when sectarians agree to log their activities over a limited period, revealing exactly how they distribute their time among such activities as prayer, collective worship, study, witnessing, work,

---

[8] An outstanding instance of a study completed without the co-operation of a movement's authorities and, indeed, despite some attempts at hindrance, is R. Wallis, *The Road to Total Freedom: A Sociological Analysis of Scientology* (London: Heinemann, 1976). A similar, but unsociological instance is provided by D. and H. Parker, *The Secret Sect* (Pendle Hill, NSW: D. and H. Parker, 1982) (a study of the Cooneyites). In an early phase of my own work, I was privileged to have the vigorous co-operation of local congregations of the Elim Church, but I was refused access to archival material at Elim Headquarters: not surprisingly, the Church did not like what it subsequently saw as a one-sided account of its protracted and embittered process of schism: see Wilson, *Sects and Society*, pp. 39–56. The subject still rankles with Elim officials: see D. Cartwright, *The Great Evangelists* (Basingstoke, Marshall Pickering, 1986), 138. For the reaction of the other party in The Schism, see A.W. Edsor, *George Jeffreys: Man of God* (London: Ludgate Press, 1964), 90–114; and id., *Set Your House in Order* (Chichester, New Wine Press, 1989), 77 ff.

[9] For an example of the result of such co-operation by sectarians, see various studies of Jehovah's Witnesses, particularly J. A. Beckford, *The Trumpet of Prophecy* (Oxford: Blackwell, 1975), and the entire issue of *Social Compass*, 24/1 (1977).

[10] The Unification Church made some such materials available for the excellent study by E. Barker, *The Making of a Moonie: Choice or Brainwashing?* (Oxford, Blackwell, 1984).

personal maintenance, and so on. This technique, sometimes known as a 'time-budget', is of most value in the study of communitarian sects, in which members are virtually full-time religious.[11]

Sociological studies of sectarianism have been as many-sided as the foregoing indication of the abundance of sources and methods suggests. They have varied between attempts to provide a total documentation, analysis, and interpretation of a movement in all its social dimensions, to more narrowly focused studies in which one specific facet of sectarian life has been the primary concern. To study the sect as a total social entity involves providing an account of its teachings and their provenance; of the movement's origins as a separated body; of the course of its development; of the character and transmission of leadership; of the source of its appeal; of its methods of recruitment; of the nature of 'conversion'; of the social composition of its constituency; of the maintenance of social control; of its economic structure; of the extent to which children are retained in the movement; of its capacity to motivate and mobilize its members; of the relationship of ideology to organization; of the movement's social ethos; and of its relation to the wider society and to other movements, among perhaps other items.[12]

The attempt to depict the sect as a total community has attracted sociologists particularly in the case of communitarian sects, in which members create a real living community, often on the principle of holding all things in common. Such a sect offers itself virtually as an alternative pattern of social organization to that of the wider society. Such sects constitute a society in microcosm, and they have attracted not only social theorists but also social reformers who have looked at such movements as Utopian experiments. Essentially, sects of this kind have sought to replace the major differentiated institutional framework of the complex social system with what might be called the communal alternative,

---

[11] This measure of co-operation was accorded by Belgian Moonies: see K. Dobbelaere and B. Wilson, 'Het sektarisch antwoord op het begrip vrije tijd: het tijdsbudget van Belgische Moonies: een Gevallen Studie', *Vrijetijd en Samenleving*, 4/2 (Aug. 1986), 133–65.

[12] For examples of sociological work dealing with many, but perhaps rarely with all of these issues, see, *inter alia*, Wilson, *Sects and Society*; Beckford, *The Trumpet of Prophecy*; O'Dea, *The Mormons* (Chicago: University of Chicago Press, 1957); and on Seventh-day Adventists, M. Bull and K. Lockhart, *Seeking a Sanctuary: Seventh-day Adventism and the American Dream* (San Francisco: Harper and Row, 1989).

a (usually quite small) persisting social group in which the dominant divisions of the economy, the polity, conflict resolution, custom, education, and socialization are dissolved and relocated in a primal network of relationships. The sect, in this instance, becomes virtually a reconstituted and ethicized tribe. The Reformation sects of the Hutterian Brethren and some Mennonite communities represent relatively unselfconscious examples of experimentation with this type of solution.[13] Among many eighteenth- and nineteenth-century experiments, mainly in America, the Rappite community (at its different locations) was a much more self-conscious endeavour in an otherwise not dissimilar genre, and one which inspired Robert Owen and other would-be reformers of the social system.[14] The twentieth-century Bruderhof of Eberhard Arnold (which eventually sought affiliation with the Hutterites) was a totally self-aware movement largely of middle-class intellectuals in search of the honesty and immediacy of a peasant and artisan lifestyle away from the iniquity of the wider social system.[15]

As might be expected, examples such as these are extreme cases: whilst all sects maintain a level of tension with the world, few can completely adopt the techniques of insulation and isolation that were available in the unsettled areas of the eighteenth- and nineteenth-century United States, and few seek so directly to organize a way of life which so completely rejects the institutional framework of the wider society. The communal alternative is radical, but many sects that do not espouse communitarianism, and which see it as neither ideologically mandatory nor socially expedient, none the less tend to evolve alternative systems, often

[13] On Hutteries and Mennonites there is now a considerable literature, but see especially J. W. Bennett, *Hutterian Brethren: The Agricultural Economy and Social Organization of a Communal People* (Stanford: Stanford University Press, 1967); J. A. Hostetler, *Hutterite Society* (Baltimore: Johns Hopkins University Press, 1974); and his *Amish Society* (Baltimore: Johns Hopkins University Press, 1963); H. L. Sawatsky, *They Sought A Country: Mennonite Colonization in Mexico* (Berkeley and Los Angeles: University of California Press, 1971); and J. Séguy, *Les Assemblées Anabaptistes-Mennonites de France* (Paris: Mouton, 1970).

[14] On the Rappites, see K. J. R. Arndt, *Georg Rapp's Harmony Society 1785–1847* (Philadelphia: University of Pennsylvania Press, 1965); and on Robert Owen's connections with Rapp, see J. F. C. Harrison, *Quest for the New Moral World: Robert Owen and the Owenites in Britain and America* (New York: Scribner's, 1969); and A. Taylor, *Visions of Harmony: A Study in Nineteenth-Century Millenarianism* (Oxford: Clarendon Press, 1987).

[15] For an account, see B. Zablocki, *The Joyful Community: An Account of the Bruderhof* (Chicago: Chicago University Press, 1971).

eschewing the facilities of the wider society. They dissociate themselves entirely from the political system, neither standing for office nor voting. They seek to settle their own disputes (and resort to law often only to protect their right to a separate way of life). They keep their children out of state education as much as they can, either because they reject intellectual values, which is commonly the case, or because they have evolved a system of their own which they regard as uncorrupted. And some sects even seek to sustain alternative therapeutic facilities, which may engage in conventional medical practice, or, more commonly, may challenge medical science by offering spiritual, mental, or faith-healing. Practically all sects reject secular recreation and entertainment, organizing the leisure time of their own members, often in the pursuit of specifically religious concerns. All of these issues are taken up from two different perspectives in Chapters 2 and 3—the one specifically concerned with the relation of sects to the state, and the other discussing more explicitly the sources of tension generated by the sect's rejection of the institutional provisions of the wider society.

The characteristic sectarian tendencies towards the creation of an alternative society have been a major source of hostility toward sects in the general population. Whilst reformers have sometimes extolled and even imitated the patterns of living evolved by sects, in general, separatist organization has been regarded as parasitic rather than as experimentally instructive, the very differences instituted by sects being seen as an affront to normal assumptions and arrangements. Yet such sects have sometimes served as virtual if unintentional social laboratories in which certain rudimentary aspects of social organization can be more readily observed than in the general population. Communitarian groups of long persistence display distinctive patterns of fertility; they have been observed to perpetuate certain genetic traits; and in matters of speech-patterns, customs, and even in their musical styles, they have unwittingly preserved from the process of change their own distinctive forms of congregational activity.[16] Paradoxically, such

[16] An early study of fertility among the Hutterites was J. Eaton and A. Mayer, *Man's Capacity to Reproduce: The Demography of a Unique Population* (Glencoe, Ill.: Free Press, 1954), and of the incidence of genetically inherited mental disorders, J. Eaton and R. J. Weil, *Culture and Mental Disorders* (Glencoe, Ill.: Free Press, 1955). A recent study relating to manic depressive disorders is by J. A. Egeland *et al.*, 'Bipolar Affective Disorders linked to DNA Markers on Chromosome 11' *Nature*, 325 (26 Feb. 1987). Researchers into Tourette's syndrome, an inherited condition

segregated communities have not only been unconscious conservators but they have also at times shown a remarkable capacity for innovation and a practical ingenuity stimulated by the isolation that they have imposed upon themselves and the need to work out their own techniques for economic organization and social management.[17]

The last-mentioned phenomena have, of course, drawn the attention of various social scientists in addition to sociologists— demographers, psychiatrists, and musicologists among them. There are other specific issues that have brought sects to the attention of the public and of students of sectarianism. The economics of sect organization, like the economics of religion generally, has yet to be developed, but where unique patterns have been perceived, sectarian financial management has received some attention. Among the cases that have been examined have been the extraordinary cycle of capital accumulation, land-purchase, and the subdivision of communitarian settlements among the Hutterians;[18] the attempts, first at communitarianism and later at the development of sophisticated corporate financial control among the Mormons;[19] and the mobilization of resources, and the techniques of both street fund-raising and business enterprise in the Unification Church.[20]

When, exceptionally, sects have engaged in political activities, or have sought to attain sectarian goals by political means, they have attracted both public and academic attention, and most conspicuously in recent times in Northern Ireland, although older and more militant examples are of course to be found in the general history of

causing a nervous tic, common among the Amish, have used the community as a research laboratory: *Economist* (25 July 1987). On music, see for the two communities, Hostetler, *Amish Society*, pp. 123–9, and his *Hutterite Society*, pp. 169–72.

[17] The Shakers exemplify this capacity, see E. D. Andrews, *The People Called Shakers* (New York: Dover, 1963), 113–29.

[18] See Bennett, *Hutterian Brethren*.

[19] On early communitarianism among Mormons, see the brief account in F. M. Brodie, *No Man Knows My History* (London: Eyre and Spottiswoode, 1963), 105–9: see also, L. J. Arrington, *Great Basin Kingdom* (Cambridge, Mass.: Harvard University Press, 1958); and for the corporate activities of modern Mormonism, J. Heinerman and A. Shupe, *The Mormon Corporate Empire* (Boston: Beacon Press, 1985).

[20] For a short account of the financial affairs of the Unification Church, see D. G. Bromley, 'Financing the Millennium: The Economic structure of the Unificationist Movement', *Journal for the Scientific Study of Religion*, 24/3 (Sept. 1985), 253–74.

millenarian movements.[21] Without actual political action, sects have, however, more commonly sought redress less by legislation than by litigation, taking their concerns to law. They have sought to get protection for the right to lead a different way of life from the majority and to be exempted from normal social and civic obligations, most notably in such matters as compulsory military service; obligatory membership of trades unions; and the obligation to salute national flags or to sing national anthems on public occasions.[22] On the affirmative side, they have fought for their right to be recognized as charities and to benefit from the fiscal provisions which, in many countries, are associated with being recognized as religious and thus as bona fide charitable concerns.[23] Chapter 4 examines the difficulty which the courts have experienced in applying the abstract principles of religious non-discrimination, specifically in the matter of charitable status and the rights and concessions normally available to those who seek to undertake public worship, within a framework of law that has admitted in only a limited measure the application of those principles. Chapter 5 takes this issue further by exploring in more detail the circumstances of one particular sect in its attempt to regain from the authorities its status as an organization capable of operating as a religious body trusts that must be deemed charitable.

This brief review of the range of controversial issues (some of them very general, others highly specific) that sects present for investigation in itself indicates the appropriateness of different research strategies to open up different problems. The more narrowly focused concerns may not appear to demand the same intimate acquaintance with sect life that general studies certainly require, and yet even for the former a measure of empathic

[21] A recent conspicuous example is the Free Presbyterian Church of Ulster, and more particularly its leader, the Revd Mr Ian Paisley. See S. Bruce, *God Save Ulster: The Religion and Politics of Paisleyism* (Oxford: Clarendon Press, 1986).

[22] The struggle of Jehovah's Witnesses to establish, *inter alia*, their rights not to salute national flags, is documented in D. R. Manwaring, *Render unto Caesar: The Flag-Salute Controversy* (Chicago: University of Chicago Press, 1962); see also, J. Penton, *Jehovah's Witnesses in Canada: Champions of Freedom of Speech and Worship* (Toronto: Macmillan, 1976). On various other legal issues relating to religious minorities as these have developed in various countries, see J. A. Beckford, *Cult Controversies* (London: Tavistock, 1985).

[23] See, for various related issues, J. Neumann and M. W. Fischer (eds.), *Toleranz und Repression: Zur Lage religiöser Minderheiten in modernen Gesellschaft* (Frankfurt-on-Main: Campus Verlag, 1987).

understanding is important, perhaps no less than a commanding knowledge of factual events or of the authority relations that prevail. That empathy is acquired only by participant observation, which is perhaps the core method of enquiry into sects and the key to understanding them. Whilst a great deal can be learned by the use of questionnaires, and even more by interviews, shared participation provides the emotional context without which sectarian values and attitudes cannot be adequately plumbed and appraised. Whilst in other areas of social life, a questionnaire may suffice to yield all that is needed by way of factual information (and provide some, albeit much less reliable, indication of opinions and values), religion, in its emotional, evaluative, and cognitive dimensions, is a more profoundly serious concern than any other, and sectarian religion represents an intensification of this characteristic. The bald questionnaire, without a previous apprehension of the emotional tone, the implicit values, and the assumed facticities of life for sectarians, would produce only a travesty of reality if, indeed, it met with any sort of response at all. To understand in more than a formal and notional way why—to take specific examples from two different sects—Jehovah's Witnesses object to the demand that they should salute a national flag, or should accept a blood transfusion; or why Exclusive Brethren do not eat at the same table with non-Brethren, and object to the registration of their names in association with those of outsiders, would be impossible without participation in these movements. A simple questionnaire enquiry without preparatory participation would fail to discover, and so would distort, the nature of these sectarian dispositions, and thus be worse than useless. If this is the case for the understanding of such specific issues, it is clearly much more so when the general ethos and life activities are the focus of enquiry.

As a research technique, participant observation is not unproblematic. It is more of an intuitive art than a learned skill, and not everyone can readily adopt the role of observer, which requires a capacity to develop a measure of sympathy with sectarians whilst retaining a certain detachment. What is learned by this technique may not be wholly replicable in the way that is expected of scientific method: results are in some degree dependent on the personal capacities of the researcher, and on the balance that he can strike between simultaneous identification with his subjects and distantiation from them. At its best the technique yields more than is forthcoming from informants, since the participant observer has an implicit comparative perspective and engages in interpretative but self-conscious reconstruction of what he learns from the vantage point of a being with a foot in two worlds. He must be patient, sensitive, alert, and responsive to the situation, but his responsiveness must be subject to certain self-imposed constraints.

The role makes considerable demands on emotional and social stamina, which can induce a real strain. This is most acute when the researcher has concealed his identity and purpose from his subjects by pretending to be a prospective convert or a neophyte. The dual role is likely, in such circumstances, to become almost unsustainable. The investigator is pretending to espouse values that are radically different from those which his scholarly purpose prescribes for him. He is likely to have difficulty in maintaining the deceit, and he may—in my view, should—experience anxiety about the dubious ethical implications of the strategy that he has adopted.[24] One might, indeed, suppose that the successful, assured, and untroubled concealed participant observer would produce results the integrity and sensitivity of which would be open to doubt.

Normally, participant observers reveal their purposes to the sects with which they seek to work, and indeed certain areas of enquiry would be closed off were they not to do so. The 'revealed' participant observer has less difficulty in retaining his primary commitment to the values of his discipline: he is less likely to 'go native', to adopt the world-view and the values of his subjects. The middle point between sympathy and detachment is not, even so, easily struck: excessive sympathy, whilst it may not lead to conversion, might result in a work unduly sentimental; too much detachment will yield only a distorted caricature of the subjects.

Participant observation is a time-consuming procedure. It cannot in itself be precisely 'programmed', and it cannot be accelerated. The investigator has to find his group, gain admission, become accepted at meetings, learn to mix easily, devote himself to learning the argot and apprehending the emotional range of his subjects, and he must learn in matters of dress and comportment how to 'fit in' to

---

[24] For an account of role strain whilst a concealed participant observer, see D. E. van Zandt, 'Ideology and Structure in the Children of God: A Study of a New Sect' (University of London Ph.D. thesis, 1985). See also the perceptive and informative discussion of 'the moral career of a research project' by R. Wallis, *Salvation and Protest: Studies in Social and Religious Movements* (London: Frances Pinter, 1979), 193–216.

group expectations. He has to learn a repertoire of sensitivities which may be far from being native to him; he must know what subjects to avoid, and the terms in which other matters can be taken up. Ideally, he will achieve near total immersion, but this can occur only slowly, and there is no easy point at which he can safely decide that he has learned all he can. Even determining whether what he has observed is normal or incidental takes some time. And then, diminishing marginal returns set in sooner or later: and yet, sometimes, what can be learned at the margin may turn out to be of great importance. Sociology, however, is a distilling discipline, tending to reduce the mass of observations into analytical propositions that can be summarily stated (in this differing from the phenomenological approach): extensive participant observation may be apparent in the final product only in the sense of authenticity that comes through the published accounts of the work that has been undertaken.

The research sociologist cannot become and does not seek to become a sectarian, but he can get closer by participant observation than has ever been possible for historians. Although sect members will—at one level—always know more about sectarian life than will the investigator, participant observation opens the way for empathic understanding, for acting with, worshipping with, feeling with, and perhaps even living within a sect, and this adds a dimension of social knowledge from which the historian is precluded. Conversely, just as it would be a betrayal of academic commitment to become a sectarian, in certain respects the sociologist can—at a different level—know much more about a sect than its members are ever likely to know. He has the advantage of comparative analysis, by which he might interpret the various aspects of sect life in the light of what he knows of other sects and the general probabilities of sect dynamics.

The more usual methods of social enquiry—interviewing, the use of questionnaires, and of informants (as well, of course, as recourse to written records and published materials)—needs little specifically to be said about them. In all these procedures, the researcher does not merely collect what happens to have been preserved, rather he actively stimulates data.[25] What he obtains is not

---

[25] Curiously, at least one historian has objected to this aspect of sociological research: see G. R. Elton, *The Practice of History* (Sydney: Sydney University Press, 1967), pp. 72–3.

unsolicited and random, but the result of systematic, indeed strategic probing. He needs not to speculate, as a historian often must, about possible motivations and intentions: he can enquire directly about them, and he can cross-check the responses to his questions. There are hazards in the use of questionnaires, and the total reliability of respondents can never be assumed or ensured, but, by and large, sectarians constitute a public that is almost certainly more honest and more conscientious than the general population. Indeed, the participant observer who undertakes interviews may often find himself overwhelmed with information as he is pushed into the role of acting almost as a cathartic agent. Sectarians are necessarily deeply preoccupied with their distinctive way of life, and they may find it a relief to talk to the outsider about things that deeply interest them both (even if from quite different perspectives) without the constraints and conventions that obtain in the group life of the sect itself. The sympathetic stranger who 'knows about us' may have disclosed to him much more than a social investigator can reasonably expect or deliberately elicit.

Chapter 9 discusses the question of motivation, and exemplifies what can be learned by interviewing members of a sect about their own appraisal of how they acquired their current commitment and just what it means to them. The procedures of enquiry in that chapter and also in Chapter 12 are appropriate in acquiring an understanding of minority religious commitment at the most fundamental level, at the grass roots. (It may be noted *en passant* how rarely those who readily condemn sects and sectarians have ever engaged in first-hand enquiry of the kind on which these two chapters are based.) Several of the papers in this volume, however, afford a different view which might, not unparadoxically, be called a macrocosmic view of sectarianism, by providing a broad, comparative delineation of certain general sociological patterns and processes. The course of evolution of sectarian movements, dealt with in Chapter 6, perhaps best illustrates this genre. The topic is one that has attracted recurrent attention and has been the subject of various generalizations. Only a broad comparative perspective enables us to see just what are the probabilities for sect development and what circumstances condition them. Such elaborate comparative analysis, which seeks to encompass many different movements and to illustrate common processes occurring in diverse cultural contexts, is perhaps the archetypical end-product of sociological enquiry, which marks off the work of the sociologist from that produced by historians and anthropologists. Yet, sociologically desirable as are such comparative analysis and the generalizations that flow from it, work of that kind, to be useful, can be only as good as the detailed studies on which it must ultimately rest. The detailed investigations of Chapters 9 and 12 are examples of one type of microcosmic study which contribute to the stock of basic information on which our generalizations rest.

Sociological enquiry depends on the co-operation of respondents. Religious bodies generally are disposed to some secrecy of operation, and this tendency is intensified in many sects. The sources of this reserve are several. In the first place sectarians regard religion as very much a matter of sovereign personal conviction which is no one else's business. Many sects have also experienced misrepresentation by journalists and even by judges and public officials. Third, the methods of sociological enquiry ineptly introduced may induce the sense that the investigators see their subjects as deviants or at least as oddities, and sects as a form of social pathology. The purposes of enquiry may remain incomprehensible to sectarians, and, indeed, even the most judicious display of impartiality and objectivity may appear to them as commitment to quite alien, perhaps inimical, values. Finally, there is the threat that the tolerated but inquisitorial stranger, with his divergent value-orientations, may seriously disturb the faith of members.

When sects resist sociological (and even more emphatically, psychological) enquiry, they do so with the apprehension, even if without the full comprehension, that there is a strong tendency within the social sciences towards a certain reductionism: religious commitments are taken at less than their face value and are seen as epiphenomena to be explained by reference to social, economic, or psychological causes. Since, in most sects, the member seeks to be seen as someone the primacy of whose religious convictions predicates his total social being, his comportment, relationships, and his involvement in, or abstention from, the operation of the wider social system, he must of necessity resist, and probably resent, the suggestion that his religious predilections are influenced or even determined by his social origins and circumstances. The sect has its own self-explanation and justification, and although the investigator cannot unreservedly accept such statements just as they stand, he does well to take them fully into account as first data that are due his respect. Since sects often reject conventional scientific wisdom and are often explicitly anti-intellectual, the theoretical formulations of social causation must always appear to sectarians at best as error and at worst as sin. And all of these considerations indicate the delicacy with which the sociologist must proceed if sects are to be studied and explained, and if these radical unconscious experiments in living patterns are to be understood.

Passing mention has been made of data derived from informants, and such sources have been of value with respect to sects no less than to tribes. Carefully used, the material that the informant supplies can become a basis from which to address more pertinent questions to sect leaders, and even if it is not in itself wholly accurate, it can be a lever with which to stimulate sect authorities to correct the record. Informants who are merely contacts and who have no personal motives for what they tell are to be preferred to those who, for their own purposes, seek to use the investigator. The disaffected and the apostate are in particular informants whose evidence has to be used with circumspection. The apostate is generally in need of self-justification. He seeks to reconstruct his own past, to excuse his former affiliations, and to blame those who were formerly his closest associates. Not uncommonly the apostate learns to rehearse an 'atrocity story' to explain how, by manipulation, trickery, coercion, or deceit, he was induced to join or to remain within an organization that he now forswears and condemns.[26] Apostates, sensationalized by the press, have sometimes sought to make a profit from accounts of their experiences in stories sold to newspapers or produced as books (sometimes written by 'ghost' writers).

Much of the foregoing discussion of methodological issues, despite passing allusion to the millions of adherents of the three or four largest sectarian groups, has proceeded to discuss sects as if they were small, almost single congregations. That, indeed, was often assumed in the early sociological work on sects. Such small associations still exist, but more typically today sects have

---

[26] On 'atrocity stories' as a genre, see A. D. Shupe, jun., and D. G. Bromley, 'Apostates and Atrocity Stories', in B. Wilson (ed.), *The Social Impact of New Religious Movements* (New York: Rose of Sharon Press, 1981), 179–215; and D. G. Bromley, A. D. Shupe, jun., and J. C. Ventimiglia, 'The Role of Anecdotal Atrocities in the Social Construction of Evil', in D. G. Bromley and J. T. Richardson, (eds.) *The Brainwashing/Deprogramming Controversy: Sociological, Psychological, Legal and Historical Perspectives* (New York: Edwin Mellen Press, 1983), pp. 139–60.

numerous congregations, often internationally distributed, and some of them control elaborate corporate structures and complex ancilliary services—most conspicuously the case with the Seventh-day Adventist Church, the Church of Jesus Christ of Latter-day Saints, and the Unification Church, even if other movements, such as the Brethren and the Christadelphians, persist with minimal organizational arrangements.

Whilst local sectarian life, in whatever movement, may still be appropriately studied by the methods discussed above, and whilst those studies are still essential for an understanding of what it means to be a sectarian, the large-scale sect has dimensions and facets that are comprehensible only by the use of quite different techniques and with the availability of quite different data. Large modern sects have their internal hierarchies and their bureaucratic administrators who follow routinized career patterns. Without returning to sacerdotalism, they have, none the less, evolved a type of internal professionalism. Their periodicals have often acquired a public relations role, no longer revealing, as was the case with small nascent sects, the internal tensions and difficulties within a movement. Instead, they put forward a bold but bland face to the world, in which problems, power struggles, financial arrangements, and even theological arguments are concealed not only from the outside enquirer but also from the ordinary rank and file of the faithful. Sociologists do not always gain ready access to the inner operations of these organizations, but a considerable amount of semi-sociological commentary sometimes emerges from within the sect, which, in its complexity, fails to maintain that coherent monolithic character assumed of sects. Some members become critical or contentious and may produce a literature which, whilst not directly sociological, and certainly lacking those criteria of ethical neutrality, detachment, and scientific method in terms of which sociology makes its claims, none the less provides the sociologist with some primary insights and certain data on which sociological analysis might proceed.[27]

Certain sects have, then, evolved into organizations which, in many respects, are quite unlike the Troeltschean model of

[27] Important examples of this type of internal critical literature are, in Mormonism, *Dialogue: A Journal of Mormon Thought* (begun in 1966); and, within Seventh-day Adventism, *Spectrum: A Quarterly Journal of the Association of Adventist Forums* (begun in 1969).

sectarianism. In part, this development reflects the much more avowedly pluralistic character of modern society: the old dichotomy of orthodox church and deviant sect ceases to apply. Inevitably, in consequence, the methods by which sects are to be studied undergo adaptation. There is one other important feature of the contemporary situation that should not escape notice. Sects, in time past—and the term was easily assumed to imply this—represented divisions within and separations from the dominant form of the Christian church. Today, there are many new religious movements which, in some respects, are much like sects but which in others differ radically from them. They tend to be of exotic provenance, extra-Christian or post-Christian. They do not seek specifically to correct existing Christian ideas as these are presented by the established churches, and they may regard Christianity as being not so much erroneous as merely irrelevant. They tend to be less anti-intellectual, and often offer rather a superior form of intellectual enlightenment, invoking supposedly scientific, religiously eclectic, or distinctly oriental systems of knowledge. Their appeal has been to a young public less rooted in traditional culture, less disposed to fight against it than to ignore it. Whilst sectarians are likely to be or, of choice, to become socially marginal, as society undergoes change so do its margins and its conceptions of marginality. The more recent religious movements have recruited those whose marginality may be more temporary, a function of generational change, affected life-style, and the new dissolution of coherence in the once firmly clustered criteria of social status. Some of these movements are much more accessible to sociological enquiry than were the old sects. They may accept a great deal of modern culture. The points at which they diverge from the wider society are different, and their distinctiveness is cast in different terms. So it is that the study of these movements, loosely grouped with and similar to sects, may call for some variation or augmentation of established assumptions about sectarianism and of the methodologies appropriate to its study, even though we may suppose that the fundamental canons of the social scientific perspective will remain essential to the enterprise.

The final section of this volume explores some of the issues brought forward by the various New Religious Movements. Already in the two and a half decades since the earliest of these movements emerged, they have stimulated a literature that promises to exceed in volume and diversity the corpus of older sociological studies of sectarianism. But, just as these movements are themselves more volatile and, in some cases, appear to be more ephemeral than traditional sects, so may be the literature devoted to them. Even so, they have opened up new areas of study, have brought forward new problems, and have offered, as one scholar has perceptively put it, a new 'perspective for the understanding of society'.[28] Chapter 10 considers some broad issues relative to this new wave of minority religion, and Chapter 11 deals specifically with the adversities which they will need to surmount if they are to survive, whilst Chapter 12, as already indicated, applies microcosmic techniques to one such movement in one particular locale. The final chapter in this volume returns to an issue intimated in Chapter 4, namely the problem for legal purposes of defining 'religion'. The matter is, however, more than a merely technical forensic concern, and the examination of the particular case of Scientology—surely, one of the most controversial movements claiming to be a religion—is made the point of departure for a tentative attempt to illustrate what may be discerned as a secular trend in religion (and, without seeking to pun, a secularizing trend). It opens up the question of whether, if we are competently to discuss religion and to develop adequate categories, we do not need a language that is liberated from the constraints of one particular cultural tradition. This case-study is intended to bring into the sharper focus of one, albeit extreme example, some of the problems that confront legislation and litigation, and by the same token confront society generally, in relation to religious issues when new forms of self-styled religions are coming into being.

[28] E. Barker (ed.), *New Religious Movements: A Perspective for Understanding Society* (New York: Edwin Mellen Press, 1982).

Part I

Survival:
The Sect Against The World

2
Sects and the State:
Some Issues and Cases

IN most Western countries, religious sects—and the term is used to include what are more generally referred to as new religious movements—are generally accorded at least formal equality before the law. Paradoxically, it was the first secular state, the first state which did not embrace specific religious principles as part of its legitimation, that is to say, the United States, which became also the first guarantor of religious freedom. The religious diversity of immigrants gradually compelled those states, such as Virginia, Massachusetts, and Connecticut, which had given privileged or established status to one religious denomination, to accept the equality of all faiths. Even in the United States, however, complete toleration has at times been in jeopardy;[1] while in other countries the extension of religious freedom has been patchy and uneven. None the less, the general course of development throughout the Western world has been clear. The principles of freedom of thought, conscience, and religion, including the freedom to change one's religious beliefs, and to manifest one's religion in worship, teaching, practice, and observance, are embodied in the European Convention on Human Rights, which was signed by fifteen states in 1950.[2] A more encompassing resolution was adopted in 1981 by the General Assembly of the United Nations, which called for the

[1] As an example of persisting intolerance in the United States, see D. R. Manwaring, *Render unto Caesar: The Flag Salute Controversy* (Chicago: Chicago University Press, 1962). The Witnesses objected to the obligation of children in public schools to salute the national flag, and in the patriotic days of the Second World War suffered considerable hostility in consequence until they won their right to exemption in the courts.

[2] The European Convention for the Protection of Human Rights was signed on 4 Nov. 1950, and 'came into force' on 3 Sept. 1953. Article 9 declared: 'Everyone has the right to freedom of thought, conscience and religion; this right includes freedom to change his religion or belief, and freedom, either alone or in community with others, and in public or private, to manifest his religion or belief, in worship, teaching, practice and observance.' The Convention was subsequently affirmed in a joint declaration of the European Parliament, Council, and Commission on 5 Apr. 1957.

elimination of all forms of intolerance and of discrimination based on religion or belief. That resolution embraced the principle of equality before the law and the right of freedom of thought, conscience, religion, and belief, and set out a number of principles respecting the right of assembly; the maintenance of charitable institutions; publications; teaching; donations, and so on. Even those countries that for centuries prohibited any religious expression other than that of the officially recognized church—Italy, Spain, Portugal, and Greece, for example—have, during the last three decades, steadily granted concessions and even legal rights to sects that were formerly banned. United Nations' resolutions and those of European Conventions do not, of course, have the force of law for their participating members, but they reflect the spirit of expanding religious toleration which in broad measure has been evident throughout the Western world.

Despite these developments there are still instances of religious repression and discrimination, and some sects remain the object of widespread social opprobrium and official disapproval. Those who, on the basis of a distinctive set of beliefs, hold themselves apart from the generality of people face periodic censure and contempt. The Press in particular, when it has no 'real' news concerning politics or the economy, indulges without excuse in the denigration of one sectarian group or another. The public appears to have a persisting appetite for sensationalism about religion and, perhaps second only to sexual scandal, sensational, or sensationalized, stories about religious minorities are the stock in trade of newspapers, and not only in Britain.[3] Where the Press feeds the public with such material, it is scarcely to be expected that the state, despite pious injunctions from international bodies pronounced at a high level of generality, will take a radically different stand.

It must, of course, be conceded that sects adopt a posture of protest against the wider society. However moderate its doctrines may be, the very fact that the sect stands apart from the majority may be taken as an implicit rebuke to others. And often, sectarians go further and become explicit critics of contemporary society, its

---

[3] See, for examples of the Press coverage of new religious movements, the two papers: K. Dobbelaere, G. Voet, and H. Verbeke, 'Neue religiöse Bewegungen im Spiegel der belgischen Presse', in J. Neumann and M. W. Fischer (eds.), *Toleranz und Repression: Zur Lage religiöser Minderheiten in modernen Gesellschaft* (Frankfurt-on-Main: Campus Verlag, 1987), 230–44; and G. Ambrosio, 'Neue religiöse Bewegungen in Italien', ibid. 313–35.

ethos, organisation, and its dominant preoccupations. At times, that criticism extends to the state itself. But few modern sects contend overtly and aggressively against the state *tout court*. The implications of teachings and prophecies concerning the overthrow of temporal princes are not normally drawn out to the point where they become manifestly seditious, much less a call to action.[4] Sects are generally quietistic in this respect, even if they espouse anti-state doctrines, and even allowing (in most cases) for their vigorous evangelism. Usually, when a sect finds itself in direct opposition to the state the issue in contention is not the sect's generalized hostility but some quite specific concern. In modern times, sectarian allegiance is rarely mobilized, at least in modern advanced societies, 'for the sect' and 'against the state' in any transcendent way, much as many sects reject, at a theoretical level, the present dispensation of things. The issues of contention are normally well defined and may even be well rehearsed over a period of years of covert antagonism on a particular point between a sect and particular agencies of government. To take an extreme example, the hostility between the nineteenth-century Mormon Church and the federal government of the United States over the matter of polygamy extended over several decades and brought Mormons into bloody conflict with the state, and yet, at a more general level of Mormon comportment and ethos, there can be no doubt that the Church espoused in very conventional terms the dominant values that were firmly entrenched in the American way of life.

The Mormon example indicates that even sectarian organizations that in general accept and endorse the prevailing values of the secular culture, may, none the less, on certain crucial issues find themselves in open conflict with government. Less dramatically, but in illustration of the same point, there is the lobbying which, in time past, Christian Scientists have undertaken in defence of medical freedom (a generalized demand which embraces the freedom sought for their own form of healing practice), in respect of which they opposed state compulsion in the matter of medical treatment, for example, of children. Yet, such specific issues apart, there can be no doubt of the general posture of Christian Science in its broad

---

[4] A remarkable historical exception in British history occurred in the activities of the Fifth Monarchy Men in the 1650s and 1660s: for an account, see B. S. Capp, *The Fifth Monarchy Men: A Study in Seventeenth-Century English Millenarianism* (London: Faber, 1972).

affirmation of secular culture. Thus, even sects that are sometimes labelled 'world-affirming'[5] are not exempted by that general orientation from the possibility of engaging in conflict with the agencies of the state.

For a sociologist, following the usual procedures of his discipline, it might be tempting to put forward a theoretical scheme indicating the convergence of circumstances that produce state–sect tensions by differentiating types of state and types of sect. Such, however, is the variation of states and sects, and such the idiosyncracy of the specific issues on which conflict might occur, that a theoretical formulation of this kind would be at least premature, and perhaps less useful than a brief review of empirical cases. Certain very general points about types of sect and types of state may be indicated but, beyond this, the primary focus must be on the types of issues that are productive of conflict.

It might well be thought, if we are to distinguish among sects, that those movements that are avowedly adventist, and which lay primary stress on the expectation of the early second advent of Christ (or on some other soon-to-be-realized millennial programme), would be those which experienced the keenest tensions with the state. After all, their expectations are for the early overturn of the present system of government. Conversely, it might be expected that those sects that I shall call 'introversionist', that is, sects that withdraw as fully as possible from the wider society, and which make the cultivation of in-group purity their primary concern, would, by virtue of insulating themselves from the impact of governmental agencies as thoroughly as possible, escape occasions of confrontation.[6] Such a neat formulation does not, however, mirror empirical reality. The millennium (or the advent) is by no means always the issue on which conflict with the state arises even for vigorously millenarian sects: the millennium is, after all, hypothetical and in the practical day-to-day life of the sect other issues are more immediate. The millennium promises total confrontation, of course, but the sect cannot afford such confrontation —at least, cannot afford it yet; but other issues may symbolize its distinctiveness. For example, considering the categories of sects,

---

[5] This concept is introduced by R. Wallis, *The Elementary Forms of the New Religious Life* (London: Routledge, 1984).

[6] For a fuller discussion of 'introversionist' (and other types of) sects, see B. Wilson, *Religious Sects* (London: Weidenfeld and Nicolson, 1970).

it might be supposed that the Seventh-day Adventists would experience particular tension with the state precisely because the advent is the *raison d'être* for their separate existence as a movement. In fact, even in developing countries, where the state is often relatively fragile and its officials consequently sensitive to criticism, for example in Zambia, all the evidence suggests that the real cause of recurrent conflict between this sect and the state arose from the Adventists' refusal to work on their Saturday sabbath rather than from their preaching of the imminence of the second advent, in which they surely believe.[7] Or again, Jehovah's Witnesses today experience much more conflict with the authorities because of their refusal to accept blood transfusions than because of their very intense and virtually single-minded preaching of the imminence of the appearance of God's Kingdom. Or, to provide an example of the vulnerability to conflict of an introversionist sect which, theoretically, ought, by virtue of its conscious policy of insulation from the wider secular society, to be able to avoid all direct involvement with the state, we may take the case of the Hutterian Brethren in Alberta. The Hutterites seek to establish their own segregated farming communities where they hold all things in common. None the less, public hostility is aroused among other Albertans by this very policy of vicinal segregation and collective settlements. Legislative action has been mounted against the Hutterites because other citizens are afraid of the increasing concentration of these sectarians (who have a very high fertility rate) whom they see being able to acquire political influence through the ballot box. And such fear exists even though the Hutterites do not vote. Today, the state has prohibited the establishment of new Hutterian communities within a certain radius of their existing settlements.[8]

Turning to types of state, one might suppose that all liberal democratic states would have a record of expanding tolerance for sectarian bodies. In practice, it is the liberal, democratic, *secular* states, such as the United States and Japan, which manifest the

[7] This was the finding of J. M. Assimeng, 'A Sociological Analysis of the Impact and Consequences of some Christian Sects in Selected African Countries', (University of Oxford D. Phil. thesis, 1968).

[8] For general accounts of the Hutterites, see J. W. Bennett, *Hutterian Brethren: The Agricultural Economy and Social Organization of a Communal People* (Stanford: Stanford University Press, 1967); and J. A. Hostetler, *Hutterite Society* (Baltimore: Johns Hopkins University Press, 1974).

greatest degree of tolerance. Liberal democracies in which there is an established or privileged religion are, for various reasons, just a little less tolerant, and here one might list Britain, Sweden, and France. Totalitarian states in the Eastern bloc, and states with constitutionally protected religions, specifically Islamic countries, and to some extent Israel, curtail religious liberty in various ways, whilst sects also encounter tensions in one-party states, particularly so for those sects that oppose 'earthly powers' and the members of which refuse to join political parties. In one-party states, refusal to support the party is easily regarded as disloyalty to the state itself. Thus, Jehovah's Witnesses, who preach obedience to the state as long as that obedience does not conflict with primary obedience to God, have clashed with the authorities in such one-party state as Malawi and Zambia, and the armed conflict of the Zambian authorities and the Lumpa Church in 1964 also arose because Lumpa Church members refused to support the majority party (although in this instance tribal rivalries were also a contributory factor).[9]

My present concern, however, is with liberal democratic societies that subscribe to the principles embodied in the United Nations resolutions and the affirmations of the European community. In Britain, this commitment to fundamental equality before the law long antedates these recent declarations, of course, and one of the *obiter dicta* of Justice Romilly from the last century is much cited to the effect that the law does not discriminate among religions.[10] The toleration of what used to be called 'dissenters', and which was specifically extended to Quakers, Roman Catholics, and Jews, and less explicitly to the multifarious religious groups now operating in the United Kingdom, went beyond the mere provision of rights of assembly and worship, but included also various privileges. In particular, these movements were permitted to establish charitable trusts; they were granted exemption from payment of local taxation (rates) in respect of properties used exclusively for religious worship; and they were gradually accorded a variety of concessions pertaining to rights of conscience.

[9] Information on the Lumpa Church is drawn from *East Africa and Rhodesia*, 20 Aug. 1964; the *Report of the Commission of Inquiry into the former Lumpa Church* (Lusaka: Government Printer, 1965); and for background information, R. I. Rotberg, 'The Lenshina Movement of Northern Rhodesia', *Rhodes-Livingstone Journal*, 29 (June 1961), 63–78.

[10] For a fuller discussion of these issues, see below, Ch. 4.

Obviously, such rights and privileges depended on the sect's conformity to the law, and in particular the sect has been required not to provoke public disorder, to endanger health or morals, or to infringe the rights and freedom of others. The problem that arises, stated in very general terms, is the point at which these various qualifications come into operation. Sects that take some pride in their general support for the law may find themselves attacked for disturbing public order or for acting in ways contrary to public policy. The subjects that are then raised may give rise to the assertion that a particular movement is outside the bounds of bona fide religion, and hence is ineligible to enjoy the privileges or the tolerance generally accorded to religious bodies. We can distinguish several points at which the teachings and practices of sectarians may bring the sect into conflict with state authorities. There are:

1 issues in which the sect directly challenges the authority of the state;
2 issues in which sect teachings are held to be contrary to specific aspects of public policy;
3 issues in which it may be alleged that adherence to the sect or its teachings endangers the rights even of those individuals who are its members;
4 issues in which the authorities seek to defend conventional morality and to protect the general public.

We may examine each of these areas of conflict between sect and state in turn.

For practical reasons, it is relatively rarely the case, at least in liberal democratic societies, that a sect openly and explicitly challenges the authority of the state. We have noted already that many sects do claim that the transcendent obligation of members is to obey the will of God as the sect understands it, and that, should divergence arise between the law of men and the law of God (or such other supernatural agencies as the sect takes to be authoritative) then the latter must prevail. It has not been uncommon for sects in the fundamentalist Christian tradition to invoke those texts of Scripture which prophesy the degradation of kings or of the governments and principalities of this world. Nowadays, mere teaching of this kind, without exhortation to action, is unlikely, at least in the West, to induce any reaction from the authorities, and it must be remembered that Christian sects generally acknowledge an obligation to obey magistrates and to 'render unto Caesar'. The conflicts that arise in this area tend to be more specific. Conscientious objection has been perhaps the principal item in contention, since many sects seek this particular right of conscience (albeit on somewhat varying grounds), and in general exemption from military service has been increasingly readily accorded in Western societies. Patriotism is no longer the unquestioned virtue that it was considered to be even thirty years ago. Groups other than, and more vociferous than, religious sectarians have in recent years paraded a more outspoken anti-patriotism, claiming the right to conscientious objection to military service as but one among various demands for freedom from state constraint. Their prominence has relativized the position of those sects that object to military service, and they are now sheltered from exposure by those within the main-line churches and by politically motivated conscientious objectors who occupy much more public platforms and who canvass their consciences more vigorously and with arguments more threatening to the integrity of the state.

The types of issue in which the teachings and practices of a sect might contravene public policy are potentially numerous. Three areas in which problems could arise may be readily distinguished. It is public policy in many countries today to forbid active discrimination on racial or sexual grounds. Religious groups are in their nature discriminatory organizations, at least as between believers and non-believers. In various respects, for example in the matter of participating in certain rites of public worship, such as Holy Communion, religious bodies discriminate on ritual and moral grounds. An individual who is unconfirmed (or who is not a clear potential candidate for confirmation) is normally excluded from partaking in Communion: again, at least technically, an adulterer might, in many Christian denominations, be refused Communion and be excommunicated from his church. Religions also impose punishments (penances) on those who transgress their rules. Clearly, there is room for conflict with the public authorities in the matter of discrimination, but at present the subject is unclear and, one might say, in certain cases, to which reference will be made below, that the authorities have deliberately, and perhaps necessarily, fudged some of the issues. For the moment, let us take three issues that are less complex. The state has prohibited racial discrimination. Most Christian sects have no problems on this score, and today the

mainstream of Christianity and also of sectarian Christianity is free
from racist ideology or practice, even though what is today called
racism prevailed in some Protestant denominations in the past—
particularly at the time of the American Civil War—persisted in
Mormonism until the late 1970s, and may do so still among
extreme Calvinist movements in South Africa.[11]

Many sects, however, are distinctly anti-racist, offering a
radically different basis on which to categorize mankind: fundamentally, albeit often with variations, as 'saved' and 'damned'.
Some, among whom should be included Jehovah's Witnesses and
the Unification Church, are particularly proud of their capacity to
incorporate peoples of all races as equals in every respect. Yet,
latently, racist ideas linger in the Christian inheritance, and because
of their literalism and intensity these ideas are likely to persist in at
least the background thinking of some sectarians. Many Christian
groups assume that the promises made by God to the Jews as a
chosen people were transferred to Christians as the new heirs of
God by virtue of Christ's offer of salvation. A basis of biological,
indeed racial, discrimination transformed into spiritual discrimination, lies within Christianity, and perhaps persists among ultra-
orthodox Jews, in the quasi-sectarian communities that exist in
various metropolitan cities in the Western world, who have never
disavowed the elitist racial status which their Scriptures claim for
them. Paradoxically, Christian groups may also manifest a specific
racism in the anti-Semitism of which they are sometimes accused,
and evidence of which has been gathered by sociologists. The basis
for this orientation lies in the attribution of culpability to the Jews
as instigators of the crucifixion of Christ.[12]

[11] The founder of Mormonism, Joseph Smith, Jun., faced with the problems of
establishing the Church's attitude towards American Negroes during the period
when his migrating movement had temporarily sought to settle in the 'border' state
of Missouri, claimed to have received a divine revelation which, whilst affirming the
blessedness of the Negro race, declared them to be cursed as appertaining to the
priesthood of his Church. Since all Mormon males become priests, this verdict gave
to Negro men a very secondary status within the Church, and was almost
tantamount to their exclusion. Smith's revelation operated throughout the history of
the Church until the late 1970s, when the then President received a new revelation
which brought Mormon Church practice into conformity with prevailing anti-
discriminatory attitudes. See K. J. Hansen, *Mormonism and the American
Experience* (Chicago: Chicago University Press, 1981), 179–204.

[12] For an empirical investigation, see H. E. Quinley and C. Y. Glock (eds.), *Anti-
Semitism in America* (New York: Free Press, 1979), 94–109, where the Christian
roots of anti-Semitism are discussed.

There is one other strand of Christian thought that might be said to come close to a form of racism: the teachings designated as British Israelism (or, in America, sometimes as Anglo-Israelism). This doctrine seeks to identify the British (or more generally the Anglo-Saxon) race as the literal descendants of the ten lost tribes of Israel, to whom all God's promised benisons will one day accrue. These ideas have never given rise to a distinctive sect but they have been accepted by some within various sectarian movements, exerting their fascination for the early Southcottians, for some leading Christian Scientists, and for the founder of the Elim Pentecostal Church and, subsequently, of the schismatic movement that he also brought into being. Outside the commonly acknowledged Christian family of churches and sects, some of the teachings of the West Indian Rastafarian groups which now operate in Britain and perhaps in other parts of the Western world are ostensibly racist, and the 'prophet' of the movement, Marcus Garvey, called himself a Fascist.[13] Here, of course, the preferred race is negroid. Despite all these traces of racism among contemporary sectarian groups, racism is not one of the charges for which sects are generally indicted.

Discrimination with respect to sex is self-evidently much more commonplace in sectarian movements. Christian organizations frequently reserve all leadership positions for men and do so on the basis of biblical principles or at least on the example of biblical models. Sexism is not however an issue specific to sectarianism, since there is a much more entrenched and well-canvassed preference for men over women within the Roman, Anglican, and some other churches, and as yet the 'equal opportunities' legislation has not been applied to the clerical professions. Of course, the charge of sexism might also be made against a number of non-Christian religions that now flourish in the British Isles.

In various other specific ways, religious minorities may stipulate practices that contradict public policy. To cite one example: that cult of Sikhs founded by Govind Singh exhorts a type of militant religious attitude that is unusual in, say, the Christian tradition. Some of the obligations on a Singh, or Lion, are summarized as the five 'Ks', one of which is that men should at all times wear a

[13] On Garvey, see E. D. Cronin, *Black Moses: The Story of Marcus Garvey and the United Negro Improvement Association* (Madison: University of Wisconsin Press, 1955).

dagger.[14] A dagger is an offensive weapon, and under the normal criminal law anyone wearing a dagger might be subject to punishment. I do not know how obedient to this rule are modern-day Sikhs of the Singh cult in Britain, nor do I know whether policemen stop and search unwary Sikhs in the way that they stop unwary motorists to administer breath-tests to check the extent of alcohol consumption, but clearly there is here an example of a religious injunction that might well be held to be contrary to public policy.

The third type of issue that might bring sects into conflict with the state relates to matters on which the fundamental right of an individual might be held to be infringed by the sect or by his own adherence to sect teachings. These matters involve the paternalism of the welfare state, which claims the right or the duty, under certain circumstances, to protect individuals from their own conscious preferences with respect to their own beliefs, practices, or commitments. There is some continuity here with those issues on which the state has taken up a distinct position with regard to protecting people, or certain categories of people, in relation to such matters as the consumption of alcohol, tobacco, drugs, or pornography, but in general the state has been cautious in its dealings with religion, and has not yielded to the demands sometimes made that it should compile a register of sects or publish advice regarding their probity or desirability.

Not infrequently the justification for demands that the state should act against or in circumscription of particular sects rests on the assumption that the sect can, in some way, be differentiated from the members who comprise it. It is readily taken for granted that, within a sect, there are those who in certain ways compel or control others. In reality, whilst in some sects there are powerful leaders, this is by no means always the case. That there may be collective exercise of constraint is apparent, but the extent to which the individual member acquiesces in such measures of social control must be the subject of subtle scrutiny. The constrained individual in one situation will often be one of those exercising constraint in other circumstances, and the question of conformity may itself be very much at issue in what it means to be a member.

---

[14] For a discussion of the tradition of the Khalsa brotherhood and its origins, see W. H. McLeod, *The Evolution of the Sikh Community* (Oxford: Clarendon Press, 1976).

The typical examples of this category of conflict include the demand, frequently voiced, for public action against sects that look to the conversion of adolescents as their main strategy of recruitment. The accusation of 'brainwashing' has become familiar, inept as that term certainly is when applied to religious sects.[15] The state cannot, however, act specifically to meet the general allegation that sects 'brainwash' new recruits. Although the Unification Church lost a libel action in which the allegation of 'brainwashing' was very much the central issue, the charge has certainly not been proved. Since such an allegation has not been and perhaps cannot be proved, there is a strong tendency for this indictment to lead to a demand for more extensive action against the sect—action going far beyond the immediate implications of what the ill-defined (and perhaps, relative to religion, indefinable) charge of 'brainwashing' might suggest. A process of escalating allegations occurs, facilitated by the emotive connotations and factual vagueness of the term 'brainwashing', which culminates in the general proposition that the sect's teachings do not really constitute a religion, and that, therefore, the movement ought not to enjoy those privileges generally accorded to religions. Whether a particular movement is or is not a religion is a crucial question relative to claims for conscience and toleration, but such a question cannot be determined by reference to the specific techniques of disseminating doctrine and attracting converts. In the intensification of the Press campaigns against the Unification Church in the early 1980s, allegations were made that that movement was not an authentic religion, that it jeopardized the well-being of the young, and engaged in deceptive practices in recruiting members and soliciting donations. After years in preparing its case against the Unification Church, the Attorney-General's office finally conceded, in 1988, the weakness of their position, dropped their legal proceedings to deprive the Church of its charitable status, and agreed to pay its costs.

A second and conspicuous example of the way in which the state seeks to protect the individual from the sect arises with respect to children in those sects in which specific forms of child-care

---

[15] Brainwashing, so-called, has become the subject of a considerable literature, but see D. G. Bromley and J. T. Richardson (eds.), *The Brainwashing/Deprogramming Controversy: Sociological, Psychological and Historical Perspectives* (New York: Edwin Mellen Press, 1983); and for a particular study, E. Barker, *The Making of a Moonie: Choice or Brainwashing?* (Oxford: Blackwell, 1984).

provided by the state are rejected on religious grounds. Here, of course, one has an instance of leaders (namely, parents) and followers (namely, children). When parents object to medical treatment—because they believe in faith-healing, or because they are Christian Scientists, or because, in the case of Jehovah's Witnesses, they renounce blood transfusions—the state has taken upon itself powers to act.[16] In the United Kingdom, children may be made wards of court on a temporary basis whilst in hospital in order that medical treatment (including blood transfusions) deemed necessary by the state may be administered despite the sectarian preferences of the parents. Of course, the parents are legally powerless to intervene in such a case, and the sect must accept and accommodate as best it may such enforced 'sinfulness'. Jehovah's Witnesses whose children are given blood transfusions are not put out of fellowship, and Christian Scientists declare in such instances that the patient recovers in spite of medical treatment, and not because of it.

A similar type of situation, also affecting children, arises in cases that come to court in which parents of differing religious persuasions contest the proposition that allegiance to a sect will distort or restrict a child's education. Such cases have not been uncommon. Courts in Britain have made judgments that have implied that the fact that one parent was a sectarian was in itself sufficient to decide that the other parent, merely by virtue of being non-sectarian, was to be preferred as the custodian of the child.[17]

[16] An account of the question of blood transfusion among Jehovah's Witnesses is given in M. Penton, *Apocalypse Delayed: The Story of Jehovah's Witnesses* (Toronto: University of Toronto Press, 1985), 153–4.

[17] In one such case, the decision of the justices, who had granted custody of a 5-year-old boy to the (non-sectarian) father in preference to the mother who was one of Jehovah's Witnesses, was reversed on appeal. Hollings LJ, granting the mother's appeal, said, 'When the justices granted custody to the father they stated that despite the recommendation in the welfare [officer's] report that the mother should have custody, they were concerned that if that were done she would probably indoctrinate the child and he would be isolated from society and be prevented from leading a normal, full and varied life.' His Lordship referred to the comments of Scarman LJ in re T (Minors), unreported 10 Dec. 1975, who had said, 'We live in a tolerant society. There is no reason at all why the mother should not espouse the beliefs and practices of Jehovah's Witnesses . . . There is nothing immoral or socially obnoxious in the beliefs and practice of the sect. There is a great risk, because we are dealing with an unpopular sect, in overplaying the dangers to the welfare of these children inherent in the possibility that they may follow their mother and become Jehovah's Witnesses . . . It does not follow that it is wrong or contrary to the welfare of the children that life should be in a narrower sphere, subject to a stricter religious

Paradoxically, when both parents are sectarians of the same persuasion, the law does not see religious commitment as sufficiently injurious to the well-being of the child to interfere.

The paradoxes presented by the law when the state acts with respect to religion do not end here. There is a celebrated case in which the state has acted to prevent a sectarian (using the term broadly) from being discriminated against because of the requirements made of him by his religion. In this case, which was finally settled in the House of Lords, the judgment pronounced that a headmaster of a *Christian* school was guilty of *racial* discrimination in debarring a turban-wearing Sikh from his school (although it was acknowledged that Sikhs who did not wear turbans were readily admitted to the school).[18] But, as already indicated, religious bodies are, in their nature, discriminatory. They make specific demands of their votaries and they disenfranchise those who fail to meet these requirements. In this case, the judiciary acted to guarantee the 'racial' rights of an individual who was conforming to the demands of the religious minority to which he belonged. But it did so by declaring that his religious group was in fact a 'race'; ignored the fact that turban-wearing is an obligation accepted only by some orthodox Sikhs; and ignored the possibility that such an interpretation of the law might allow some other religious groups that have a long-sustained distinctive life-style to claim the status— a privileged status in British law—of being a race. It is not my present purpose to enquire why (particularly since it has no distinctive biological origin) a religious group should have been held to be a race, but the case makes apparent in high relief the anomalous situation in which the modern state at times acts to preserve certain highly discriminatory values, such as those

---

discipline and without parties on birthdays and at Christmas . . . It is essential to appreciate that the mother's teaching, once it is accepted as reasonable, is teaching that has got to be considered against the whole background of the case and not as in itself so full of danger for the children that it alone could justify making an order which otherwise the court would not make' (*The Times*, 19 June 1980). Lord Scarman notwithstanding, prejudice by the state's officials against sects has persisted, as this quoted case indicates.

[18] For this case, *Mandla (Sewa Singh) and Another* v. *Dowell Lee and Another*, see, for the Court of Appeal hearing, *Weekly Law Reports*, 19 Nov. 1982, 932–50; and for the House of Lords hearing which reversed the Appeal Court judgment, *Weekly Law Reports*, 8 Apr. 1983, 630–2. *The Times* Law Report was published on 25 Mar. 1983. There is also a brief account in St. J. A. Robilliard, *Religion and the Law* (Manchester: Manchester University Press, 1984), 162–3.

cherished within religious bodies, whilst in other cases it acts (in the spirits of the laws against racial discrimination) as if all men were in some sense interchangeable and equal units.

The fourth type of instance in which sects might conflict with the state are those in which not the individual sectarian but the general public is to be protected and its conventional morality defended. Let me offer two examples under this heading: sexual regulation and therapeutic claims. Some sectarian groups organize their communal life in ways that diverge radically from those of the wider society; and where sexually unusual patterns have prevailed, public outrage has sometimes occurred. Accusations of free love or sexual promiscuity have often been made against many communal groups, sometimes without justification. On the other hand, some sects have adopted attitudes to sexual behaviour which the general public regards with disapproval. Typically, communitarian groups, in which all things are held in common, have discovered that once private property is eliminated then a major bulwark of, and perhaps even the need for, conventional family organization is removed. Communitarian sects face the need for sexual control and a system of orderly relations between the sexes but find themselves free to develop patterns that may significantly differ from the system of family structure as it has evolved in Western society. Thus it is that such sects have so often been accused of instituting (and, very occasionally, have indeed instituted) free love and group marriage.[19] More typically, they have either sought to impose celibacy, as did the Shakers, the Rappites, and the Amana Society in the United States, or they have retained monogamous marriage whilst distributing family functions to communal agencies (for example, the rearing of children) as among the Hutterians.[20]

By virtue of their concern to maintain a separate way of life, many sects that have not been communitarian but which have tended to gather as insulated communities have accepted variants

[19] The most celebrated instance of the practice of group-marriage by a sect occurred in the elaborate system of selective intercourse implemented at the Oneida Community of John Humphrey Noyes: see J. McK. Whitworth, *God's Blueprints: A Sociological Study of Three Utopian Sects* (London: Routledge, 1975), 120–31.

[20] For the Shakers, see Whitworth, *God's Blueprints*; and E. D. Andrews, *The People Called Shakers* (New York: Dover, 1963); on the Rappites, see K. J. R. Arndt, *Georg Rapp's Harmony Society, 1785–1847* (Philadelphia: University of Pennsylvania Press, 1965); and on the Amana Society, B. H. M. Schambaugh, *Amana That Was and Amana That Is* (Iowa City: State Historical Society of Iowa, 1932).

of conventional marital and familial norms, and this, perhaps more than any other single tendency, has rendered them vulnerable to social opprobrium and the threat of state interference. Mormon polygamy in the nineteenth century is the most conspicuous case. More recently, the techniques of recruitment adopted by the Children of God (later known as the Family of Love), and by the Melchior sect in Belgium, in which women members were enjoined to seek to attract new male converts by the offer of sexual companionship ('flirty fishing', so designated by the Children of God) have created tensions between these sects and the wider society, and have induced calls for state action against them. Perversely perhaps, the general public sometimes finds obligatory celibacy as practised by other sects almost as offensive as promiscuity. The obligatory celibacy required of Moonies whilst they serve their initial apprenticeship in the Church, and the fact that each member awaits the decision of the Revd Mr Moon respecting the identity of his or her future spouse and the date of the wedding, are matters that have been raised by the mass media in their frequent condemnation of the Unification Church.[21] But these issues remain matters of public rather than state concern, since if individuals are credited with free choice, part of their freedom must be to permit unconventional practices. Indeed, in a society where sexual permissiveness is widely canvassed, at least by the entertainment industry, and is widely reported (in the tabloid Press) of socially prominent individuals, and in which there are ethnic minorities among whom arranged marriages are still common, it must be evident that there can be little ground for state interference with sects that espouse a code of sexual morality which diverges from that which judges, the main-line churches, and, in their moralizing moments, the mass media, assume to be normative and normal.

The protection of the general public is also at issue when it can be shown that a religious movement makes false representations and unsubstantiated claims. There are various directions in which this might occur—for instance, in the solicitation of funds for undisclosed or falsely stated purposes or by religious bodies that fail accurately to identify themselves in terms readily understood by those who are approached. One of the grounds on which the Attorney-General

[21] The most detailed account is Barker, *Making of a Moonie*.

mounted the subsequently aborted legal action in which he intended to challenge the right of the Unification Church to charitable status was that Moonies deceived members of the public about the movement's identity. The Moonies, it was suggested, represented their work as Christian missionary work, and the government case depended, in part, on contesting the accuracy of the designation 'Christian'. To make his point, the Attorney-General would have been obliged to define that term, and the case could readily have taken on the character of a heresy trial. Although protecting the public from deception remains an object of public policy, in practice, where religious belief is concerned, empirical evidence is often scarce, and it is difficult to pronounce on what constitutes legitimate beliefs and how beliefs shall be appropriately categorized.[22]

An issue of perhaps wider incidence concerns the promotion of religious therapeutic practice. By no means all sects offer specific methods of therapy, but some make therapy their primary focus of appeal, sometimes being relatively undemanding of adherents in other respects. Clearly, it is open to people to follow any system of therapy that they choose: the issue of potential conflict arises when unsubstantiated claims are made for certain religiously canvassed therapeutic techniques; when specific techniques are believed by the medical authorities to be actually harmful; or when such medically unapproved techniques are preferred to orthodox medicine in the treatment of children or dependents. A considerable part of the legal trouble that has arisen for Scientology has been occasioned by the therapeutic claims of the movement; and the grounds advanced as justification during the late 1960s and 1970s for the ban on those who sought to enter Britain to study Scientology related to government disapproval of the movement's therapeutic system, rather than to any sort of official restriction of its religious beliefs and practices.

There is one species of problem arising between the modern state and the sect which is not easily encompassed in the foregoing categories. It arises as a by-product of social policy in the implementation of which the interests of deviant minorities are not taken into account. Two instances come from Sweden, but they have their parallels elsewhere. Both are situations that affect the

---

[22] See Ch. 3 below for the account of the judgments of the Australian High Court on this issue.

affairs of the movement known as Exclusive Brethren, an introversionist sect which withdraws as fully as possible, short of
segregated, vicinal, communal organization, from all involvement
with the wider society. The first example relates to officiation at
marriage ceremonies. The Brethren, who are not a corporate body,
and who are firmly opposed to the idea of an official clergy, would
like to marry according to their own preferred procedures. In
Britain, such an arrangement is relatively easily achieved, since it is
premises that are licensed for weddings, and the trustees of such
properties may appoint any of their number to perform marriages
subject only to the incorporation in the service of the approved
form of words and the due registration of the performance. In
Sweden, ordained ministers are licensed to perform marriages, but
the Brethren reject any idea of an ordained ministry. At present, the
problem is stuck in a bureaucratic stalemate. The second illustration relates to labour law. Swedish governments of recent decades
have evolved an incorporated paternalistic state, and one area in
which legislation has progressively rigidified the structure of
Swedish social organization has been with respect to labour. All
those involved in work must belong either to a union or to an
employers' confederation: there is a double closed shop throughout
the whole economy. Brethren refuse to belong to any organization
of which Christ is not the head, and thus they have conscientious
objection to being drawn either into unions or into employers'
organizations. Many Brethren run small businesses, often family
concerns, but because they reject membership in either type of
organization, they risk total embargo from both unions and
owners.

In Western liberal democracies, the general trend in recent
decades has been for increased religious toleration. To put the
matter at the minimum, one may observe that politicians generally
have become loath to engage in religious disputes. The reluctance of
the government to see parliamentary time devoted to the potentially
divisive issue of the use of the old Prayer Book which its advocates
were seeking; the granting to the Church of England synod of
enlarged legislative powers over the Church's affairs; and the
increased assertion that religion and politics are quite separate
spheres—all testify to the trend. Yet, there have been a number of
conspicuous instances, some of them mentioned above, in which
the agencies of state and sects have become embroiled in conflict.

Government law officers and the Charity Commissioners[23] have pursued one or another religious movement, and government has, at times, relentlessly refused, even when good opportunity has presented itself, to relieve sects of certain disabilities under which, given their conscientious scruples, they are at present obliged to suffer.[24]

In Britain, a small but vociferous minority of secondary political figures have persistently spoken out against minority religions, and the Press, given its sensitivity to the issue of the freedom of publication, has been remarkably insensitive about the freedom of religion. There have been calls for the registration of religious bodies, and demands (mostly, but not entirely unheeded) for legal action against so-called 'cults' and the withdrawal of concessions conferred by the charitable status which most of them enjoy. Anti-cult movements, principally stimulated by the incidence of conversions of (mainly middle-class) young people, have sprung into being, some of them not disavowing extreme and even illegal tactics to 'rescue' by unlawful detention young converts who are then subject to 'de-programming'. The British authorities have tended to be wary of anti-cult groups of this kind which approximate the role of vigilantes. Instead, they have provided financial support for a neutral agency, INFORM, which seeks to mediate relationships between distraught parents and their converted offspring.[25] On the Continent, governments have shown less impartiality. In Germany, the federal authorities have published material opposing new religious movements, and have subsidized an anti-cult organization, *Aktion für geistige und psychische Freiheit*. In France, a parliamentary commission of inquiry was instituted, and an agency,

[23] See Ch. 4 below for an account of the refusal of the Charity Commissioners to register the trusts of the Exclusive Brethren.

[24] Members of the Exclusive Brethren pressed the government at the time of the debate on the Criminal Justice Bill in 1988, to strengthen the provisions by which judges might, on conscientious grounds, excuse Brethren from jury service. The government resisted an amendment at the report stage of the Bill, defeating it by 209 votes to 205: *Hansard*, 20 June 1988, 871–93.

[25] INFORM was established at the initiative of Dr Eileen Barker of the London School of Economics, whose research into the Unification Church had made her uniquely aware of the problems arising from the conversion particularly of young people. This neutral agency seeks to promote better understanding between leaders of new religions and parents, and receives financial help from government and from the Church of England.

L'Association pour la defense de la famille et de l'individuel is provided with state subsidies.[26]

It appears that the emergence of the new religious movements, the cults as their detractors choose to call them, has, if not arrested, then at least hindered the general process of increasing religious toleration. In some way, these movements appear to tax the basic premisses on which toleration rests: at least some of them, and perhaps some of the older-established sects, went further in their departure from the assumptions of public good and individual well-being than the agencies of state were prepared to countenance. It appears that the limits of religious toleration are vague and uncertain. Governments, prompted by the media and by parents, distrust new movements, perhaps because of their exotic provenance; in part because of their strong appeal to the young; and because of their unconventional lifestyles and the total commitment that they command. At the same time, there is government resistance towards making concessions to those of tender conscience. The liberal pronouncements of international bodies remain largely rhetorical gestures directed perhaps more at the Eastern bloc and the Third World than towards the condition of tiny religious minorities in the West. The ambivalence on the topic is evident in the occasional counter-proposal such as the Cottrell resolution approved by the European Parliament in 1984.[27]

Thus the broad process of toleration which may be traced historically is less even and more circumscribed than may at first sight appear. That may be because the real motor in the engine is not the recurrent advocacy of greater religious freedom, but is rather the wider and more structural phenomenon of secularization, the process by which religion loses its significance for the operation of the social system. As religion loses its consequence for the economy, the polity, the judicature, education, and social relations generally, so attitudes of religious indifference become normal. Up to a point, religious minorities benefit from what has become official and virtually institutionalized indifferentism.

[26] J. A. Beckford, 'Cult Controversy and Conflict', *Sociological Analysis*, 42/3 (1981), 249–64.

[27] The resolution brought by a British MEP, was based on a 'Report on the Activity of Certain New Religious Movements within the European Community', PE82/322 (fin. 22 Mar. 1984), and recommended measures of surveillance of such bodies. The resolution was passed on 22 May 1984, by 98 votes to 28, with 26 abstentions.

Beyond that point, particularly when they are the victims of Press sensationalism or of the inertia which, with respect to powerless minorities, indifferentism also encourages, they may continue to experience opprobrium or disregard. The toleration that such sects enjoy probably and paradoxically owes more to the rationalization of modern societies and its implicit marginalization of spiritual concerns than to the liberalism which those societies espouse as part of their civic creed, as becomes evident from an analysis of the conflicts between states and sects.

3

Sects and Society in Tension

IT is a commonplace to refer to the cultural situation in Britain as one of religious pluralism, in which a notional and pervasive orthodoxy has been fragmented by various currents of diversified religious belief and practice. In some measure that pluralism has existed for centuries, of course, but it may be important to note that two divergent tendencies have been at work. Whilst new and exotic religions have been introduced, certain older forms of religious diversity have lost their distinctiveness. The terms in which we had become accustomed to think of religions other than orthodoxy— 'nonconformity' and 'dissent'—have become anachronisms, not only because we have largely abandoned the idea of religious conformity as a norm, but also because bodies once seen as radical departures from the norm have gradually come to be regarded as only marginally different. (This has occurred as a consequence of secularization, changes in social structure, amalgamations, and the general effect on Christianity of the introduction of much more markedly alien religions.) The social bases and the theological import of those old religious differences have been largely eroded as more radical departures have relativized the position of the erstwhile 'dissenters', as Muslims, Sikhs, and Hindus have moved into British society. What once were challenging and even dangerous rivals to orthodox faith have become more or less acceptable variants within a generalized, and perhaps increasingly colourless Christianity. 'Nonconformity' and 'dissent' have virtually dropped out of the nation's (non-legal) vocabulary. The reality of such divergent 'nonconformity' persists only in minority sectarian movements.

Although sociologists use the term 'sect' in a completely neutral and non-pejorative sense, for the public at large, and especially for the mass media, the word remains, as for a long time it was for the Church, a term of opprobrium. Almost by definition, as commonly used, the term 'sect' (or 'cult') implies the likelihood of tension with society. Whereas once 'sect' was seen as explicitly an opposition to 'church', today, in a secularized society where the major denominations have grown closer together, the sect is seen more sharply as a challenge to society at large. The challenge is not to conventional religious beliefs so much as to the general, secularized social mores. The sect is seen less as a combatant in religious issues than as a deviant and abnormal religious threat to conventional, generally a-religious social practice. Sects thus become an issue of social rather than of explicitly religious concern.

The Character of Sectarianism

A sect is a self-consciously and deliberately separated religious minority which espouses a faith divergent from that of other religious bodies. For present purposes, the term 'sect' is not confined to minor deviations from the traditional Anglican faith, but is employed to encompass also those minority movements sometimes referred to as 'cults' or as 'new religious movements'. Each sect is, in greater or lesser degree, unique, and although sects may be grouped as families by reference to their historical origins, or classified by doctrinal position, organizational structure, or other, sociological criteria, my present concern requires no such classification.[1] Rather, one may allude on the one hand to the general attributes of all such movements, or on the other hand to the particular instances of tension between society and one given sect.

Within the general exclusivistic framework of Christianity, the sect challenges, usually explicitly, the adequacy of the teachings, explanations, religious practices, social mores, life-style, and ethos of all other religious bodies, and of the public at large. Typically, the sect claims to provide better access to salvation than is elsewhere available, and does so by virtue of a monopoly of truth, commitment to, and belief in which are normally indispensable conditions. We may leave aside the variety of specific concepts of salvation, noting only that these range from bodily or mental healing to elaborate prospect of the transmigration of the soul, the resurrection of the body, or reincarnation: the common denominator is always the promise of present reassurance in the face of baleful or untoward phenomena or events. Whatever specific terms it employs, the sect is always an agency of salvation.

[1] For a typology of sects which has at times been used as a basis for classification, see B. Wilson, *Religious Sects* (London: Weidenfeld and Nicolson, 1970), 36–47.

Salvation, although usually (and in the Christian cases, always) predicated for an afterlife, has, however, implications for present life. Two aspects of this concern for salvation are worth noting. First that the conditions for the attainment of salvation imply a range of taboos and injunctions for everyday living: and second, that the realization of life in obedience to those strictures is also in some meaure in itself seen as an at least partial achievement of salvation. The sect becomes a location for the experience of salvation as well as an agency of promise. Sects generally do not only extol the virtue of their moral demands and their significance in the moral economy, but they also emphasize the joy available from fulfilling those demands. Christian sectarians readily suggest that this life may already be heavenly; that life in the sectarian community is a foretaste of God's goodness; that they have already claimed a healing experience; are building God's Kingdom; or are cultivating perfection for God, in whose service alone is perfect joy. Thus, each sect sustains an explicit culture—a repertoire of what shall not be done and what shall be done. Since many of these interdictions and injunctions run counter to the cultural assumptions of the wider society, sects are always likely to experience tension whenever their affairs impinge, as they often must, on those of the world outside.

Sectarian Alternatives

The sect is, then, canvassing either an alternative way of life or, at the least, exemptions from the normal obligations of the wider society and alternatives to a specific range of its facilities. The generality or specificity of those alternative arrangements varies from one sect to another, from those which establish well-insulated communitarian settlements to others that are concerned merely to advocate a 'better way' with respect to one particular element of society's operation. Some sects seek to establish a way of life and a pattern of social relations which permit the group to function as a community, or on the model of community, even though the conditions for genuine communitarianism are not easily found in Britain today. The classic communitarian or near-communitarian sects exploited the free or cheap land available in the unsettled terrains of eighteenth- and nineteenth-century America and Russia: such conditions, in which vicinal isolation reinforces ideological insulation, have rarely been available in contemporary Britain. Even so, some sects in Britain have sought to re-create living communities, even if they have also recognized that not all their members could be embraced in this pattern of organization. Among groups which have experimented with such communal structures are the, originally German, Bruderhof founded by Eberhard Arnold; the Anthroposophists; the International Society for Krishna Consciousness (Hare Krishna Movement); the Unification Church (Moonies); the Emissaries of Divine Light; the Bugbrooke Community; and the Findhorn Community.[2]

Such total communities seek to reduce tension with the wider society by removal from it; but near neighbours inevitably become aware of them, and although relations are not always bad, there may be occasions for expressions of disapproval or even hostility. The very fact of withdrawal into a sequestered enclave arouses suspicions of sinister purposes, and may be represented as a cloak for deviant, perhaps evil practices. When the moral stance of such a community also differs significantly from that of the wider society—and this is commonly the case, and is indeed justification for segregation—then this is easily regarded as evidence of evil intents. So it is that communitarianism, interpreted as the ideal solution to the problem of sustaining a distinctive ideology (and sometimes held as mandatory for its realization),[3] by no means ensures a sect that tension with the wider society can be avoided. Segregation is intended to limit interaction with outsiders, but periodically the very fact of segregation may in itself excite their

---

[2] On the Eberhard Arnold Bruderhof, see J. McK. Whitworth, *God's Blueprints* (London: Routledge and Kegan Paul, 1975); on Anthroposophists, G. Ahern, *Sun at Midnight: The Rudolf Steiner Movement and the Western Esoteric Tradition* (Wellingborough: Aquarian Press, 1984). On the International Society for Krishna Consciousness, see K. Knott, *My Sweet Lord: the Hare Krishna Movement* (Wellingborough: Aquarian Press, 1986); and, for America, see S. J. Gelberg (ed.), *Hare Krishna, Hare Krishna* (New York: Grove Press, 1983); and E. B. Rochford, jun., *Hare Krishna in America* (New Brunswick, NJ: Rutgers University Press, 1985). On the Unification Church, see E. Barker, *The Making of a Moonie: Choice or Brainwashing?* (Oxford: Blackwell, 1984). On the Findhorn Community, see P. Hawken, *The Magic of Findhorn* (London: Fontana/Collins, 1975). On Bugbrooke, see R. Curl, 'Three Christian Communities: A Sociological Study' (University of Oxford D.Phil. Thesis, 1976).

[3] For the general discussion of the relation of ideology and organization in minority religious movements, see B. R. Wilson (ed.), *Patterns of Sectarianism* (London: Heinemann, 1967).

attention, and appear almost as a challenge to investigative journalists intent on an exposé.

At the opposite extreme from sects which adopt communal life are those which concentrate their concern on the provision of one specific facility for salvation—most typically, an alternative therapy. It might be thought that such movements could operate with very little tension with the wider society, but this is not the case in practice. Challenge to any of society's institutional provisions is likely to bring a sect into conflict with the state, or with particular entrenched cadres—in these instances, with the medical profession, psychiatrists, and the Ministry of Health.[4] The modern state, whether a corporate state or a welfare state, whether totalitarian or liberal-democratic, does not readily accept unlicensed alternative agencies which provide facilities claimed to be superior to those of the state itself. Even the *laissez-faire* societies of the capitalist West, in which the promotion of privatization is extended to vital public services (transport, telecommunications, medicare, defence supply, education, for example), do not readily allow, much less approve, a radical challenge to the established scientific, technical, generally materialist assumptions embodied in the facilities and organization of modern institutions. Since sects always canvass more explicitly spiritual alternatives to one, some, or most of the institutions of the wider society, occasions of tension between sect and society, and more explicitly, between sect and state, are almost inevitable.

Not every sect seeks to be a total alternative society. Some, certainly, see their mission as providing an interim ethic for the world until the end of this dispensation and its displacement by an apocalypse and millennium.[5] Other sects see their role as being to 'build the Kingdom' on earth by instituting new ethical precepts for their followers. Still other movements—less committed to an eschatology or to post-mortem states—concern themselves with

---

[4] Thus the Church of Scientology became engaged in a running dispute with the Ministry of Health and with the National Association for Mental Health: see C. H. Rolph, *Believe What You Like* (London: Andre Deutsch, 1973); and R. Wallis, *The Road to Total Freedom: A Sociological Analysis of Scientology* (London: Heinemann, 1976), 204–5.

[5] On the relation of eschatology and morals in Seventh-day Adventism, see M. Pearson, *Millennial Dreams and Moral Dilemmas* (Cambridge: Cambridge University Press, 1990); and M. Bull, 'Eschatology and Manners in Seventh-day Adventism', *Archives de sciences sociales des religions*, 65 (1988), 145–59.

access to only a more limited form of salvation. Yet, there is a tendency at times, for groups which stand over against society to enlarge their claims, to generalize their points of distinction, and to apply more widely the legitimating principles which they invoke.[6] Sometimes, the principles which justify one particular claim (either to exemption from state demands, or privileged access to alternative facilities) are elevated into the much more general legitimations of a separated way of life. The early Mormons illustrate this tendency in their evolution of a distinctive—at certain times, communitarian—economic organization and their (subsequently abandoned) church school system.[7] The Seventh-day Adventists, in developing their educational system, their food factories, and (in America) even more conspicuously their extensive medicare facilities, provide another example. But even where such an elaborate network of alternative facilities has not been created, the attempt to defend the sect's peculiarities *vis-à-vis* the wider society has sometimes led to an extension of contention, either by the sect widening its demands for special accommodation, or by its withdrawal from a wider area of social involvement. Thus, Sikhs, after gaining the right to wear turbans and to be exempted from the law respecting safety headgear on motorcycles and as employees on public transport, eventually succeeded, in a most curious House of Lords judgment, in winning the right to wear this religiously prescribed headwear even in a Christian school. Christadelphians who, in World War I, contested the obligation to do military service, found that their arguments for exemption also entailed that, in all logic, they must in addition refuse to accept special constable duty and work in armaments factories.[8] In 1964, members of the Exclusive Brethren who were pharmacists sought exemption from membership of the Pharmaceutical Society: when refused by the House of Lords, the sect dissociated itself yet further from society by withdrawing membership from those who remained as practising pharmacists.[9]

[6] This point is made by R. Stark, 'Must All Religions be Supernatural?' in B. Wilson (ed.), *The Social Impact of New Religious Movements* (New York: Rose of Sharon Press, 1981), 159–77.

[7] For a general account, see L. J. Arrington, *Great Basin Kingdom: An Economic History of the Latter-day Saints 1830–1900* (Cambridge, Mass: Harvard University Press, 1958); and L. J. Arrington and Davis Bitton, *The Mormon Experience* (London: Allen and Unwin, 1979).

[8] On the House of Lords judgment, see Ch. 2 n. 18. On the Christadelphians, see B. R. Wilson, *Sects and Society* (London: Heinemann, 1961).

[9] The Pharmacy Bill, promoted in 1964, had the object of exempting Exclusive

Institutional Exemptions

The specific focuses of tension between sects and society may be broadly divided into issues on which the sect explicitly rejects the practices of the wider society, and issues on which the sect takes what might be called in contemporary vernacular 'affirmative action', that is to say, matters on which the sect seeks to put into operation its own distinctive values. Some of the activities and normal social obligations to which the sect objects are rejected for symbolic, some for intrinsic, reasons. Some are rejected for both. Whatever the grounds, the very fact of exercising conscious and deliberative choice respecting social arrangements may also, for at least some sects, constitute an important symbolic indicator of protest against the assumptions unquestioningly made by the generality of people. The items that are rejected, either on first principles, or in extension of them and in defence of the sect's separated circumstance, cover the whole range of society's institutions. We review them in sequence: defence, polity, economy, status, education, recreation, and health.

There is no consensus among Christians with respect to the obligation to bear arms for one's country, but pacifism is an ethical position that has been not infrequently asserted even among orthodox Christians. Not all sects are pacifist, but clearly participation in defence of the wider society may be seen as a considerable test of the extent to which the sect pursues an ideology contrary to that of the majority. Conscientious objection to military service proved a major source of controversy for several sects in Britain in World War I and, given the liberalization of social attitudes, to a lesser extent in World War II. When national feeling is high, the conscientious objector is likely to be an object of particular opprobrium. For the Bruderhof, in World War II, hostility was compounded by the fact of its German origins, to a point where the group decided to migrate to Paraguay. But pacifism pure and simple is not always the issue. Neither Jehovah's Witnesses nor Christadelphians are pacifists in the strict sense, although they are

Brethren who were practising qualified pharmacists from the requirement to be members of the Pharmaceutical Society. The Society was prepared to accept this arrangement and the Bill passed the House of Commons, but was rejected by the House of Lords: *Hansard*, House of Commons, 3 Mar. 1964, 690. 1138–9; 20 Mar. 1964, 691. 1949; 8 May 1964, 694. 1634; *Hansard*, House of Lords, 25 June 1964, 259. 321–30, 333–44; 6 July 1964, 259. 860–95.

conscientious objectors. Their objection is to fighting the wars of what have sometimes been called 'the sin powers' of this world: if a better cause were to present itself, as perhaps it might at Armageddon, then these sectarians would not hesitate to fight at Jesus's command. Here the objection is clearly symbolic and, if the cause is understood by outsiders, more likely to give rise to tension. There is, however, another function for a sect in counselling its members to object to military service: the maintenance of social distance and insulation.[10] Sectarians inducted into armies must suffer severe problems of maintaining a sense of apartness in the midst of a collectivity governed by completely alien mores, and in a system which (with even more compelling coercive power) is more emphatically totalitarian than even the most severe sect. Sects which, like the Seventh-day Adventists and some of the Brethren, reject the bearing of arms but permit non-combatant military service, may reduce the overall occasion for tension between the sect and society, but do so at the cost of increasing the experience of tension for those of their individual members who are conscripted for military service.

Bound, as are many Christian sects, by the word of the Scriptures to render unto Caesar that which is Caesar's, the interpretation of that dictum is, none the less, subject to considerable variation. Whatever general obligations of good citizenship might be accepted, and indeed enjoined, sectarians may also draw the line at even symbolic commitment to the support of the state. Jehovah's Witnesses make this most apparent in their refusal to sing national anthems and to salute national flags—although these interdictions have caused them greater difficulty in underdeveloped countries and in the United States than has been the case in Britain.[11] They, the Christadelphians, and Exclusive Brethren abstain from voting in political elections, as a further indication that they hold in contempt the rights which the state confers on its citizens. Such abstention is not in itself a cause of tension, of course, whereas the symbolic distantiation of refusing respect to the monarch might well be.

[10] For a fuller discussion, specifically related to the Christadelphians, see B. R. Wilson, 'Apparition et persistance des Sectes dans un milieu social en evolution', *Archives de sociologie des religions* 5 (Jan-June 1958), 140–50.

[11] For an account of the issue in the United States, see D. R. Manwaring, *Render unto Caesar: The Flag-Salute Controversy* (Chicago: University of Chicago Press, 1962).

Much as sectarians may hold themselves apart from the wider society in social and political activities, their attitude to economic matters is by no means so unequivocally a rejection of the practices, or even the values, of the wider society.[12] The economic orientations of sects are complex and widely variable, and we may distinguish between the economic ethic, economic associations, and economic occupations. The economic ethic espoused by each sect is by far the most complicated aspect of the response to this department of life.

Sects are by no means confined to a traditional espousal of the so-called Protestant ethic, although this may constitute a part of their dispositions. Since many sectarians eschew all contact with the wider society which is not absolutely necessary, and hold themselves apart from social activities, outside the life of the sect itself it is work which becomes the primary focus of everyday life. Like others, the sectarian must earn his living. Unlike some others, he is often committed to high principles of integrity, to keeping his word, fulfilling his obligations, maintaining his self-esteem, and proving that he is better than the generality of men and, by extension, that his faith is better than theirs. Work, in consequence, becomes a principal arena within which to give effect to these orientations, and a circumstance in which to demonstrate to others the values embraced in the sectarian way of life. Generally speaking, sectarians are committed workers, and such dedication, whilst it may at times provoke the distaste of others, does not usually create any particular social tensions. On the other hand, sectarians are not materialists and, with some exceptions (among the predominantly therapeutic sects), they are not likely to endorse achievement-orientation as such. Getting on in this world, whilst it certainly occurs as a consequence of diligence in some instances, is not a primary motivation of most sectarians. That can be seen in the rejection by many sects of any sort of training for the highest professions, as well as in strongly expressed ideas that one must not be conformed to this world, nor lured to lay up treasure where 'moth and rust doth corrupt'. It must be at once evident that members of communitarian groups have explicitly rejected the most effective ways of gaining personal wealth, whilst in other sects

---

[12] This point was cogently, if somewhat acidly, made by Mr Justice Walton in *Holmes and others* v. *Attorney-General*, High Court Chancery Division Group B 1979 H No. 1183, 11 Feb. 1981, 4 (see also *The Times* Law Report, 12 Feb. 1981).

it is often well understood that there are limits beyond which the acquisition and accumulation of personal wealth are not desirable. Thus, Jehovah's Witnesses often abandon well-paid posts and take up less rewarding part-time work in order to use their time in the work of door-to-door canvassing. Exclusive Brethren, whilst not infrequently becoming self-employed men with small businesses, none the less do not seek to enlarge their businesses beyond the point at which personal supervision and control is possible.

Decisions of this kind, whilst exposing sectarians to curiosity and perhaps ridicule, are not in themselves sources of social tension, but where a sect affirms a more radical vision of economic organization, such tension may arise. The Unification Church is committed to a new conception of economic activity and new patterns of economic organization: work must be appropriate to the building of the Kingdom which will be a transformed social order in the world.[13] In Britain, the Church's activities have not developed sufficiently for industrial plant or financial agencies to emerge, as they have in the United States, Latin America, Japan, and Korea, but there is another source of incipient social tension. Moonies, when engaged in fund-raising by selling literature on the streets, often work long hours and are recompensed only by communal board and lodging and minimal pocket money, and these arrangements have elicited sharp public criticism.

Occupations are also subject to some measure of discrimination among sectarians, but less on directly economic grounds, than on the grounds of desirability in the light of the sect's own ethic. Thus, Christadelphians would not be found as policemen or lawyers; Christian Scientists could scarcely be doctors and (although cases have been known) only with difficulty pharmacists. Entertainment, professional sport, and journalism would be seen as unsuitable areas of employment by many Pentecostal sects, among others, whilst the embargo on higher education found, for instance, among Jehovah's Witnesses, Exclusive Brethren, and the Hare Krishna movement, precludes various occupational possibilities. Although sectarians must make a living somehow, they are generally unlikely to regard making a living as a primary concern; their choice of

---

[13] For a brief account of the ideological element in the running of church-related business in the Unification Church, see D. Bromley, 'Financing the Millennium: The Economic structure of the Unificationist Movement', *Journal for the Scientific Study for Religion*, 24/3 (Sept. 1985), 253–75.

occupations is sometimes circumscribed by sectarian principles, and in the case of communitarian sects such as the Hare Krishna movement it is even more narrowly dictated.

Economic choices of this kind are not, however, a direct source of tension with the wider society, but the restriction on economic association may be. Membership in trade unions or employers' federations is prohibited by many sects. Seventh-day Adventists, Witnesses, Brethren, Christadelphians, and others eschew trade-unionism, and Brethren are no less firmly opposed to employers' federations and, indeed, to any organizations in which they would be joined in association with unbelievers. Legal actions brought by sectarians have been conspicuous in testing the rules of the 'closed shop', and in gaining for sectarians the right to work without being members of a trade union.[14] Such issues have been fiercely contested by trade unions, for whom the sectarian demand for liberty of conscience represents a fundamental challenge.

It follows from the general character of sectarian attitudes to work and economic occupations, that sects deliberately stand outside both the class structure and the status system of society. Sectarian beliefs diverge fundamentally from ideologies which emphasize class consciousness—a concern entirely alien to the sectarian *Weltanschauung*. Sects cannot be recruited for class action, and their general life circumstances and standards of comportment are themselves a radical denial of the cogency of class analysis. Sectarians consider themselves to know what their 'real interests' are, and these are not economic interests: their concern is salvation, whether it be envisaged as future bliss or contemporary safety and protection from evil.

Leaving aside members of gnostic or manipulationist sects which are usually preoccupied with therapeutic benefits, sectarians generally are disdainful of the status system of society. Sectarians have a different point of reference for assessing their position relative to others, and the general terms of social status are irrelevant. Indeed, they step aside from the conferment or the acceptance of social honour; and although, in a society in which many marked status distinctions have been eliminated, they can no longer make their rejection of status so pointed (as could seventeenth-century

---

[14] On the case in which Christadelphians established their right in appeal to the Industrial Tribunal to work without trade-union membership, see UK Industrial Tribunals Case No. 19377/76 and 19378/76 Folio No. 11/26/65.

Quakers with their use of the familiar form of address and their refusal to doff hats), none the less, the search for social honour beyond the confines of the sect is disavowed. Striving for status is regarded as a threat to sectarian integrity, as is indicated by the widespread practice of substituting for honorific titles the terms 'Brother' and 'Sister'. Among Exclusive Brethren status symbols (cars larger than strictly necessary, women's head-dress other than head-scarves) are specifically prohibited.

Understandably, it is in the ideational domain that sects experience perhaps most tension with the wider society. The modern liberal democratic state permits adult citizens to believe what they like, but the state is by no means so permissive with respect to the education of children. All sects have an evaluation of knowledge which diverges from that of the secular state and its institutions, and many of them reject the factual basis of some areas of the school and university curriculum. Some sects, notably Jehovah's Witnesses, Exclusive Brethren, and the Hare Krishna movement, discourage involvement in public education beyond the obligatory school age, being particularly distrustful of higher education (except perhaps in purely technical crafts and skills). Christian groups of a fundamentalist persuasion (and this accounts for many sects) disbelieve in evolution and the basic premisses of all the natural sciences and perhaps of all the social sciences. For these sects, arts subjects are often no less suspect, since literature in particular is perceived as purveying values contradictory of the moral injunctions of faith. Novels, plays, opera, and ballet are often distrusted, and in some movements subject to prohibition.[15] To some extent, the natural sciences, evolutionism apart, are more acceptable than the humanities, stained as these are with the alien values of secular history, profane and immoral people and pursuits, or the traditions of a church which is seen as an agency of corruption.[16]

There are sects which challenge general educational provision on only a narrow front. Seventh-day Adventists have a relatively highly educated membership, with a very high percentage of medically educated people in their ranks. Only in the limited areas of biblical

[15] As examples, see the account of the attitudes of Elim Pentecostalists and Christadelphians in Wilson, *Sects and Society*, pp. 85–8, 289–92.

[16] For a fuller discussion, see B. R. Wilson, 'Sectarians and Schooling', *School Review*, 72/1 (1964), 1–21.

understanding and in their disapproval of arts subjects are they disposed to challenge general educational wisdom. Christian Scientists have no quarrel with education as such but, and in this respect they have a position in common with other New Thought movements, they necessarily regard the traditions of rational empirical enquiry as of no more than limited value. These groups organize their own teachings as alternative bodies of knowledge; they do, however, imitate the language of science, and even replicate the general higher educational system in establishing grades, patterns of instruction, and lecturing programmes. These movements are less opposed to learning than fundamentalist sects (Pentecostal and Holiness movements, for example), which adopt an anti-intellectualist stance that contrasts sharply with the pseudo-intellectualism of sects which, in the service of their sectarian ideologies, imitate the structure and style of secular educational institutions and arrangements.

Sectarian caveats concerning the content of education have generally been resolved by the sect instilling in its young members the idea that sectarian truth is always to be accepted against secular wisdom, and by choosing to have their children exposed only for as long as is legally mandatory to those parts of general education to which the sect objects. In the optional areas of education, in religious instruction, in extra-curricular activities and recreation, sectarian scruple has more room for exercise, and in this area the distinctiveness of their religious positions becomes more obvious. Christadelphians, Jehovah's Witnesses, Exclusive Brethren, and Pentecostalists will generally seek to keep to a minimum the involvement of their children in such school activities as plays, sports, outings, holiday tours and clubs. For sects of this kind, the time is too precious to be 'wasted' on what are seen as frivolous pursuits: because the time is God's; because serious concern for religious matters is what counts; or because the advent is imminent, children are to shun voluntary involvements in school, and are to seek their friends and to spend their time elsewhere.

These attitudes to recreational activities in school are, of course, sustained in the home and the neighbourhood. Children are to keep themselves apart from all outsiders, and whilst play may not in itself be prohibited, most sects have some idea of what constitutes wholesome play and direct their children to that. Not uncommonly, books, games, puzzles, general knowledge quizzes, and jigsaw puzzles with religious themes are produced, so that play time may be instructional in religious facts and values. Secular entertainment is spurned for the most part, and although not all sects have firmly stated rules about such matters as watching television, or even attending the cinema and theatre, these things are carefully monitored, and overmuch indulgence is clearly perceived as being contrary to the religious ethos. Paradoxically, although recreation is in every sense an area of voluntary choice, it is precisely because sectarians do not choose what others choose, hold themselves apart in their use of leisure time, and—gnostic and therapeutic groups apart—associate only with each other rather than with non-members, that sects elicit some of the strongest reactions from the general public. The child-centred society is inclined to see prohibitions respecting children's play activities as wilful deprivation. These tensions may, however, also be fired by latent feelings of guilt on the part of parents who find it easier and pleasanter to indulge their children than to exercise discipline.

Finally, the ancient association of health and religion renders healing an issue of particularly acute tension for those sects that have teachings pertaining to bodily or mental health. By no means all movements espouse a special doctrine of healing. Some, such as the various Brethren bodies, regard the healing tradition of early Christianity as having been a particular faculty available only in the apostolic dispensation. The Seventh-day Adventists, whilst not entirely ruling out the possibility of healing by faith through God's will, gradually became so committed to medical missionary work that their ministry is, today, intimately associated with regular scientific attitudes to health as represented (marginal aspects of diet aside) by orthodox medicine. Jehovah's Witnesses, whatever biblically based theories they may have with respect to causation of illness, normally accept medical treatment—with the one important reservation which has caused recurrent difficulties for the movement, namely, their prohibition (since 1945) of blood transfusion.[17]

Faith-healing has had its advocates and practitioners in both the mainstream churches and sects, but some sects have made faith-healing a major claim to the credence of the public. Revival

[17] For a succinct account of Jehovah's Witness teaching concerning blood transfusion, see M. J. Penton, *Apocalypse Delayed: The story of Jehovah's Witnesses* (Toronto: Toronto University Press, 1985); 153–4.

campaigns have, in particular, been the occasions for demonstrations of faith-healing, but among Pentecostal sects, some of which were themselves spawned from revivalist traditions, faith-healing has been canvassed as a continuing faculty bestowed by God on some spiritual people, together with the exercise of the other gifts of the Spirit as described in 1 Corinthians 12.[18] A similar position is taken by the Restorationist (House Church) movement.[19] Today, faith-healing is rarely pressed to the point of conflict with medical practice, even though some sects, particularly among Pentecostal groups, formally urge their members to seek divine healing before having recourse to medicine, and regularly also claim divine cures in cases which have remained unrelieved by medical treatment. Spiritualist groups take much the same sort of stance towards orthodox medicine, and there has been controversy with the medical profession particularly when spiritual healers have sought (and sometimes gained) admission to hospitals from local health authorities.[20]

Movements which claim a special gnosis, as do Christian Science, New Thought movements, and Scientology, often also claim a special faculty of healing. Although curative theories differ, these groups tend to assert that true healing occurs only under their ministry and not by materia medica.[21] Christian Science, in time past, has been the most vigorous exponent of such a monopolistic theory of mental healing, and there have been serious cases in which practitioners of Christian Science have been in trouble with the law when their patients have died. Scientology is more narrowly concerned with the improvement of mental ability by the use of a psychotherapeutic technique which dissipates mental blocks. Claims for this technique have brought the movement into dispute with the public at large, the courts, and the Ministry of Health.[22]

[18] The teaching and attitudes of the Assemblies of God, the largest Pentecostal sect in Britain, are given in G. Allen and R. Wallis, 'Pentecostalists as a Medical Minority' in R. Wallis and P. Morley (eds.), *Marginal Medicine* (London: Peter Owen, 1976), 110–37.

[19] For a general, albeit popular, account of these movements, see A. Walker, *Restoring the Kingdom: The Radical Christianity of the House Church Movement* (London: Hodder and Stoughton, 1985).

[20] See G. K. Nelson, *Spiritualism and Society* (London: Routledge and Kegan Paul, 1969), 171–2.

[21] See on this point, A. E. Nudelman, 'The Maintenance of Christian Science in Scientific Society', in Wallis and Morley (eds.), *Marginal Medicine*, pp. 42–60.

[22] See Wallis, *Road to Total Freedom*, and Rolph, *Believe What You Like*.

These then, reviewed in relation to major institutional areas, are the ways in which sects seek exemption for their votaries from the general facilities and obligations of the wider society. In some measure, they have won gradual recognition for their distinctive claims to 'opt out' of a variety of activities, and in some parts of the world they have been significant contenders in establishing rights of conscience.[23] It is, however, less in those areas where sects seek exemption than in those matters in which they make an affirmative stance that tension has most markedly arisen. These issues have been outside the realm in which negotiation has had to be undertaken, and they manifest much more powerfully the sense of the distinctiveness of sectarian values. We may distinguish three general areas: public comportment; proselytizing; family relations, all of which bring a sect into situations in which public hostility may be awakened.

The Affirmative Sectarian Ethic

Except in the relatively rare circumstances in which a sect is vicinally isolated, its members of necessity conduct their business among the general public, and their comportment may become a matter for public scrutiny. Distinctive dress, speech, diet, and behaviour may mark out adherents from others. Hare Krishna devotees often adopt Indian costume; the Salvation Army dresses in uniform for public display; Exclusive Brethren, when going to meetings (which occur at least once daily), wear cardigans and open-necked shirts, and their womenfolk wear headscarves. Since the five-day week was instituted, the Saturday sabbath observance of Seventh-day Adventists and the Worldwide Church of God (the followers of Herbert Armstrong) is no longer the same source of the friction which, for employers, it once was. None the less these are all devices of boundary maintenance for the sect: devices which establish who is included but which also make clear who is excluded. By their use, social distance is reinforced.

It is, however, in proselytizing activity that sectarians become most obvious to society at large. Not all sects sustain a programme of the active canvass of outsiders, but those which do generally earn thereby an unfavourable reputation with the wider public.

---

[23] See Manwaring, *Render unto Caesar* and Penton, *Jehovah's Witnesses in Canada* in which a large number of legal cases are cited.

The techniques of Jehovah's Witnesses in their house-to-house 'witnessing', and of Mormon missionaries have been widely experienced. Hare Krishna adherents are often visible on the streets (although recently they have sometimes abandoned their distinctive apparel) and, in many big cities at least, many people have encountered Moonies. The obtrusiveness and the intrusiveness of all these groups is perhaps a major source of public irritation: movements which proselytize by less confrontational methods (for example by campaigns in public halls, leaflet distribution, and commercial radio evangelism) produce less tension. Even so, the very fact that sects are seeking to convert people gives rise to a vague disquiet among the public at large. People resist the idea that they ought to be changed, and attribute dubious motives to those who wish to effect such change. It is widely asserted, particularly by the relatives of converts, that those who have undergone a conversion experience have in some way been 'got at', have been misled, duped, taken advantage of, or have, in contemporary parlance, even been 'brainwashed'. Converts who later apostacize regularly explain their conversion in terms either of diminished personal responsibility ('they came when I was depressed'; 'under strain', 'experiencing difficulties') or of deception, exploitation, and manipulation. This is the limited repertoire of motives which allow the apostate to claim his own self-esteem and to reclaim his reputation with others.[24] The Press, the anti-cult organizations, and the de-programmers virtually rehearse reclaimed converts in these reinterpretations of their earlier religious choice.

Paradoxically, it may be noted in parentheses, minority religions are likely to suffer a bad reputation whether they are active in recruitment or not. Sects which do not actively seek new members—the Exclusive Brethren are the prime example—are regarded as secretive and as having something to hide:[25] those

[24] See A. D. Shupe, jun., and D. G. Bromley, 'Apostates and Atrocity Stories: Some Parameters in the Dynamics of Deprogramming', in Wilson (ed.), *The Social Impact*, pp. 179–215.

[25] This was the implication of the Court of Appeal judgment in 1982, in which the Brethren lost their case against Broxtowe Borough Council which had denied the Brethren exemption from local rates for their meeting-rooms on the grounds that, since no invitation was extended to the general public to participate in worship, these places did not constitute places of 'public worship'. The judges upheld this view, making some form of invitation to the public the decisive criterion of a place of public worship. Law Report 7 Dec. 1983, Court of Appeal, *The Times*, p. 17. See Ch. 4 below for an account.

which do seek to convert outsiders are seen as a threat to 'normal' life.

Family relations might be thought to be the most secluded area of social life, in which sectarians, like others, might enjoy privacy as security from interference. In practice, it is divergence in family-life patterns and norms which appears to arouse the greatest degree of tension between sects and the wider society, including the state. Within the family, sect members are free to live in accordance with their own moral norms, yet the very fact that their moral assumptions differ from those of society at large is a source of tension. History indicates that sects, because their moral codes differ, have often been accused of licentiousness. Some sects certainly have set conventional morality aside in the name of freedom, pleasure, or by adopting antinominian positions: the Rajneesh movement is the best-known of recent cases. The Children of God (later known as the Family of Love) clearly run counter to society's moral predilections, with their belief that truly to love one's fellow men the believer ought to extend to the outcast and lonely not only food, a caring disposition, but companionship, including, if need be, sexual compassion.[26] In Britain, certainly, sects of this type have been exceptional.[27] But it is not only sects which explicitly reject society's moral code which provoke tension by their unconventionality. Any institutionalized departure from the taken-for-granted values of the wider society may suffice to arouse indignation. Thus, Moonies are condemned at times—much as were Roman Catholic orders in late nineteenth-century Britain with respect to vows taken by neophytes—because converts commit themselves to a life of chastity until they marry: the ascetic sexual mores of most Christian sects are generally interpreted by journalists and media men as 'repression'. The inevitable

[26] On the Children of God, see R. Wallis, *Salvation and Protest: Studies of Social and Religious Movements* (London: Frances Pinter, 1979), 74–90; and D. E. Van Zandt, 'Ideology and Structure in the Children of God: A study of a New Sect, (University of London Ph.D. Thesis, 1985).

[27] A celebrated instance which no doubt to some extent lives on in folk memory (much as do Jonestown, the Charlie Manson cult, and Benjamin Purnell of the House of David in the United States) was the Agape Community at Spraxton, Somerset, led successively by Henry Prince and J. H. Smyth-Pigott. On this sect, there are only popular works: C. Mander, *The Reverend Prince and His Abode of Love* (Wakefield: EP Publishing, 1976); D. McCormick, *Temple of Love* (London: Jarrolds, 1962). On the House of David, see R. S. Fogarty, *The Religious Remnant* (Kent, Ohio: Kent State University Press, 1981).

conclusion is that it is not so much the actual content of their practice that causes sects to be objects of opprobrium and the focus of social tension, as the fact that they choose to take up decisive moral positions which differ from the relaxed indifferentism of the wider society.

In public disputes about sectarian practice, the allegation is often made that sects 'break up families'. This is a particularly frequent assertion in the mass media, and one that is sometimes taken up by politicians. Such tension is most often engendered by new movements—Moonies, Krishna people, or the Children of God—but the principle at issue is one known to many sects. When an individual joins a minority religious movement, he is likely to find the beliefs and the moral norms of his relatives no longer acceptable. He may then choose to live in closer association with his fellow religionists than with his kinsfolk, feeling religiously committed to a new lifestyle which replaces the habits and practices of his former life.[28] These are normal consequences when someone is converted to a religion that retains any of its pristine earnestness, rigour, and moral obligation. If the convert cannot persuade his parents, spouse, or children to embrace his new convictions, the charge is readily made that the religion itself is responsible for 'breaking up' that family. This crude interpretation of the situation meets the demand for sensationalism characteristic of the Press in its reporting of minority religions. Disagreement about religion or about the morality which faith enjoins may well cause people to go their separate ways: yet, it is perhaps a measure of the secularity of contemporary British society that separation or divorce in consequence of marital infidelity, incompatibility, or cruelty occasions much less public and media indignation than separation following religious disagreement.

There are, of course, other types of case in which this same charge of breaking up families is made. Sects such as Jehovah's Witnesses and Exclusive Brethren follow the practice, long since instituted among Methodists, Mennonites, and others (which, however, with their diminishing religious rigour, they have now largely or wholly abandoned), of banning, 'disfellowshipping', 'withdrawing from', or 'putting out' the wayward member.[29]

---

[28] For a detailed exposition, see Barker, *Making of a Moonie*.
[29] On practice among Jehovah's Witnesses, see Penton, *Apocalypse Delayed*, pp. 89–90, 299–300; for the Brethren, see Ch. 5.

Scientologists, too, albeit not on biblical grounds, have practised a not dissimilar form of 'disconnecting' relations with those they deemed hostile to their beliefs. These practices are fundamentally similar to Roman Catholic excommunication. When a member is put out, those remaining in the sect withdraw normal social intercourse in pursuit of biblical prescription on the subject. In a tightly knit sect, the wayward member is, of course, cut off from friends as well as from kinsfolk, and this is, no doubt, a severe punishment. The public, led by the Press, is quick to judge such action as too severe and to regard such cases (which are, however, relatively rare) as evidence that the sect 'breaks up' families, despite the self-evident fact that deliberately to break up families must be very much to the detriment of any religious body.

One other aspect of family relations in sects particularly incites attention: the upbringing of children. In a youth-orientated society, in which attitudes to children have become progressively more positive, and child-rearing ideologies increasingly permissive, the maintenance by sectarian families of more stringent discipline and of attitudes to children easily labelled 'Victorian', becomes a subject of vociferous complaint. Some sects—for instance, Christadelphians—inherit a hyper-Calvinist doctrine which, at least originally, maintained that before the age of discretion and believer's baptism a child had no prospect of afterlife salvation; and even though today Christadelphians themselves might demur about this teaching, it has undoubtedly shaped Christadelphian attitudes towards child-rearing. The occasions on which sectarian attitudes to children become public are not—certainly not—cases of indictment for cruelty. More typically they occur in two instances: when, because it is seeking to take advantage of tax concessions (seeking, that is, charitable status), a sect's general polity and policy is under review; or, more generally, when parents disagree about religion and the custody of their children is at stake. It is then commonly argued by the non-sectarian or ex-sectarian parent that he or she should have custody because, it is alleged, if left in the care of the sectarian parent, the child's upbringing and education would be seriously distorted. In the case of Exclusive Brethren, the burden of complaint is that their children are kept apart from others; are not given holidays or taken to places of entertainment; and that their education is terminated at the minimum age (except for narrowly technical courses). Much the same is said against

Jehovah's Witnesses, to which it is added that the children are deprived because the sect does not acknowledge Christmas and birthdays. Few issues arouse such strong sentimental concern, and although in recent years judges appear to have become less prejudiced, these items have been invoked in cases in which custody has been given to the parent leading an acknowledged immoral life simply because the other parent was of a sectarian persuasion.

Sources of Tension

The votaries of many sects do maintain standards of behaviour which excel those of both other religionists and secularists: they are generally punctilious in obeying the law, in the payment of taxes, in conscientiousness and integrity at school and work, but they are rarely given credit by the media, the courts, or the public for their orderly comportment. Such matters are not newsworthy, and their various good works—the hostels of the Salvation Army, the (much less extensive) Home Church work of the Moonies, and the reclamation of drug addicts and wastrels by many movements—go unsung. Sects are news only when they are objects of opprobrium. It is, of course, news reporting, with all its negativity, which forges public opinion—and at times even the opinion of judges. The pejorative language of the media in reference to sects has not been extensively studied in Britain, but there is no reason to suppose that it differs much in character, extent, and bias from that which has been revealed by scholars to be normally used by the media in Belgium and Italy.[30] Sects and new religious movements make news only when there is supposed scandal or sensation to report; in the 'human stories' of apostates or the anguish of parents about children exposed to sectarian influence (whether as converts or as offspring). Sects are a source for induced tension—of a kind unequalled even when children are drawn into or exposed to crime or drug addiction. Sectarianism is a negative issue, and news about

[30] K. Dobbelaere, G. Voet, and H. Verbeke, 'Neue religiöse Bewegungen im Spiegel der belgischen Presse' in J. Neumann and M. W. Fischer (eds.), *Toleranz und Repression: zur Lage religiöser Minderheiten in modernen Gesellschaft* (Frankfurt-on-Main: Campus Verlag, 1987), 230–44; and G. Ambrosio, 'Neue religiöse Bewegungen in Italien', ibid. 313–35, but on Britain see the analysis of J. A. Beckford and M. A. Cole, 'British and American responses to New Religious Movements', a paper delivered at XIX Conférence internationale de Sociologie des Religions, Tübingen, 1987.

it becomes almost serialized as what have been called 'negative summary events', in which negative stereotypes are carried forward from one news item to another.[31]

No outsider, least of all the detached sociological investigator, can consider any one sect—much less all sects—to be prescribing and practising the ideal way of life. There may be movements which merely pose as religions, and others which, although genuinely spiritual, succumb to devious measures and resort to ill-advised policies. That is to be expected. Overall, however, there can be no doubt that sects sustain levels of comportment which—according to the moral prescripts of society—are generally well above the average. Yet, the negative image that has been projected recently is such that the long tide of legislation which has steadily over three hundred years extended the measure of toleration to dissenters now appears to be in danger of being stemmed or even reversed. In the 1970s, the Charity Commissioners froze the charitable trusts of the Exclusive Brethren, and refused to allow them to register any new ones—a decision which the Brethren were finally able to overthrow in the courts.[32] Subsequently, one local government authority decided to levy rates on a Brethren meeting-room on the technicality that, since no invitation was issued to the public at large, the rooms were not places of public worship.[33] For three years the Attorney-General engaged in preliminary preparation to bring an action to challenge in the courts the charitable status of the Unification Church, before abandoning the project as insupportable. Yet, despite all this, there can be no vestige of doubt that both the Exclusive Brethren and the Unification Church are bona fide religions with highly devoted followings. What then induces these occasions of confrontation of government and sects? It can only be supposed that particular sections of an 'interested' public— apostates and, in the case of the Unification Church, anti-cult groups—have actively campaigned against these movements. They have been greatly aided by the Press, and the hostile climate produced in the wake of the People's Temple disaster at Jonestown,

---

[31]This term, coined by K. E. Rosengren, P. Arvidsson, and D. Sturesson in 'The Barsebäck Panic: A Case of Media Deviance' in C. Winick (ed.), *Deviance and the Mass Media* (Beverly Hills: Sage, 1978), has been employed effectively to characterize media coverage of many new religious movements by J. A. Beckford, *Cult Controversies* (London: Tavistock, 1985), 231–47.

[32] An account of this case and its background is presented below in Ch. 5.

[33] See n. 24 above.

Guyana. The Press is not always able to distinguish one movement from another, and readily and illicitly links events in one movement with those in other totally unrelated movements. Negative summary events are not always confined to accounts of one movement: they are easily transferred from one to others.

Even though the media in modern Britain have created a hedonistic climate in which sexuality (the individual's own or the reported sexual activity of others) has been virtually reinterpreted as entertainment, none the less, the intrinsic content of sectarian moral practice might create little hostility were it a strictly private option. For someone to lead an ascetic life is a matter of public (and media) indifference, but when a community or a movement sponsors such a life-style and canvasses it, then fear is engendered. Moral panic arises not only in the well-celebrated contexts of wayward, delinquent, and criminal deviance, but also even from the active example and advocacy of more rigorous conformity to traditional moral ideals than is sustained by the not-so-moral majority. For many, the sect is perceived as an affront, a godlier-than-thou commitment which they readily charge with hypocrisy, but which may awaken a latent sense of inadequate performance, guilt, and even moral envy among those who retain, as many may, half-conscious ideals of 'being good'. In consequence, the sect may be seen as a more explicit threat to the young than the amorphous, unorganized subcultures of easy sex, drink, drugs, and petty crime, simply because the sect is overt, organized, and legitimate, and active in its canvass.

The young sect seeks to challenge comfortable and conventional moral assumptions, and demands of the general public (in a way in which main-line churches do not) that they consider radically the meaning and purpose of living. It constitutes a moral minority in the body of a society in which there is moral flux, in which social organization is less and less underwritten by moral prescriptions and in which there is increasing tolerance of dispositions once labelled 'immoral'. The sect emerges as a type of reassertion of community values in which moral consensus—albeit sometimes in totalist mould—is re-established. In any but a fully *laissez-faire* society tension between such a moral minority and the amoral majority is likely to recur.

4

Old Laws and New Religions

'DISCRIMINATION' is a word that, in recent decades, has acquired distinctly pejorative connotations, and modern societies, at least in the West, have made laws to prohibit discrimination in various departments of social life. It might be supposed, particularly in light of recurrent international expression at the very highest political levels that even in matters of religion, formal discrimination had finally become a thing of the past. If men have the right, as these international tribunals proclaim, freely to believe, practise, and teach whatever religion that each of them chooses, it may well be supposed that complete religious equality has been attained. Citizens may claim equal rights regardless of their religion, and different religions are said to be equal before the law with respect to the facilities that they may enjoy and the rights that they may exercise.

The empirical evidence, however, is that in few countries, if any, is such equality the reality. It is perhaps most nearly approached in societies that are formally secular—secular, that is, in the sense of being committed to official neutrality in religious matters, as is the United States of America. It is perhaps furthest from attainment in societies that are constitutionally secularist—that is, anti-religious, as in the Soviet Union—or in societies that are constitutionally committed to the support of one religion, as is Pakistan. The consciously created state—such as the United States—may, after all, order its affairs in accord with abstract, rational principles, but most modern states—those of Western Europe, for instance—are what may be designated as continuing societies, not consciously created so much as merely evolving from pre-political systems. These societies inherit a customary commitment to a particular tradition of religious faith which is identified with the political, social, and cultural patterns of the people's way of life. That religion may have acquired formal legal status and—often by a process of the accretion of custom, as well as by legal enactment—may have accumulated a wide variety of privileges and assumed, unchallenged, and even automatic rights. Such religions, understandably enough, are preferred religions, enjoying advantages not available to other faiths, or, if available, then available only as concessions. The rational principle of religious equality is almost everywhere qualified by the actual historically determined practices, procedures, and dispositions of each society and of its people. The law in any country is not quickly responsive, and perhaps not at all responsive to those bland and unexceptionable pronouncements, somewhat facilely promulgated by international organizations, which commend religious freedom on the basis of abstract, general, rational, and liberal assumptions about what a society might be like.

Beyond this disparity between the exhortative formal resolutions of international bodies on the one hand, and social actuality on the other, lies the question of just what constitutes a proper religion. To propose the general principle of religious non-discrimination presupposes that we all agree what religion is, what it requires, and what constitutes religious belief, practice, and organization. Obviously, in all modern democratic societies there is an acknowledged measure of religious diversity. The range of variation of what is often called religious pluralism is considerable in countries like the United States, Australia, and Britain, but much more marginal in countries such as Belgium or Sweden. But even states which accept in principle the idea of religious pluralism may define it within parameters limited by historical considerations from which the contemporary situation is relatively remote. Beyond these parameters lie the penumbral areas of alien religion and quasi-religion.

The issues bring liberal, albeit abstract, principles into direct contention with concrete, historical, and traditional cases. In some measure, this confrontation occurs in all societies, even those in which political revolution has facilitated total constitutional revision and the endeavour to formulate state laws in accordance with rational principles. But these issues are particularly acute in societies in which evolution rather than revolution has been the pattern of social development—and perhaps nowhere are they more apparent than in Britain, where old laws and new religions today experience an uneasy coexistence. The diversification of religious expression and belief is ill accommodated by the existing laws, but there is little likelihood—pressure on parliamentary time being what it is—that new legislation will be enacted. England is a society torn between the egalitarian principles that proceed on assumptions of formal rationality that all religions are to be treated equally, and the actual received tradition of one entrenched and privileged religion, in relation to which all other faiths are, in a sense, merely tolerated and implicitly regarded as misguided, wayward, inferior, or errant forms of faith. The English law courts, today, regularly affirm that the law does not discriminate among religions, but deals with each impartially. In fact, as I shall seek to show, impartiality is quite impossible, given the historical context of the assumptions on which much English law relating to religion was—and continues to be—based. Those assumptions are implicit where they are not explicit, both in statute law and in the body of case law and interpretation of statutes which constitute so large a part of the English legal tradition.

The religion described as 'by law established' in England is that of the Church of England, of which the reigning monarch is the temporal head. Twenty-four bishops and two archbishops of the Church have seats in the House of Lords, the upper house of the legislature, and the state is involved (albeit less so than formerly) in the appointment of bishops in the Church. Although not supported by taxation or by financial assistance from the state, the Church of England enjoys special status and the prestige of its historical pre-eminence and association with the monarchy as the official church of the nation. Over three centuries since the first Toleration Act of 1689, many of the provisions which, for the Church of England, were presumptive rights, have been accorded by formal legal enactment as privileges and concessions to other religious bodies. Among these privileges are the protection of the law from interference with religious services; the right to conduct marriages on their own premises according to their own rituals; to exemption from local taxes on their property, for which properties of the Church of England are automatically exempt; and, by registering their trusts as religious, and hence as charitable, to escape most forms of national taxation. To qualify for these concessions, all self-styled religions, which historically, and in the legislation still, are alluded to as 'nonconformist' or 'dissenting', must be able to establish their credentials as bona fide religious organizations.

My discussion focuses on a limited range of concessions for which religious bodies in England might qualify, which are, however, automatically conferred as rights to that church which is by law established. Although the issues themselves may appear to be of very limited consequence—may indeed, when set in the wider context of religious and political liberty, appear as trivial—none the less, they constitute a prism through which the spectrum of issues of vital importance to religion in modern society may be perceived. Clearly, in a liberal democratic society the laws do not prescribe what people shall or shall not believe. In this sense, there is religious freedom and equality. Within the limits of the common criminal law, people are free to engage in activities in pursuance of their beliefs and in the open attempt to persuade others to believe and to act similarly. The law becomes involved only in respect of the extension to each religious body of the privileges that various enactments have made available for religions which establish their eligibility.

The situation, and the problems which arise, are similar to those of other countries: the law becomes involved either in defining religion or in according recognition to associations which claim to be religious. That this type of concessionary law is open to abuse is evident, as became apparent in post-war Japan, where liberal laws permitted a large number of organizations to register as religions, even though they were in fact businesses, laundries, or restaurants using 'religion' as a front in order to obtain tax concessions. Japanese law was subsequently changed to eliminate these bogus organizations. However, even while putting aside such flagrant abuse of law, the determination of what is legitimately religious remains a serious issue. Commercial activities *per se* certainly do not necessarily establish a case against an organization, since many churches engage in commercial and even financial activities of one kind or another: the issue turns on quite different, less directly forensic, and more explicitly sociological considerations.

What an English court of law must do in determining the application of these laws is to apply the formulations of legal statutes by interpreting the actual intentions of the legislators with due regard to the ways in which those intentions have been interpreted in earlier litigation. In the case of religion, however, it is apparent that what English lawmakers often had in mind was a provision of far narrower application than the range of instances to which the law is now applied. At the time when the various statutes affecting religion were passed, the diversity among religious bodies in England was much less than it is today. Those laws assumed that, although there were various forms of 'dissent' and 'nonconformity', virtually all of them were, none the less, confined within the Christian tradition, and that Christian precepts and concepts were applicable. The terminology was Christian, or at least monotheistic. The courts have not infrequently said that it is not their business to define religion, and they have at times openly acknowledged their lack of competence to do so, and yet judges must apply laws which assume that courts know what constitutes religion and its attendant phenomena. Again and again, the courts find themselves seeking expert advice about particular 'self-styled' religious movements, with a view to determining whether they are religious and whether the principle implicit in particular laws—laws which quite clearly conceived of religion much more narrowly—can be said to apply to them.

The privileges for which religious organizations are eligible in England are:

1 charitable status, which allows the organization to operate without being subject to most forms of national direct taxation;
2 exemption for their religious buildings from payment of local taxes (rates);
3 the licensing of buildings to permit the performance therein of marriages in accordance with the religious rites of that particular religious organization;
4 registration of buildings as 'places of religious worship' which is in itself a prima facie claim to other privileges.

To extend these privileges to a particular organization the appropriate authorities must be satisfied on various points. The authorities concerned, however, are not one centralized department of state: they are discrete and separate agencies which do not work in conjunction with each other. Registration is a matter for the director of Population Censuses and Surveys, the Registrar-General, who must be satisfied that the organization is religious, and that its buildings are used for activities that he regards as 'religious worship', before he will register a building. Dependent on such registration is the facility for the organization to employ its own officials to conduct legally binding marriage ceremonies for its members. Registration will influence (but not dictate) the decision of local government officers with respect to granting exemption from payment of local rates. Those local government agencies enjoy a certain autonomy in rating decisions, although they may be influenced by general policies pronounced by the government through its Department of Environment. Charitable status is granted by yet another agency—the Charity Commissioners, a separate, quasi-legal body, which is independent of government control—and is awarded to a trust set up by a religious body providing that it promotes religious instruction. Recognition as a charity confers the major tax concessions that are available to religious organizations.

Many of the cases that have been brought before the courts have been brought by organizations seeking to be declared 'religious' and to have their religious services recognized as worship. Thus courts have to settle how 'religion' is defined and what is conceived to constitute 'public religious worship'. When charitable status is disputed, the courts apply various criteria, which have grown up over the course of hundreds of years. They are not logically set forth; they overlap and are interdependent, and lack suitable external and objective points of reference. If charitable status is to be conferred, it must be possible first to declare a movement to be a religion: but no exhaustive or definitive indicia of religion are incorporated in the law itself. In general, the case has been satisfied by showing that the beliefs of a movement may be said to be 'monotheistic'. Whatever else may constitute religion (and the courts are hesitant about all else) the courts accept that monotheism is religion. The second criterion is that the movement's beliefs and practices should not be 'subversive of all religion and morality'. Disregarding the contradiction between a positive finding for the first desideratum and the possibility of applying neutrally the whole of the second, it is clear that if the courts consider that a movement subverts morality (however that may be defined) then they will declare that it cannot qualify for charitable status. Thus, to obtain charitable privileges, the activities of the organization must be ruled to be for the public benefit, and the law assumes that whatever conduces to advancing religion is, indeed, for the public benefit.

The question of what constitutes 'public worship' is handled in a way which is also beset with difficulties. Worship is held to consist in attitudes of submission, reverence, adoration, and actions which manifest these dispositions, as well as acts of propitiation and prayer. The law dictates that certain privileges are accorded only if what is undertaken is *public* worship, however, and what, in effect, has been disputed before the courts has been whether this phrase means 'for the public', 'by the public', 'in public', or by a group 'of the public' who, however, are self-selected. The points of contention in all these various issues have been brought to the attention of academic advisers to the courts—comparative religionists and sociologists of religion. The courts have heard them but, inevitably, since there is much to dispute, they have not always heeded them.

The Definition of 'Religion' by the Courts

Judges have at various times acknowledged their incompetence to settle the matter of what constitutes religion: none the less, they must come to some sort of decision in order to settle each specific case. They have laboured with various biases, particularly that of strong religious conviction: there is no doubt that the original legislators, in extending privileges that were once the monopolistic prerogative of the Church of England, also had very limited ideas of how far a religion could deviate from that of the Anglican Church if it was to be counted as a religion at all. Although charitable trusts include the advancement of religion as one of the legitimate and eligible goals of a charity, in effect at times that goal has been so narrowly interpreted that 'religion' has been taken to mean 'Christianity', and Christianity has at times been taken to mean Anglicanism. Thus in 1754, Lord Hardwicke ruled that the teaching of Judaism was not a charitable object, and applied the funds which the testator had left to provide instruction in Judaism instead to the provision of instruction in Christianity (*De Costa* v. *De Paz*). Commenting on this decision in a subsequent case (*Re* Bedford Charity, 1819), Lord Eldon concluded that 'it is the duty of every single judge presiding in an English Court of Justice, when he is told that there is no difference between worshipping the Supreme Being in Chapel, Church or Synagogue, to recollect that Christianity is part of the law of England'. That that spirit is not entirely dead became apparent in the way Lord Comyn commented in the libel action brought by the Moonies against the *Daily Mail* in 1981, but judges have reduced this bias steadily over the years. Yet the 'bias' (I use the word neutrally) is legitimate in the sense that it is often evident in the legislation itself—and was built into the intentions of legislators. In *Bowman* v. *Secular Society* [1917] AC 406, 429, 443, the House of Lords ruled that it was not criminal or unlawful to deny Christianity, and allowed a gift to the Secular Society to be valid, but, in appraising the general situation, one of the *obiter dicta* of Lord Parker was that 'a trust for the purpose of any kind of monotheistic theism would be a good charitable trust'. In so saying, he echoed the principles advanced by Lord Macnaghten for charitable trusts; the law had come to recognize that 'any form of monotheistic theism is a religion'.

Monotheism however is not regarded by comparative religionists or sociologists of religion as an exhaustive definition of religion, and the English courts have not as yet explicitly recognized non-theistic (or polytheistic) faiths to be religions. Although religious bodies of these persuasions may actually enjoy privileges granted to religions, whether they would be confirmed in these privileges if they were challenged at law is unclear. When pressed, the courts return to formulae which apply to Christianity, Judaism, and Islam, but not to the other great world religions. They say, as said Dillon J., 'It seems to me that two of the essential attributes of religion are faith and worship: faith in god and worship of that god'—to which he added the definition given in the *Oxford English Dictionary*, 'A particular system of faith and worship . . . Recognition on the part of man of some higher unseen power as having control of his destiny, and as being entitled to obedience, reverence, and worship.'[1] The inclusion of 'worship' and the references to 'a god' indicate that cultural bias, and historical bias, still persist in judicial thinking. Of course, it could certainly be said that such bias was also in the minds of the legislators who have framed the various laws, so that judges, wittingly or otherwise, endorse the intention and the specific meaning of those who made the law, as they are obliged to do. Yet, they continue to affirm the principles of impartiality of the law as among various religions. They affirm, and regularly reaffirm in these cases the principle that 'As between different religions, the law stands neutral',[2] and that 'The Court does not favour one religion more than another. The Court is not a tribunal equipped to determine whether the doctrines of any branch

---

[1] *Re* South Place Ethical Society: *Barralet* v. *Attorney-General* [1980] IWLR 1565.
[2] Lord Reid, *Gilmour* v. *Coats* [1949] AC 426, 458.

of the Christian Church, or any Christian denomination or sect, or any non-Christian religion are true or false and does not attempt to decide that question.'

The law in England affects and may also be affected by legal decisions in those other countries which have similar legal systems, and decisions elsewhere respecting the charitable status of religion have been settled on very much broader principles of interpretation of the law than have cases in England. Thus, in Australia[3] the High Court sought to come to grips with the issues in a spirit manifestly more liberal than any judgment that has as yet come from English courts. In that case, Mason A. C. J., and Brennen J. acknowledged that minority religions had to be protected. They declared:

The chief function in the law of a definition of religion is to mark out an area within which a person subject to the law is free to believe and to act in accordance with his belief without legal restraint . . . Religion is . . . a concept of fundamental importance to the law . . . A definition cannot be adopted merely because it would satisfy the majority of the community or because it corresponds with a concept currently accepted by that majority . . . The freedom of religion being equally conferred on all, the variety of religious beliefs which are within the area of legal immunity is not restricted.

They held that

for the purposes of the law, the criteria of religion are twofold: first, belief in a supernatural Being, Thing, or Principle; and second, the acceptance of canons of conduct in order to give effect to that belief [though canons of conduct which offend against ordinary laws are outside the area of any immunity, privilege, or right conferred on the grounds of religion].

They further maintained that even if a religious leader were a sham and a charlatan this would not invalidate the fact that his followers had a religion:

charlatanism is a necessary price of religious freedom, and if a self-proclaimed teacher persuades others to believe in a religion which he propounds, lack of sincerity or integrity on his part is not incompatible with the religious character of the beliefs, practices, and observances accepted by his followers.

In the same case, two other judges, Wilson and Deane JJ. set out several indicia of religion, after having rejected the idea that a

---

[3] High Court of Australia, *Church of the New Faith and Commissioner for Payroll Tax*, Oct. 1983.

supernatural being was an essential element of religion. They declared that the indicia of religion must be discovered from empirical observation of accepted religions and said:

One of the more important indicia of 'a religion' is that the particular collection of ideas and/or practices involves belief in the supernatural, that is to say, belief that reality extends beyond that which is capable of perception by the senses. If that be absent, it is unlikely that one has 'a religion'. Another is that the ideas relate to man's nature and place in the universe and his relation to things supernatural. A third is that the ideas are accepted by adherents as requiring or encouraging them to observe particular standards or codes of conduct or to participate in specific practices having supernatural significance. A fourth is that, however loosely knit and varying in beliefs and practices adherents may be, they constitute an identifiable group or identifiable groups. A fifth . . . is that the adherents themselves see the collection of ideas and/or practices as constituting a religion . . . All of these indicia are satisfied by most or all of the leading religions: it is unlikely that a collection of ideas and/or practices would properly be characterized as a religion if it lacked all or most of them . . .

It is clear that the thinking of these judges reflects both an awareness of the existence in society of a much wider range of religious commitment and belief (than was acknowledged in legislation) and also that the way in which to interpret the law must have regard both to sociological evidence and to sociological methods of enquiry (empirical observation of social phenomena). Yet it is also clear, in the English case, that if the function of judges is to interpret law in accordance with the intentions of legislators, then in England, a much narrower conception of religion might be said to be appropriate, until such time as laws themselves are repealed and new ones made.

Definitions of 'Worship' by the Courts

Two issue have arisen for different religious groups in recent years which have involved the courts in definitions of 'worship'. Organizations may obtain privileges by having their buildings registered as places of religious worship, and by being recognized as places of 'public worship' by local government authorities. In 1970, the Church of Scientology brought a court action to cause the Registrar-General to register as a place of 'religious worship' one of their chapels, which he had previously refused to do. The court ruled that the Registrar-General was certainly not bound to accept the word of those seeking registration that their organization did indeed constitute a religion. In that case Lord Denning said:

We have had much discussion on the meaning of the word 'religion' and of the word 'worship' taken separately, but I think we should take the combined phrase 'place of meeting for religious worship' as used in the statute of 1855. It connotes to my mind a place of which the principal use is as a place where people come together as a congregation or assembly to do reverence to God. It need not be the God which the Christians worship. It may be another God, or an unknown God, but it must be reverence to a deity. There may be exceptions. For instance, Buddhist temples are not properly described as places of meeting for religious worship. But apart from exceptional cases of that kind it seems to me the governing idea behind the words 'place of meeting for religious worship' is that it should be a place for the worship of God. I am sure that would be the meaning attached to those who framed this legislation in 1855.[4]

And Lord Justice Buckley opined:

Worship I take to be something which must have some at least of the following characteristics: submission to the object worshipped, veneration of that object, praise, thanksgiving, prayer, or intercession . . . I do not say that you would need to find every element in every act which could properly be described as worship, but when you find an act which contains none of these elements it cannot, in my judgment, answer to the description of an act of worship.

The partiality of the law in this instance is clear: it conceives that 'worship' must imply an object of worship. Yet 'worship' is not an unchanging phenomenon in society. As conceptions of deity change, so do conceptions of worship, and in movements which do not proclaim a supreme being—Buddhism for example—what is done at religious gatherings is clearly not 'worship' in this narrow sense of the term. The language in which the term 'worship' is current is language of a particular culture and particular time-period. The term is built into various laws, but religious activities come to take on a different nature, no longer encompassed by the term 'worship' as traditionally understood. Concepts change: worship once involved sacrifice, but were any religious group today to seek to reinstitute sacrificial forms of worship, they would

---

[4] R. v. *Registrar-General Ex parte Segerdal* [1970] 2 QB 697.

assuredly fall foul not only of the law relating to the registration of religious buildings, but of the criminal law itself. Yet, our laws relating to what constitutes religious practice are stuck with a time-bound and culture-bound set of assumptions about the necessary character of religious activities.

Lord Denning acknowledges that Buddhism may be an exception, and Buddhist temples *are* registered and exempted from rates in England. But why should there be exceptions: if one exception be granted, does this not open the way for others? Or does it imply that the very basis of assumption on which the law rests has become, with the passage of time, unduly narrow? Again, it must be evident that not all Christian groups undertake worship in the form postulated by Lord Justice Buckley and yet they enjoy privileges of registration and rating exemption. Quakers provide a cogent example of a sect which does not meet to supplicate, praise, give thanks, or manifest submission to a deity. Christian Scientists provide an example of a movement in which the idea of deity is considerably de-anthropomorphized, as Mind, Principle, Spirit, to which older conceptions of ritualized worship are clearly inappropriate. Contemporary Protestant theologians redefine God in impersonal terms, as an ultimate concern, a ground of being, and explicitly reject the idea of a personal God 'out there': with such changed conceptions, traditional notions of worship become anachronistic. The term 'worship' implies a personal relationship— a sense of personal commitment and obligation. It characterizes personal dispositions and becomes inappropriate when the personal element disappears from the prevailing conception of the super-natural. Even the general public, when its reactions can be assessed (for instance, however inadequately, by opinion polls) steadily abandons ideas of a personal God in favour of conceptions of a more abstract kind. In the recent survey of European Values, covering ten European countries, it was shown that although 75 per cent of people professed belief in God, only 32 per cent professed belief in a personal God: the majority of believers conceived of God as some type of abstract agency. Abstractions do not require worship: is there not something incongruous about worshipful acts to an impersonal force?

The other recent case affecting worship relates to the Exclusive Brethren. One local government authority in England disputed in the early 1980s whether Brethren meeting-halls were in fact places of public worship, on the grounds that outsiders were given no indication that the halls were used for worship—there was no sign, no notice-board, or other indication: they held that these halls were, in effect, places of private worship and hence, ineligible for exemption. Whereas older legislation affecting dissenters gives the impression that any such self-designated congregation might in itself constitute a sufficient 'public', recent legislation (perhaps influenced by the laws on charities which, however, were not specifically at issue in this case) implies that 'public' means open to the public, in some sense providing a public benefit. In earlier cases, it had already been established that the rituals of an enclosed order are not charitable since they fail to amount to public benefit,[5] and that the rituals of such an order do not constitute public worship.[6] It was established in the Mormon Temple case[7] that 'public worship' must be something more than the congregational worship of an existing community. The Temple was ineligible for rating exemption because it 'was not open to the public at large but only to a selected class of the Mormon sect known as "Mormons of good standing"'. Lord Reid said: 'In my view, the conceptions of public religious worship involves the coming together for corporate worship of a congregation or meeting or assembly of people, but I think that it further involves that the worship is in a place which is open to all properly disposed persons who wish to be present.' The Brethren, however, were not enclosed, did admit members of the public who turned up, even though they certainly did not issue a general invitation nor especially encourage outsiders to attend. The Court ruled that there must be some form of invitation for religious worship to constitute 'public religious worship'. Lord Justice Stevenson said:

worship must be made public . . . there must be signs to indicate at least the place is a place of religious worship . . . and that the public would not be trespassing if they entered but have permission, expressed or implied, to go there. Such signs may be given by the building itself . . . Many, if not most, churches, and chapels, indicate their nature and the nature of what goes on inside them by their style of architecture or religious symbols or the ringing

[5] *Gilmour* v. *Coats* [1949] AC 426, 458; and also *Cocks* v. *Manners* (1871) 12 Equity 574.
[6] *Association of Franciscan Order of Friars Minor* v. *City of Kew (Australia)*, Victoria Law Reports [1944] 199.
[7] *Henning* v. *Church of Jesus Christ of Latter-Day Saints* [1964] AC 420.

of a bell, as well as by notices of services on a notice board, or in leaflets or a newspaper, or by speakers preaching and appealing to the public in the open air or by house to house calls.

As will be evident, many of the 'signs' are indeed specific to the Christian religion: and yet, Britain is now a multi-religious society in which the meeting-places of many faiths do not at all resemble a church, nor are in the habit of announcing their activities either by bell or printed notice.

Other groups could be affected by this Appeal Court decision respecting the Brethren. Ultra-orthodox Jews would not welcome the 'unclean' into their synagogues, yet those synagogues are exempted from the rates. On the basis of this decision, they have no claim for exemption—although no doubt they will continue to receive it since local government is unlikely to take action, particularly since these Jews are highly concentrated in certain districts. Similarly, Zoroastrians, of whom there is a community in London, would have no claim to exemption, since their movement is entirely closed—outsiders cannot join, and no one can be converted to a faith where all participants are of necessity inborn.

Thus, although the law claims not to distinguish between one sect and another, it is apparent from these cases that there is a historical inbuilt bias. The Acts by which privileges were conferred were concessions, extending little by little to other religious groups the privileges once enjoyed by the Church of England alone. But the ecclesiastical principles on which the Church of England was formed differ radically from those on which sects came into being (or which are implicit in the Asian religions which now flourish in England). The polity of the Church of England was Erastian: it was assumed that everyone belonged or 'ought to belong'. Sects, on the contrary, were self-selected dissenters. The Church of England conceived of itself as having a 'public service' commitment in its activities—the Church prayed for the nation. Sects, in contrast, provided for those who deliberately stood apart: they never regarded themselves as committed to provide for everyone. Even those sects which were anxious to recruit—and this is not a universal feature of sects—did not expect to recruit everyone. They conceived of themselves as standing apart from the wider society; they had an implicit minority consciousness as a 'gathered remnant'. It is evident that the law actually prefers certain types of sect because of the assumptions it makes about the public nature of worship—assumptions rooted in Anglicanism. If a sect is concerned to convert the public, it is shown greater favour at law: sects which are not interested in converting outsiders are the ones likely to fall foul of the law relating to exemption from rates, and to have more difficulty in claiming charitable status. Oddly, although the law prefers proselytizing sects, this can scarcely have been the preference of the Church of England or of the legislators (most of them undoubtedly members of that Church): the intention of the legislators can hardly have been to provide preferential privileges specifically for those sects most actively working in competition with the Church of England. One other contradiction may be noticed in passing: the Law Courts have recognized the Exclusive Brethren as a body entitled to charitable status, because their religious work is counted as for the public benefit, and so exempted from national taxation; but the Appeal Court dealing with the separate issue of exemption from local rating, rejected the idea that worship in Brethren meeting-halls was 'public' and denied them local exemption from rates. Thus whilst the High Court dealing with the charitable status of the Brethren regarded their activity as for the public benefit, the Appeal Court hearing the entirely separate case respecting their places of public worship regarded their worship as being insufficiently for the public benefit to qualify for exemption from local taxes. (For the record, it may be noted that subsequently the Brethren modified their practice, and erected notice boards indicating that their meeting-rooms were places of public worship.)

In Conclusion

The cases that have tested the laws pertaining to religion in England have not all arisen from religions that are very new. Some continue to arise from older and more traditional sects, but the new religious movements are likely to present a more radical challenge to the various laws that pertain to religion—laws so randomly scattered and so lacking in consistency that they cannot remotely be designated as a 'legal framework', much less a 'legal system'. Religious choice can be expected to widen as modern populations become increasingly detached from specific geographical locations and distinctive historical roots. That detachment from indigenous culture has many causes, not least among them the processes of migration from one country and one culture to another, and the rapid acceleration of social, geographic, and diurnal mobility within a given country. The idea that a given people inherit a common culture and a common religious tradition becomes more and more of a fiction, yet it is a fiction embodied within the law. The radical contemporaneity of modern mass media of communications, the decline in the general influence of the past over the present, and the future-orientation of modern institutions makes ever more questionable the concepts entrenched in legal enactments and promotes an inevitable process of legal obsolescence. The law becomes less and less relevant to actual social phenomena, but it remains remarkably durable.

We may perceive two simultaneous processes at work. Rational principles are increasingly advocated and, since they confirm the patterns of social organization that are everywhere advancing, these precepts are taken as normative. At the same time, there are persistent demands that innovative systems of belief and practice that define themselves as religious should be banned, restricted, or disprivileged. (We need only to recall such cases as the restrictions imposed on Scientology in Victoria, South and Western Australia, England, and the United States; or the recent history of the Rajneeshis in India and America; the police raids on Moonie premises in France; the curious indictment of the Revd Moon on tax charges in America; and the sustained efforts to preclude unpopular movements from the concessionary privileges that are notionally available to all religions.) Attitudes and episodes such as these will no doubt recur, but, given the current processes of social change, they rest on the basis of cultural assumptions that are increasingly dubious.

One facet of this problem which is refracted through the prism which the law holds up to social phenomena, is that the bodies which, in any normal sociological usage, conform to the designation 'religious', fall outside the reference of those rather limited, culturally determined concepts that are built into the law (and to some extent into everyday usage). The law tends to have a limited view, requiring that all religions be necessarily recognizable by reference to established or received traditions: thus, the law of England maintains its distinct monotheistic bias with its attendant assumptions about the necessary style and forms of religious activities, entrenched in the law as 'worship'. Only with the employment of more abstract categories, capable of subsuming a range of intrinsically somewhat divergent, but in principle functionally similar phenomena, will parity before the law be achieved for different religious groups. If equality before the law is what is sought—and the judges themselves have regularly endorsed the idea that the law is neutral with respect to religion—then, culturally specific terms like 'deity', 'worship', and all the connotations of anthropomorphism will need to be replaced by more encompassing abstract concepts.

One might, however, raise one further question. Is absolute equality before the law—whatever the lip-service to the concept—always what is wanted in respect to religion? One can envisage two radically divergent positions: the formally rational position adopted by high-level (but remote) international agencies: that as all men are to be regarded as equal, their religions also should be so regarded. The simplest solution for the legal approach to religion for those of this persuasion would be for all religious privileges to be swept away, permitting the law to abandon the attempts to decide on concessions by defining what qualifies as 'religion' or as 'worship'. The alternative, conservative contention is to suggest that it is appropriate that the law of any country should seek to reinforce historical cultural values, the spiritual inheritance of the people, and to protect these in the face of the mounting pluralism of what might be held to be morally disruptive phenomena which bring uncertainty, contradiction, and unrest in the religious and cultural sphere. In continuing, as distinct from created societies (in Europe as distinct from the United States) there is a persisting cultural tradition rooted in a religious past and sustained by a variety of normative attitudes: although equality before the law may have become a desideratum in the modern shape of those societies, there are certain received assumptions about the lengths to which that principle might be applied. For those who take this position, the crucial question is whether the law can divest itself of substantive normative conceptions of religion without undermining the sense of social cohesion and identity. For those of this persuasion, there is, and has to be, a social *parti pris* with respect to the extent to which it is desirable—by way of the extension of privileges—to encourage new and various systems of belief and practice. The presumption is that morality and religion are not merely a matter of observing what people do and then bringing law into conformity with these patterns of actual behaviour, the position advocated by Justices Wilson and Dean in the Australian High Court in 1983, but rather of sustaining a received system of norms which direct the shape of social life. In short, in this view the law is seen as an agency which embodies an historical and continuing sense of the general will: it requires that citizens (who in England, at least, are also seen as 'subjects') should in their various dispositions, including the spiritual, be supportive of the society. In the English law, as it now stands, both strands can be detected—the strong affirmation of principles of showing no favour to one religion rather than another, and the actual cases in which preference for the integrity of historical culture continues to be manifest. One may yet ask how long the spirit of the old laws will resist the challenge of the new faiths.

5

A Sect at Law:
The Case of the Exclusive Brethren

As in all human associations, at some time or another troubles arise within religious movements. Sectarian religion is serious religion: it determines an entire way of life, and when dissension occurs within a sect, or between a religious minority and outside bodies, it is likely to attract public attention (indeed, the dissentients themselves may seek the notice of the press, take their grievances to law, or seek to gain the ears—and the voices—of MPs). Sects are not racial minorities, and no anti-discrimination act forbids prejudice in matters of religion: for those so minded, religious prejudice is still a free and even an exciting ride. To journalists, religious dissension is scandal that provides titillating copy, while MPs have, at times, been not beyond seizing the opportunity for quick publicity by expressing easy indignation about particular sectarian beliefs or practices when these can be advanced as issues of public concern. In general, this is as far as the fuss goes, and governments increasingly recognize that religion is, for them, of limited importance and rarely worth their direct involvement. Government indifference is of little solace to sects which become the victims of hostile publicity campaigns; and even governments are not beyond the influence of the media in such matters and may go further in acting against minorities than actual circumstances warrant, as the case under review here amply illustrates. For leaving aside the privileges accorded to that church which is 'by law established' even though the law in England is not supposed to discriminate among religions, equal treatment is, none the less, not guaranteed. Actions affecting religious movements may be undertaken at official, but subpolitical, levels to which neither the public at large, nor the victim in particular, has any easy access, and in the counsels of which they can exert virtually no influence except by tortuous processes of law. The recent treatment of a religious minority by the Charity Commissioners is a case in point.

The Charity Commissioners cannot, of course, in any way directly determine the validity of the particular beliefs that men espouse, nor condemn the practices that they pursue in the exercise of their religious faith: but they do exert a perhaps quaint, indirect influence on religious freedom by virtue of their competence to decide about the charitable status of trusts. Religious movements may, indiscriminately, seek a variety of privileges at law, the principal one of which is to have their trusts recognized as charitable, and so escape normal tax liabilities. The Charity Commissioners have considerable discretion with respect to the trusts that they register: but religion is presumed at law to be charitable, and, if challenged, trustees have to establish to the satisfaction of the Charity Commissioners (or, on appeal, beyond them) that their purposes are religious; that they are not subversive of religion and morality; and that the operation of the trust will be in the public interest and for the public benefit. The Charity Commissioners have no power to revoke a trust, but they can refuse to register one. In a recent case, this is indeed what they did, following an unprecedented procedure in which the Commissioners authorized a quasi-judicial inquiry into the religious movement concerned—the group known as the Exclusive Brethren.

The Exclusive Brethren is the name given (by outsiders) to those among the so-called Plymouth Brethren who, in the mid-nineteenth century, joined John Nelson Darby (1800–82) in forming a Christian fellowship which they believed to be based on strict biblical principles. The term 'exclusive' was applied because these brethren maintained that it was essential for those who believed in 'the Truth' to separate from all others, and to admit to their 'breaking of bread' only those who agreed in all doctrinal matters, and who subjected themselves to the same social and moral discipline. The first beginnings of the Brethren movement occurred in the 1820s, when Darby, then an Anglican clergyman in the Church of Ireland, began meeting with others who shared his serious doubts about the validity of Anglican orders and, indeed, about the biblical warrant for any sort of clerical class. These early Brethren were men of education and social position—twelve of the earliest Brethren were, or were training to be, Anglican clergymen (in England and Ireland); five were ministers in Nonconformist churches; a number had private means, including five with titles, and another eight were, or had been, commissioned officers.

The early Brethren believed that, by separating from what they regarded as the unwarranted and unlegitimated system that was represented by the organization of churches, they possessed an adequate basis for the unity of all properly motivated Christians. Initially, they saw no need for any but the simplest pattern of organization, and their separation from all existing churches was not conceived as a negative decision, but rather as the only basis on which the unity of true Christians could be established. Like many other movements that came to be regarded as sectarian, the Brethren began with a profound and deeply anti-sectarian sentiment, and they still reject the designation 'sect'. They sought to restore what they saw as the biblical pattern of order which would allow them to live in conformity with the will of God, and which had been corrupted by the development of the ecclesiastical systems of existing churches.

This early conception of Christian fellowship, based on minimal organization, proved within the course of a decade and a half to be inadequate for the maintenance of an integrated separate community. Brethren came to differ on whether the basis of unity was to be tested by the common life they followed, or the common 'light' (i.e. doctrine) to which they subscribed. Who should be admitted to the breaking of bread ceremony? Darby held that true Christians should separate not only from the churches, which were corrupt, but also from those who were impure in faith or morals. The principle of separating from evil became for him and his associates the essential basis for Christian unity and common fellowship. The movement split in the 1840s on this question of the 'closed table', and Darby's party became known as 'exclusive' in contrast to those Brethren who imposed no such test for admission to the communion table, thereafter known as 'Open Brethren'.

The governing principle of the exclusive fellowship was the biblical injunction to separate from evil, and over the movement's history there have been several occasions when differences of doctrine have led to the perceived need to separate, and hence to schism. Indeed, the recognition of this firm principle led the Brethren to expect that there would be a need to assert their purity by vigilance and perhaps division. Darby wrote, in 1880, 'The assembly purges itself'; and periodic and sometimes ramifying divisions occurred at various times. Unrighteousness and false doctrine had to be judged, and that judgement had to be made in the assembly. Those from whom the movement separated, those who were 'put out', had opportunity to repent and, on repentence, to be restored if the conscience of the assembly so determined, and Darby emphasized that 'the discipline of putting away is always done with the view of restoring the person who has been subjected to it, and never to get rid of him'. This discipline was itself essential to the fellowship: it was the bond which it could not do without, for apart from the possibility of restoring the 'evil' individual, discipline secured and maintained the purity of the fellowship.

The exclusive party was never a large movement. It had assemblies throughout England and Scotland, in the United States and other parts of the English-speaking world, and on the continent of Europe. It provoked relatively little public notice (although Darby's theological writings on the second advent and on matters of biblical prophecy, collectively known as 'Dispensationalism', came to exert very wide influence among fundamentalists of various denominations). The several schisms that occurred in the nineteenth and early twentieth centuries, were certainly occasions for anguish and bitterness but they occasioned no general public concern or comment.

That the Brethren have in the past been prone to schism does not in itself affect the present issue, except to make evident the consistency of the principle of separation over the movement's history. Despite these divisions, a clear line of descent can be traced from those in fellowship with Darby through a line of successors of 'leading Brethren' to the present day. To distinguish this fellowship from various schismatic groups, it has usually been known by the names of its leaders, and particularly by the name of the leader at the time of the most recent division. In 1959 and in 1970 the Brethren suffered schisms, and the continuing majority party were known as 'Taylorites', since James Taylor, jun., an American businessman, was their leader on the occasion of these two divisions. Their opponents, who do not now constitute an organized fellowship of the same strength, and many of whom are dispersed, became known as 'anti-Taylorites'.

Schism within the movement brings problems about the ownership of property, and it is often manifested in divisions within families that were formerly united in the one fellowship. Both consequences ensued among the Brethren during their various divisions. The schisms of 1959 and 1970 occurred as the distinctive

ethical stance of the fellowship was vigorously reasserted, particularly in the injunction to keep themselves separate from the
world. Social conditions had changed, a more permissive morality
was finding expression in the outside society, and the traditional
separatist ethic of the Brethren had now to be applied to issues
which the leadership regarded as new perils. Such things as
television had come into use in the outside society, and had been
accepted by some Brethren. Now the fellowship was enjoined to
eschew it in the spirit of their original ethic (which had always
prohibited theatre-going and cinema-going). Various organizations,
such as professional bodies and students' unions, acquired the right
to make membership obligatory for the relevant sections of the
population, and the call was now made for Brethren to consider
whether they could be involved in these associations without
contravening the scriptural injunction not to be 'unequally yoked'
with unbelievers. Sharing a dwelling with non-Brethren had always
been contrary to the group's norms, but in the 1960s this principle
was extended to the avoidance of sharing a front door (in an
apartment building), and the injunction against 'commensality with
outsiders' was reaffirmed. These interdictions may be regarded
as attempts to reinforce existing principles in changing social
circumstances.

Some members of the fellowship felt the reassertion of these
demands and their application to new issues as a hardship, and
their dissent led to departures and schism. Yet there was agreement
and acceptance by the majority. Thus, of some twenty-eight
pharmacists, all but one gave up their pharmaceutical practices
when the House of Lords declined to permit qualified professionals
to practise unless they continued to remain enrolled as members of
the Pharmaceutical Society (even though the Society itself was
prepared to accept this arrangement). Those who remained in the
fellowship saw the dissension which occurred over these new
applications of the movement's traditional puritan ethic as a
process by which the fellowship would be purged of laxness in
upholding the cardinal principle on which the Brethren had
historically and recurrently taken their stand—the separation from
evil. The obligation of a Christian was to stand apart from the
world by avoiding all associations not only with those outside the
fellowship, but also with any brother who lapsed into immoral
habits or who had espoused false doctrine. From the beginning, the

fellowship has maintained itself as a sanctified community, apart from the world and the churches. The recurrent difficulty has been the correction of Brethren who fall into worldly ways or who teach erroneous doctrine. When such a case occurs, the Brethren seek, in accordance with Darby's prescription, to correct the erring brother. The Brethren recognize that all are capable of falling into error and of committing sin. Usually, minor matters of misconduct are easily corrected with the help of other Brethren. When there is persistent wrong-doing or false teaching, the local assembly becomes concerned, and if the case cannot be resolved by rebuke, then an unrepentant individual is said to be 'shut up', a term used to indicate that he is not admitted to the Brethren's meetings, and in particular, to the meeting for the 'breaking of bread'. One who fails to repent is then 'withdrawn from' or 'put out', and any brother who fails so to dissociate himself from the unrepentant himself becomes subject to the same form of censure. Little as such measures might be appreciated by outsiders, they are well understood by those who have committed themselves to the fellowship as something unfortunate but essential to the maintenance of its purity. None the less, the renewed vigour with which, in the late 1950s and early 1960s, the principles of purity were reasserted gave rise to tensions and divisions within congregations and within families.

Division within families is a subject that can be quickly elevated into a matter of general public concern. The Brethren are not the only religious movement to have been subjected in recent years to considerable abuse and misrepresentation by the mass media because family members differ on matters of religious belief. Most of the cases which the media take up are of young individuals who are recruited to some little-known but demanding religious fellowship; but the case of the Brethren is rather different. Although they undertake some street preaching, urging on men their need for salvation, they are not active in endeavours specifically to recruit converts to their own fellowship. The circumstances in which the Brethren attract media attention occur when they withdraw from one of their number who has failed, in one way or another, to maintain the standards required by their religious fellowship, and when that withdrawal involves members of the deviant's own family.

In the early 1960s, the press made much of the divisions among the Brethren, recounting, in exaggerated form, instances of families divided about such matters as the movement's prohibition of television, and of young people whose families would no longer eat with them at the same table. Some of those who were 'put out' wrote to their MPs, who asked questions in Parliament, aroused the interest of the media, and some of whom urged that James Taylor, jun. (an American), be refused entry to Britain to visit the members of the fellowship here. Nothing was done. Following the more decisive schism that occurred in 1970, the anti-Taylorites again opened the campaign against the fellowship, and, in a more effective if less public strategy, complained to the Charity Commissioners, and so to the Attorney-General.

The Attorney-General of the day, through Standing Counsel, decided to commission a quasi-judicial inquiry, using the Charity Commissioners to summon evidence about the affairs of the Brethren. Neither the Attorney-General nor the Commissioners could interfere with the actual religious practices of the Brethren, of course, but they could form a view of whether the trusts created by the Brethren had a religious purpose. Mr Hugh Francis QC was given the task of undertaking the inquiry and reporting on the Brethren. He reported in November 1975, and he drew on evidence supplied principally by the anti-Taylorites. He did not see the need to make a definitive finding on matters of fact—and, indeed, one may doubt the adequacy of any strictly legal procedures to do that. He did not interview the correspondents who supplied him with written evidence, nor did he seek to elicit the response of those who remained in the fellowship by putting these complaints to them. The evidence was submitted without cross-examination of those who had supplied it. The report was thus not intended to test the truth of allegations: it was offered as 'an opinion of counsel'. Mr Francis concluded that, in his opinion, the teachings and practices of the Brethren were contrary to public policy, and he subsequently appeared on television to say that their teachings were likely to cause distress and unhappiness.

The Charity Commissioners regarded the report as inconclusive. While they were not convinced that the Brethren's doctrines on such matters as separation from evil should influence charitable status, the action that they did take had the effect of creating great difficulties in the normal conduct of the sect's affairs. The Commissioners decided to approve no more schemes for dealing with property affected by the schism, and to permit no further

registration of charitable trusts. The Brethren's freedom to worship
as they chose was unimpaired by this decision; but it did seriously
impede the administrative activities of the movement on which
their effective religious freedom in some measure depended. The
Commissioners' difficulties in deciding how to deal with existing
trusts that were at issue in congregations affected by schism can be
readily appreciated. The reasons for refusing to register new trusts
is much less clear.

That decision appears to be questionable on two grounds. First,
if the Exclusive Brethren were sustaining principles that they had
maintained in the past, it seems unreasonable to suggest that,
whereas before the schism they were entitled to be deemed a
religious movement competent to register charitable trusts, after the
schism they were no longer to be so regarded. Second, if the
Brethren were now held to be engaging in activities or practices that
were subversive of religion or morality, or not in the public interest,
then the question that arises is whether those practices were unique
in religious history and unparalleled among other religious movements that had registered trusts, or that might do so.

To test whether there were grounds on which the Charity Commissioners or the Attorney-General might refuse the registration of
a trust, the Brethren brought an action as a test-case, and that
action was heard in February 1981. The action required the
Attorney-General to consider whether the trust that the Brethren
sought to register was invalid and not charitable because the
movement was 'not a religion', or was 'subversive of all religion
and morality', or was 'not in the public interest'. The case was
heard before Mr Justice Walton, and the Solicitor-General appeared
for the Attorney-General.

In the event, the Solicitor-General produced no evidence to
suggest that the Brethren's teachings and practices did not constitute a
religion, and indeed—given the Brethren's commitment to biblical
authority, their attempt to regulate their lives according to biblical
requirements, and the institution of acts of worship commanded in
the Bible—it would have been difficult, without impugning almost
all, if not all, Christian churches and sects, to have done so. At an
early stage of the plaintiff's evidence, the Solicitor-General went
further, and conceded that the sect was not subversive of religion
and morality. None of the evidence which had been the basis for the
Charity Commissioners' decision to refuse registration of the

Brethren's trusts was offered to contest this proposition. The case proceeded solely on the question of whether the trust which the Brethren were seeking to register was for the public benefit.

Until the Solicitor-General conceded these issues, in effect it was the religion of the Brethren that was on trial. Although the case hung on the matter of a trust, the ultimate, if not the immediately admissible, questions that the court addressed were (*a*) whether the Brethren's beliefs and practices constituted a religion, and (*b*) whether they were subversive of all religion and morality. Had it been decided that these beliefs did not constitute a religion, the apparent effect would have been to disallow the registration of a trust. This would in turn have affected the ownership and use of all the meeting-rooms of the movement and would have affected liability to pay local rates, while the income of the trusts might have become liable to taxation. But the wider ramification of such a decision on the equal freedom of religious movements would have been incalculable. Among religions (once the court has determined that they are indeed religions) the law does not discriminate, and earlier cases, among them one concerning a trust created by the followers of Joanna Southcott, have established that as long as a trust is religious it is valid as a charity, even if the purposes of the trust are deemed to be foolish.

The law presumes that a religion—any religion—is for the public benefit, and the test of whether the public interest is served appears to be whether the religionists engage in activities for the promotion of their beliefs among a wider public. In earlier cases, enclosed orders had been deemed to be not for the public benefit because those orders undertook no such public promotion of their teachings. What had now to be shown was that the Brethren did engage in public preaching; that they did admit outsiders to their meetings (other than to the meeting for the breaking of bread and to administrative meetings); that the complaints concerning divisions in families related (the occasion of schism apart) to rare instances; and that the Brethren as individuals comported themselves in ways conducive to good citizenship and public order. Over and above all this, it might also have been shown that, in respect to their beliefs and practices, and in particular their policy concerning separation from evil and withdrawal from evil-doers, the Brethren have not been by any means unique in Christian history.

Apart from the evidence of a number of people who had

encountered the Brethren either as neighbours, as teachers of their children, or in business, and who testified to their upright conduct, the evidence which the court heard respecting preaching, admission to meetings, and family divisions, was entirely the testimony of the Brethren themselves. The Solicitor-General cited none of the complaints on which the Charity Commissioners had acted, and which had occasioned all this litigation. At least to the non-lawyer, it must induce surprise that in effect no justification was brought forward for a serious quasi-legal decision by a government agency. Ultimately, the indications are those of a tacit acknowledgement that the Charity Commissioners had been mistaken, and, in being mistaken, had been guilty of an injustice. Beyond this, however, the case also indicates the extreme reluctance of politicians (since the defendants were political office-holders) to fight on religious issues, and their ultimate conviction that religion is not a matter of very great social consequence.

It appears that non-lawyers were not the only ones to be surprised at the absence of any effort to justify the Commissioners' decision, however. In his judgment, Mr Justice Walton commented pointedly that the evidence had been 'all one way'. He did not conceal his own opinion of the Brethren. While they separated themselves from the world, they were 'quite content to earn wages as employees': and they suffered 'from the Pharisaical position of being blown up with their own pride, believing that they and only they had the key to all revealed truth . . .'. Twice his Lordship remarked that the evidence of the plaintiffs had not been challenged by the Solicitor-General, and that therefore he must accept it. All the evidence respecting discipline came from the Brethren, he observed, 'and it may very well put the matter in a much more favourable light than it wears in reality'. Referring to discipline and the division of families, his Lordship said:

One cannot . . . as a man of the world, avoid knowing that very serious allegations indeed have been made against the Brethren in connection with these matters. These have not been in evidence before me. I, therefore, am not entitled to pay judicially any regard to them. The Attorney-General through the Solicitor-General had taken no point upon the matter, and therefore, I am forced to accept what is there stated as being the only evidence in front of me.

Just why the evidence was 'all one way' is a matter of speculation. Perhaps the complaints on which the Charity Commissioners had acted were now deemed insufficiently substantial to put forward; or perhaps the government officers preferred not to fight the 'religious battle' which, from his comments, the judge appeared disappointed to have been denied.

There was, however, other evidence on matters of religious discipline of a comparative kind which did not come from the Brethren, and which the plaintiffs had been prepared to present, but which the Solicitor-General had been unwilling to hear, and which (early in the case) his Lordship had also been disinclined to admit. The opportunity was missed to hear matter which pertained to the larger issue of religious freedom, which might have put the case of the Brethren into a wider comparative perspective, and which would have established that, in the question of discipline, the Brethren did not differ in principle from a number of other sects. If all the evidence came from the Brethren, it did so only because the Court had preferred not to be burdened with comparative evidence about other religions, which the judge had dismissed with a reference to 'dancing round a totem pole'. One need not, however, bracket the Brethren with primitive peoples in order to place their own practices in a broader context which might enlighten the seemingly obscure state of the law on matters of this kind.

The exhortation to spiritual purity goes back to the Judaic roots of Christianity and is symbolized in a variety of ritual and social acts. The avoidance of contamination may require that certain foods be tabooed; that particular places be shunned; that ritual washing, bathing, or baptism occur; or, in sects that have transformed purely symbolic gestures into practical moral guidance, that circumspection be maintained about the company that one keeps.

In 'separating from evil', the Brethren follow, in a practical way, an exhortation that is widely enjoined in religion. The injunction to maintain purity has always had greatest cogency for minority religions. Among Christians in general, the injunction of 2 Cor. 6: 17, 'be ye separate', had greatest force when they were a small and persecuted minority in an alien world, in which they could see themselves as spiritual inheritors of the claims once made for Jews, namely to be sons of God, joint-heirs with Christ. But once Christians had become the majority, the command to 'be separate' lost its force, and it was only when protesting and reforming puritan, evangelical, or fundamentalist groups re-emerged that the demand was reasserted in its full vigour.

Such movements arose in societies that were, nominally, virtually completely Christian: in consequence, those from whom they saw themselves enjoined by Scripture to 'separate' themselves were the nominally Christian community at large and the Church into which it was organized. In that Church, they found plenty to characterize as evil and corrupt, and, on examination, many of its practices could be shown to be quite unscriptural—and Scripture was, for such groups, the sole authority for Christian practice. Since the Church appeared to be deceiving men with respect to their religious duties, it came to symbolize for such sects the most profound evil of all.

Christian separatists have practised 'putting out' for centuries. They have called it by various names—withdrawal; disfellow-shipping; disowning; banning; shunning. Catholics have called it excommunication. Despite the practice of excommunication, churchmen have sometimes complained about the rigour of sectarian discipline and separation. Thus, Bishop Grindal of London complained in the late sixteenth century that Puritans refused to admit, not only other Anglicans, but even other non-separated Puritans to their services. The position taken by these early Congregationalists was essentially similar to that which has been adopted in more recent times by the Brethren, who believe that only those who act together in separating from evil properly constitute a fellowship.

Putting out the evil person is intended to be a purificatory exercise for the community rather than punitive for the individual, whose repentance and restoration is the express prayer of the congregation. Among the Brethren, ungodly activity and false doctrine are occasions for discipline, and since all male brothers are free to expound the Scriptures, and are expected to do so, the maintenance of pure doctrine has been a prime concern, and has necessitated discipline. Working to similar effect in bringing disciplinary measures into operation has been the exigent need, in changing times, to reassert received principles with respect to moral demeanour.

This concern with regulation bears comparison with the traditional requirements of the Roman Catholic orders—even though (since in an order celibacy is maintained) the moral problems peculiar to the family, and the difficulty respecting divisions that affect families, do not there arise. Restrictions in recreation, and on association with outsiders; a required measure of dedication; and the acceptance of a rule of discipline—all are common to the Roman order and to the Brethren, who, in some respects, are not unlike monks living, within the wider society, lives of intense religious virtuosity.

In putting out the wayward, the Brethren do what the seventeenth-century Quakers did. They, too, required members to consult the meeting before moving house away from the locality of one assembly into that of another. (The Quakers even required that a man consult the meeting before taking a spouse.) Those of 'disorderly walk' were disowned. The Mennonites, who today exist as several distinct denominations, some of which have hundreds of thousands of adherents, exercised a ban (*Meidung*) on those who became involved in worldly associations, and that ban operated within families much in the same way as occurs among Brethren. A Mennonite would not eat a meal with anyone who had been banned, and it has been their practice that, if one of two spouses was excommunicated in this way, then normal relations between them ceased. The principle of the ban, enjoined in the Schleitheim Confession of 1527, was reiterated in the Dortrecht Confession of 1632, Menno Simmons himself asserted this rule in the words of 1 Cor. 5: 11, 'not to associate with any one who bears the name of brother if he is guilty of immorality or greed, or is an idolator, reviler, drunkard, or robber—not even to eat with such a one' (Revised Version). Although the General Conference of Mennonites has today relaxed its moral austerity, the idea of the ban is still well understood, and its practice continues among other groups of Mennonites.

The desire to maintain purity of community by expelling the iniquitous has been practised among other Christian movements, including those that were not formed explicitly on the principle of separating from evil as the basis for their community life. The Methodists (who were, of course, not even separatists) developed a stringent set of moral requirements of their members, and in the early nineteenth century, the wayward were refused admission tickets to the all-important band meetings. Members were closely interrogated about their sins at these meetings, and could be disowned for disorderly walk, frivolous talk, whistling, and improper dress, at a time when the Methodist Conference devoted its time to stipulating such matters as, for example, the proper length of petticoats. Among other Christian fellowships that arose more or less contemporaneously with the Brethren, similar moral requirements were exacted, and similar sanctions of 'disfellow-shipping' operated. The Christadelphians, whose beginnings in Britain were in the 1840s, and whose fellowship was similar in both polity and ethos to that of the Brethren, maintained very similar canons of rectitude, disfellowshipping wayward members very frequently. Both the Christadelphians and the Jehovah's Witnesses continue today to apply very similar rules of separation and excommunication, although neither of these sects has fallen foul of the Charity Commissioners with respect to the rigour of their disciplinary procedures.

These cases provide evidence of the practice of discipline entirely comparable to that exercised by the Brethren, in movements that have been, or in some cases are still, committed to the ideal of separation from the world. On any definition, they are religions, and on existing precedents none of them would have difficulty in registering trusts for purposes deemed religious and in the public interest. All of these groups have suffered, at times, from public and press opprobrium, perhaps because the morally indifferent often feel that the demand for moral rigour is in itself an infringement of personal liberty. Yet, that a movement maintains standards and expels those who fail to live up to them is scarcely a justification for the denial of the normal rights of religious freedom, or the right to operate on equal terms and with equal concessions at law to those of other religious bodies.

Here, then, is the 'missing evidence' concerning the significance of discipline. A sect is always a voluntary body. Its members select themselves, and the leaders may exercise only very limited sanctions over their members. The sect's operation and its discipline are, in practice, always matters for general consent. As long as a movement and its leaders operate within the framework of the law, it must be accepted that members commit themselves voluntarily to certain standards of behaviour and belief, and to the consequences of departing from those standards. Within the law—and it is rare that there is transgression of the law within any religious movement—the limit of a community's sanctions against a dissident member is to expel him, and expulsion is, after all, a common method of social control in a wide variety of human organizations, from clubs, military units, and professional associa-tions to preparatory schools.

All of this does not diminish the fact that discipline is a serious matter for the sectarian himself, and particularly so in a movement in which members are closely drawn together and separated from outsiders. Such is the case with the Brethren. The anguish that has been occasioned when individuals have been disciplined and 'put out' is entirely understandable. Expulsion from the community is a severe sentence, even considered in purely social terms. When to this is added the spiritual seriousness with which membership is regarded, one sees why passion is so readily engendered. Yet, given their interpretation of evil, and their obligation to separate themselves from it, such procedures, harrowing as they are for everyone, appear to the Brethren to be unavoidable. If obedience to God, and to the way of life that manifests such obedience, is the first obligation of Brethren, transcending all social, including familial duties, then family divisions will at times inevitably occur. In taking this ground, the Brethren recall such texts as Luke 14: 26, 'If any man come to me, and hate not his father, and mother, and wife, and children, and brethren, and sisters, yea, and his own life also, he cannot be my disciple'; and Luke 12: 52–3, 'there shall be five in one house divided, three against two, and two against three. The father shall be divided against the son, and the son against the father, and the mother against the daughter, and the daughter against the mother . . .' This is a testimony, not merely of the Brethren, but of that Jesus whom all Christians claim to follow.

The Brethren presented abundant evidence of their own to put the matter of discipline into perspective, and outsiders may also confirm that, in normal circumstances, family life among them is characterized by bonds of the strongest affection. Sects generally attach great importance to the quality and the sanctity of family relationships, and of no sect is this more fully the case than it is of the Brethren, who are diligent and conscientious parents, and who maintain homes in which integrity, honesty, and the catalogue of traditional virtues remain paramount concerns. Since they eschew other social involvements, the family, reinforced by their participation in their own community, constitutes their social world. Harmonious family life is the norm for which Brethren strive, and because they do not participate in outside activities there is a heightened concentration of concern for kith and kin. The tightness of their commitments, the separation of those who sustain them, the vigilant exercise of discipline, and, ultimately and in the rare case of need, the expulsion of those who do not fit, are all of a piece, and are necessary to each other.

The unquestioned freedom in Western society for individuals or groups to maintain a distinctive, serious, and conscientious way of life, as long as the rights of others are not thereby invaded, should not be less than the very evident contemporary freedom to maintain an utterly frivolous and uncaring life. In the courts, the Brethren have fought and won this implicit democratic right. But why should they ever have had to fight at all?

Part II
Evolution, Diffusion, and Appeal

6

How Sects Evolve:
Issues and Inferences

SOCIOLOGISTS, by the principled assumptions of their discipline, are disposed to seek general laws to explain the forms and processes of social phenomena. The value of such endeavour—for enlarging our understanding, producing analytical insights, and, as a hopeful prospect, for generating predictive propositions—cannot be gainsaid. The stimulus to comparative method on which such generalizations should rest, must in itself be salutary in producing improved explanations of social phenomena otherwise explained in only narrow reference to specific data and without awareness of the probability of the occurrence of particular patterns and sequences. Yet, this search for general propositions has its dangers: it can lead to over-hasty conclusions and to formulations that carry all the apparent authority of general laws when in fact they are merely accounts of particular cases that have been unwarrantably generalized to all associated phenomena and dignified in abstract terminology. The evolution of religious movements—often represented as 'from sect to church'—is a social process that has suffered such theoretical over-generalization. In reality, there are marked variations in the development of religious organizations. Such bodies begin in diverse contexts; they embrace widely varying perspectives and ideologies; they arise in totally differing historical circumstances. There is, indeed, no normal or typical pattern of sectarian or denominational development. There are, however, some parallels, certain salient orientations, specific dispositions and conditions which recurrently influence religious bodies, and, in specific historical periods, there are broadly shared cultural contexts affecting religion, organization, and social development.

The processes of change in one movement may, then, illuminate patterns of development in another or in several others, and this we may usefully acknowledge without any commitment to a grand design of invariable and unilinear evolution. Obviously, every sect is in part idiosyncratic and unique, and where there are profound initial differences we must expect divergent developmental consequences. Again, each sect's distinctive history exhibits some purely adventitious and random features of which no general analytical scheme can take account. But beyond these two sets of items—the distinctive and unique attributes, and the specific historical circumstance—there are some common, or at least comparable, factors among sects, examination of which may yield insights into the patterns of sect development. The principal determinants of sectarian evolution may be listed under four broad headings: stance, structure, and orientation (under which heading the familiar generalized formula of 'from sect to church' may be examined); the implications of styles of leadership, and particularly of charismatic leadership; the character of organization; and the quality of denominational distinctiveness. Throughout the argument which follows the contextual aspect will intrude, but in recent times the process of secularization has had such powerful consequences for all forms of religion that this particular circumstantial influence will, in conclusion, be considered separately.

Stance, Structure, and Orientation

Many a new religious movement begins as a sect—as a separated body of believers which arises in protest against existing clerical, and perhaps also secular, authority. The sect emphasizes its own monopoly of at least the full measure of truth. It is a voluntary body, in the sense that even those born to sectarian parents must take serious steps and evince personal commitment before they themselves are accepted into fellowship. Membership is incompatible with allegiance to any other religious body. It follows that, for these separated sectaries, religion is serious: it is not a formality. It matters, and it matters more than anything else. There are concomitant obligations in respect of behaviour and life-style. Admission is by some test of merit, whether it be conversance with doctrines; moral probity; a conversion experience; or a combination of such marks of distinction. Discipline is rigorous, and there are set procedures for suspending or expelling the morally wayward or those who challenge sect teachings. In large part, sectarians stand apart from others and develop a culture distinctly their own. Sects have been a commonplace of Christianity, and, since the Reformation, they have been organized, persisting bodies.

One significant pattern of the development of religious movements is the transformation of these sectarian characteristics. Growth, in particular, affects the sect, but not all sects grow, or even seek to grow, at all periods of their life-cycle. Some decline. But even mere persistence without growth affects the stance, structure, and orientation of sects. It is important to make this point, since early formulations of the theory of sect development were propounded in rather special historical circumstances—in America after a period of uniquely rapid demographic and economic expansion. In such circumstances it was easily assumed not only that growth was normal and a continuing phenomenon, but that it would be accompanied by a steady and virtually automatic relinquishment of specifically sectarian characteristics as religious bodies matured. Sects would be denominationalized, each one becoming one among a number of movements which accorded each other mutual respect as acceptable agencies in the promotion, with only minor variations, of the essential truths of the Christian message. Erstwhile sects would acquire a ministerial echelon, and become only marginally differentiated from older Christian churches against which their original protest had been directed. The assertions of a monopoly of necessary truth would be tempered by texts about 'many mansions' and phrases emphasizing the plenitude and rich diversity of the Christian, and more especially the ecclesiastical, tradition. Halfway covenants would become the order of the day, and the in-born young would be assimilated into church membership with fewer tests, since merit would be assumed rather than standing in need of explicit proof. Religious 'succession' would be facilitated as the distinctiveness of the sectarian lifestyle was eroded. Exclusivity would be abandoned, and there would be increased participation in inter-faith and inter-church social action and co-operation. Distinctive teachings—even if of necessity retained—would become more marginal; discipline less common. Members would cease to hold themselves apart from the rest of society, accepting association at work, and eventually even at leisure, with those of other faiths, the apathetic, the uncommitted, and the frankly unbelieving.

Such a pattern of church growth appeared to be virtually a truism to H. Richard Niebuhr when, in 1929, he formulated a generalization that sects become denominations with the second generation.[1]

---

[1] H. R. Niebuhr, *The Social Sources of Denominationalism* (New York: Holt, 1929), 19.

Much in American history supported this thesis, from the erosion of rigour implied in Halfway Covenants to the examples supplied by the history of nineteenth-century Methodism, the Disciples, and the Church of the Nazarene.[2] Niebuhr attributed this process to the induction of the second generation which in itself prompted increased concern with education, and caused the transformation of what had been rebellion in the parents into orthodoxy for the children. The argument is arresting. But it is not quite compelling. Niebuhr overlooked the uniqueness of American history, as the first Christian country without an established church. In America, the denomination was itself virtually a constitutionally prescribed mode of religious structure: there were, in America, no churches in the European sense. Nor, given religious pluralism, were sects systematically anathematized. While churches had their ecclesiastical claims abridged by denominational pluralism, sects were induced to abandon separation and protest. This process was promoted by the demographic, geographic, and economic expansion of the United States, where upward social mobility became a normal expectation. In Europe, by contrast, where status distinctions prevailed, social mobility could be regarded by Emile Durkheim as in itself the dangerous expression of 'boundless desire', the source of social disruption and anomie.[3] In Europe, men were taught to know their place, and so were religious movements. In the United States, just as individuals might move up the social scale, so might religious bodies: from sects of the disinherited, they might become denominations of the respectable, conforming in posture and structure to the American religious norm. The sect aspiring to rise in the world need not remain a sect for long.

Niebuhr overlooked the uniqueness of the American context. He espoused false premises. And he ignored the contrary empirical evidence. It was a false assumption to suppose that one could talk in static terms of 'first' and 'second' generations. In all growing movements, there are always some new—first-generation—members, and they live alongside those who are the children and grand-children of earlier members. At no given time is there simply a first

   [2] On Methodists, see E. D. C. Brewer, 'Sect and Church in Methodism', *Social Forces*, 20 (May, 1952), 400–8; on the Disciples, see O. Read Whitley, *Trumpet Call of Reformation* (St. Louis, Mo.: Bethany Press, 1959).
   [3] Durkheim's influential thesis is most developed in his study of suicide in Europe: E. Durkheim, *Suicide: A Study in Sociology*, trans. J. A. Spaulding and G. Simpson (London: Routledge and Kegan Paul, 1952).

and a second generation. New converts join old sects, and often serve to keep old families in line by reminding them of the more literal aspects of commitment, and by taking less for granted the special doctrines and practices of the sect that they have voluntarily espoused.

Every sect has its own distinctive stance and orientation, and, as a matter of empirical fact, not all sects do become denominationalized. Some move only part way in that direction: some not at all. While Methodists and Disciples became denominationalized, Brethren, Hutterians, and Jehovah's Witnesses did not. Even in movements which have undergone this process, sectarian strains have not been easily or uniformly abandoned. Sometimes, as with the Disciples, there is a split between fundamentalist (or sectarian) and liberal (or denominational) factions: and sometimes such parties continue in uneasy fellowship, the one contending for original positions against the modern accommodations of the other, as, for example, among Baptists in Britain.

Denominationalization—the loosening rigour; the loss of the sense of dissent and protest; the reduction of distance from other Christians; and the muting of claims that the sect's distinctive teachings are necessary for salvation—is a current that exerts some pressure on all contemporary movements. But some resist better than others. A sect's original stance may facilitate or impede the denominationalizing process. Where there are practices and teachings that stand in sharp contrast with those of mainstream Christianity, these may act as insulating devices. For example, in Seventh-day Adventism this is the effect, at the practical level, of the movement's teaching of the seventh-day sabbath and its Old Testament dietetic code, and, at the doctrinal level, of the sanctuary doctrine and the apparent mitigation of the Protestant emphasis on justification by faith. Where such distinctive differences exist, and persist, a movement is less likely to proceed as far or as fast down the road to denominational homogeneity.

The specific orientations which favour denominationalism are the emphasis on conversion, in the sense of experiencing a radical change of heart; revivalism, in which born-again prospects are vigorously canvassed; and the subsequent intake of large numbers of undersocialized recruits. Such recruitment calls forth measures for the after-care of the converted. A pastorate may then emerge, the members of which may gradually come to look for and eventually acquire professional status, as they seek parity with ministries in other movements. The orientations which impede evolution include, first, the belief that God is shortly to act dramatically in world affairs, thus rendering any sectarian accommodation to the world both futile and unfaithful; and second, the belief that evil can be avoided only by withdrawal into the sanctified community. In the short term at least, the revolutionist expectation sets the sect over against the world, whilst introversion sustains indifferentism to the wider society. Some sects, of which the Seventh-day Adventists would be one, have participated in all three of these modal responses, and the admixture has resulted in less emphatic denominationalism than that now espoused by, say, the Methodists and the (Arminian) Baptists, but a position less sectarian than that occupied by the more avowedly revolutionist Jehovah's Witnesses or the more profoundly introversionist Brethren.

The Role of Charismatic Leadership

By no means all Christian sects begin under charismatic leadership, even in the somewhat weaker sense in which the term 'charismatic' is fashionably employed today. But enough of them have, or have had, powerful inspirational leadership to warrant a comparative exercise respecting the implications of charisma for the development of religious movements. The belief that one individual might possess divine inspiration in much greater measure than others (perhaps even to the exclusion of others) has been a persistent theme throughout human history and among pre-literate peoples. Prophets who functioned in remote periods and in cultures with limited literacy have become the heroes of religions, nations, and ethnic groups, and distance in time and circumstance undoubtedly facilitated the accretion of myth and legend, not only for the King Arthurs, Hidden Imams, and Barbarossas, but also for the founders of the great faiths, Buddha, Jesus, and Mohammed. Much of their claims rests on faith rather than well-attested record. More recent prophets, even when making claims much less strong, have found modern times much less propitious for charisma. Since the time of Hobbes, at least, the idea has been widely held that no man stands much above another, however forcefully his image may be projected. As information and communication have improved, following widespread literacy, rational-empirical argumentation, and scientific method, the claims to exceptional charisma have become more difficult to sustain. It becomes a less acceptable legitimation of leadership. Modern men are cynical, seeking empirically based explanations for individual differences, and rational solutions for social problems. Democracy, too, formally assumes that one man is the equal of another, and this democratic current even affects charisma itself: if one can have it, then, so can everyone else, according to the contemporary movement of Charismatic Renewal.[4] No longer are there special elect vessels, but anyone may expect the infusion of the Holy Spirit. The democratic impact is clear: just as in politics, everyone may have a vote, so in religion everyone may have a voice—perhaps even a voice of prophecy.

Among Christian bodies, the pre-eminent charisma of Jesus Christ has generally restrained the charismatic claims of, or on behalf of, subsequent leaders, no matter how vigorous their personalities and how effective their leadership. The relative role of any subsequent charismatic claimant has needed careful definition and special legitimation. The stronger such claims, the more has criticism been attracted. Even those for whom no very exceptional charisma was alleged—for instance, a Luther or a Wesley, men who were charismatic only in the rather weak sense in which the term is nowadays used—have suffered in our own times from radical reappraisals.[5] Their strength of character is related to psychogenetic, not divine, provenance. Reassessment, if not radical debunking, is the order of the day, even of men like these who make no special charismatic claims. If strong claims induce more severe criticism, this is intensified the more recent the purported vessel of inspiration. For modern man, prophets, if they existed at all, existed only a long time ago.

[4] For accounts, see R. Quebedeaux, *The New Charismatics: The Origins, Development and Significance of Neo-Pentecostalism* (New York: Doubleday, 1976); id., *The New Charismatics II: How a Christian Renewal Movement became a Part of the American Religious Mainstream* (New York: Harper and Row, 1983); and D. Martin and P. Mullen (eds.), *Strange Gifts? A Guide to Charismatic Renewal* (Oxford: Blackwell, 1984).

[5] On Luther, see e.g. E. H. Erikson, *Young Man Luther: A Study in Psychoanalysis and History* (London: Faber, 1958). Popular but influential studies of Wesley include G. E. Harrison, *Son to Susannah* (London, 1944), and G. R. Taylor, *The Angelmakers* (London: 1958).

Buoyed up, pehaps, by the expansive optimism of American experience, social mobility, and incipient nationalism, some of the new American expressions of Christianity were disposed to stronger charismatic legitimation than those that had arisen or which throve in eighteenth- and nineteenth-century Europe. To establish the point, one need only juxtapose roughly contemporaneous movements in the New World and the Old. In the United States, there were three highly successful new sects with powerful charismatic leadership, albeit of varying strengths: the Mormons, the Seventh-day Adventists, and Christian Science, as well as numerous charismatically led New Thought groups and— outside Christianity—Madame Blavatsky's Theosophists. There were, too, other movements strongly committed to diffused but vigorously proclaimed charisma—the Shakers, the Spiritualists, and, at the turn of the century, the Pentecostals; and, of course, there was the current of that unique but exportable American religious product—revivalism. In Europe, the movements then burgeoning or beginning were the Methodists (of several kinds), the Moravians, the Glasites, the Brethren (Open and Exclusive), the schisms of the Church of Scotland, and the Salvationists—and none of these was the creation either of a leader claiming supernatural inspiration, or of diffused charisma. Only among the Catholic Apostolics did charismatic claims find a place, and even there in a strictly circumscribed area of operation. Of course, American sects spread to Europe, and, sooner or later, some did well there, but the charismatic element was American—and perhaps (as in the case of the British emigrant Mormons) the Americanness was almost intrinsic to charisma itself.

Not all American movements depended on charisma, of course (the Watchtower movement, later called Jehovah's Witnesses, represents a different model of religious organization). But it is no surprise to the sociologist that powerful new inspiration is claimed at the periphery of Christendom rather than at its traditional centre. Indeed, the incidence of charisma in the vigorous new nation might almost be seen as a powerful if unconscious claim to make itself the new religious centre, just as later, by 1913, it was to become the economic, and, in 1945, the political centre of the Western world. Sheer facticity made those economic and political claims indisputable: but the claim to be the religious centre has no empirical referent to sustain it: it can be legitimated only by reference to the operation of the Holy Spirit inspiring an individual who then offers to guide others. Historically, it has usually been in places remote from economic and political power that charismatic claims have been most boldly made and have had greatest success. Success—in Galilee—was followed by failure—in Jerusalem. The manger, the stable, and the fishermen do not constitute a formula, but they create a model symbolism much celebrated subsequently. One may regard the periphery either as a context of unworldly innocence in which spirituality is native; or as that of unsophisticated ignorance in which credulity persists—as one will.

Locations of innocence today rarely remain such for long. Hindsight, comparison, and relativity bring reappraisals not only of charismatic claimants, but also of the psycho-sociological factors which induce susceptibility to charismatic claims, and which may even generate what we may regard as the demand for charismatic leadership.[6] It is not through mere cynical secularism, nor by random chance, that the great charismatic figures of nineteenth-century America—the Mormon leader, Joseph Smith, jun.; Ellen White, inspirator of Seventh-day Adventists; Mary Baker Eddy, founder of Christian Science; and Madame Blavatsky, the first Theosophist—should all have been accused of plagiarism, nor that all of them have been the subject, in so far as the evidence allows, of psychiatric speculation.[7] This shared fate is not coincidence: it is

[6] On the concept of 'charismatic demand' see B. Wilson, *The Noble Savages: The Primitive Origins of Charisma and its Contemporary Survival* (Berkeley and Los Angeles: University of California Press, 1975), 82–4, 99–103.

[7] The first, if implausible, suggestions of Smith's plagiarism date from as early as 1833: see F. M. Brodie, *No Man Knows My History* (London: Eyre and Spottiswoode, 1963), 419–33. For an early psychological interpretation, see I. Woodbridge Riley, *The Founder of Mormonism: a Psychological Study* (London: Heinemann, 1903). A summary account of possible plagiarism by Mrs Eddy is provided in B. R. Wilson, 'The Origins of Christian Science: A Survey', *The Hibbert Journal*, 57 (Jan. 1959), 161–70. Mrs Eddy's psychology has been discussed in many biographies, and hysteria, paranoia, monomania, and acute anxiety states have often been attributed to her. Close adherents have written unwittingly revealing accounts of her later life from which such diagnoses have been advanced: see, in particular, A. H. Dickey, *Memoirs of Mary Baker Eddy* (Boston: Merrymount Press, 1927), and C. A. Frye, *Visions of Mary Baker Eddy* (Providence, RI: 1935). Allegations of plagiarism committed by Mrs Ellen G. White are not new, but the subject has been reactivated in recent years: see R. L. Numbers, *Prophetess of Health: A Study of Ellen G. White* (New York: Harper and Row, 1976); and W. Rea, 'Walter Rea Calls for Action', *Spectrum*, 14 (Oct. 1983). Suggestions that Mrs White's visions were a result of hysteria and catalepsy were made by a well-known apostate, D. M. Canright, *Seventh-day Adventism Renounced* (Nashville: Gospel Advocate, 1914), and similar theories have been recently debated by dissidents and

part of the pattern of church growth in our times. This is how modern man explains visions, revelations, and direct supernatural inspiration. Even without the deprecatory implications of research of this kind, our contemporaries will ask of these figures, as of others, where they got their ideas, who and what influenced them. Each is taken merely as a creature of his or her time, writing into their revelations something of prevailing ideas, fashions, and preoccupations. This then, is said to explain why Smith found the lost tribes in America, and why freemasonry loomed so large in the formative development of Mormon ritual.[8] Mrs Eddy spent years seeking therapy for her ailments. Her mind cure came originally from P. P. Quimby, and when she was introduced to the language of a somewhat hybridized Hegelian idealism, which echoed elements in Quimby's thought, the contours of Christian Science were imposed on her inherited unitarianism.[9] Hers was no mystical revelation, so much as the production of a new synthesis. Not dissimilar things have been said of the health reform preoccupations of Mrs White.[10] Given the nineteenth-century American context, it is not surprising (except, perhaps, to benighted Europeans) that they should all three have found such evil in alcohol, tobacco, coffee, and tea.

It is not my intention, in bracketing together three such very different religious leaders, with their widely divergent interpretations of the Christian message, to disparage any of them individually or by association: I simply point to explicable similarities among those who emerged as charismatic figures in a given cultural milieu in the span of three or four decades. Sects and denominations do not grow according to an inevitable sequence, passing through inevitable stages regardless of the actual period of history or the actual social context. Patterns of denominational growth are in considerable

defenders of Mrs White, including a special committee of several (Adventist) medical professors convened by the Church. See W. H. Hohns, 'Was Ellen G. White an Epileptic?', *Ministry*, 57 (Aug. 1984); and D. H. Hodder, MD, and Gregory Holmes, MD, 'Ellen G. White and the Seventh-day Adventist Church: Visions or Partial-Complex Seizures', unpublished paper, n.d. On Mme Blavatsky, see R. A. Hutch, 'Helen Blavatsky Unveiled', *Journal of Religious History*, 11/2 (Dec. 1980), 320–41; and B. F. Campbell, *Ancient Wisdom Revived: A History of the Theosophical Movement* (Berkeley and Los Angeles: University of California Press, 1980), 57–61.

[8] Brodie, *No Man Knows*, pp. 280–2.
[9] Wilson, 'The Origins of Christian Science'.
[10] See J. B. Blake, 'Health Reform' in E. S. Gaustad (ed.), *The Rise of Adventism* (New York: Harper and Row, 1974), 30–49; and Numbers, *Prophetess of Health*.

part specific to times and cultures. Thus, churches persisting or growing in our times will experience a pattern of scrutiny of their claims and the charismatic claims of their founders or early leaders. There is less trust than once there was in leadership claims: leaders are cut down to human size, and their foibles, weaknesses, ambition, and *amour propre* are regularly exposed. And this not only by rivals and outsiders: reinterpretations arise among some who were brought up in the faith, some of whom expect to remain in its fellowship. Religious movements in which past leadership has been charismatically legitimated are thus likely to be undergoing particular strain. Sects which trace their origins to groups of seekers or a collective leadership, such as Baptists, Congregationalists, and Quakers, have less trouble on this score. Even Jehovah's Witnesses, despite schisms, have escaped serious traumas of what might be called charismatic deflation. Charisma is perhaps the most extreme claim to legitimacy, but it relies on faith and total trust. Once equivocation occurs, what was once a source of strength becomes an embarrassing handicap. The greater past reliance, the greater present disabilities.

Organizational Change

As a religious movement grows its organizational structure changes in ways which vary according to the theological and ecclesiastical precepts with which the church began. Ideology constrains organization in religious bodies much more than is the case in the organizationally rational world of economics, or even of law, education, or politics. In older religious movements, tradition and its accompaniments of hierarchy, status differentiation, precedent, and protocol impede processes of reorganization, as one may see from the cumbersome and protracted manœuvrings of the Church of England as it divested itself of ancient convocations and developed first a church assembly and then a system of synods, in which the laity acquired a fuller part and business a quicker dispatch.[11] New sects, at least since the early seventeenth century, have frequently begun with a powerful thrust against a clerical

[11] For a general historical survey, see K. A. Thompson, *Bureaucracy and Church Reform* (Oxford: Clarendon Press, 1970); and for a brief account of more recent developments, K. N. Medhurst and G. H. Moyser, *Church and Politics in a Secular Age* (Oxford: Clarendon Press, 1988), 57–65.

monopoly of power, and even where an ordained ministry has been retained 'the priesthood of all believers' has been a common call implicitly rejecting the division into separate classes of ministry and laity.

Some sects, particularly those arising as evangelistic movements, and especially in the United States, have evolved towards denominations, and a principal element in this evolution is the acquisition of a paid ordained ministry—a professionally religious élite. The pressures making for the emergence of such a class include the need to care for the new recruits, particularly those recruited in rallies or revival campaigns. Movements which begin as revivalistic agencies or which espouse vigorous evangelism almost necessarily acquire a paid ministry. That ministry tends to occupy the central positions in organization, even where the work is not pastoral. Ordination becomes a certification for all other power positions, no matter how remote from specifically spiritual concerns. The ministry may then come to regard itself as 'the church', and to regard the laity as less informed, and not much to be trusted with church business, organization, or policy. For their part, the laity may then divest themselves of responsibility for evangelism and administration: that becomes work for professionals—'It's their job: they are paid for it.' In extreme cases, such as in some Pentecostal bodies, lay members may even disavow much knowledge of doctrine, referring enquiries to a minister.

The extent to which tensions arise from the division between ministerial and lay echelons varies. In early Methodism, recurrent schisms occurred as lay members struggled to break the power of the ministerial class. In the British Elim Church, a power struggle occurred between the semi-charismatic revivalist leader and the increasingly bureaucratic central administration, reflecting the clash of pristine ideological commitment and organizational imperatives. The speed with which a ministry develops and acquires dominance is a function of various factors, including ideology, and the specific techniques of recruitment that a movement employs. In some sects, a separated, ordained ministerial élite is ideologically precluded. Yet, even where this is so, and where organization is minimal, as in congregational polity or among groups which explicitly reject all corporate identity, a body of administrators emerges. The cost of disavowing all centralism is the loss of effectiveness in those pursuits that require large-scale, long-term organizational arrangements: such sects tend to be those that are least likely to develop into recognizable denominational entities.

Any echelon of administrators, be it ministerial or purely bureaucratic, is likely to develop interests and concerns that diverge in some degree from those of the movement. Goal displacement is a common phenomenon of all bureaucracies. Responsibility *for* the organization soon becomes responsibility *to* the organization, and organizational imperatives may from time to time eclipse the original ideological goals of the movement. Serving the church may replace serving the faith. Apart from their concern for job protection, which normally, perhaps necessarily, arises among officials, they often develop a preference for routine over initiative, for calculable, quantitative, and often monetary criteria of performance. Beyond this, they may develop less excusable traits: concern for status; pleasure in power for its own sake; distrust of others; the desire to manipulate; and disapproval of purists who put moral rigour or spiritual values before administrative convenience.

Professionalism implies adhesion to professional, rather than denominational, values. The expertise of professionals—ministers or administrators—is necessarily shared with other professionals in other institutions. The profession becomes an alternative reference group. Thus, ministers may take as role models those in other churches, praise ecumenically those of other faiths who make a spiritual mark in the wider Christian community. They perceive the social standing, style, and dispositions of ministers in other movements, and they may even demand similar conditions of work, retirement schemes, security of tenure, and so on, to those accorded to their fellow professionals who—it might almost be said— chance to be working in other denominations. The theologically minded and those working in seminaries increasingly turn to commentaries by those in other churches, whose views they take into account in their own published work, so drawing further from the traditions of their own laity and closer to the professional concerns of the Christian ministry *tout court*. Those engaged professionally in administrative roles learn techniques of rational organization that are essentially secular—acquiring faculties in accountancy, computers, communication skills, man-management, investment, marketing and the like, all of which pertain almost as fully to religious and denominational management as they do to public or business administration, the running of hospitals,

universities, or even commercial concerns. Through such things—
necessary as they may be—secular orientations are found even at
the core of religious movements which began with very different,
much simpler, perspectives concerning the life of faith.[12]

The influence of rational techniques on the patterns of church
growth stems from the need of eighteenth- and nineteenth-century
sects, in reacting against religious traditionalism, to evolve new
structures. Needing new organizational forms, understandably they
adapted the increasingly rational methods of the secular world.
Since they rejected religious coercion, such as prevailed widely in
Europe, and superstitious sanctions, they came to depend more on
devices that were intended to induce regularity, sustain commitment, promote education, and encourage systematic endeavour.
The very name 'Methodist' captures this rational orientation very
well: religious commitment was not now to be a merely emotional
response or a consequence of superstition, evinced most effectively
at the crisis points in life; nor was it to be a consequence of
dependence on traditional forms and set rhythms (often laid in
agrarian feudalism). It was to be purposive and rational, evolutionary and ordered. Thus it was that so many of the new
movements, utilizing the benefits of literacy, adopted regular study
programmes through educational agencies (both religious Sunday
and Sabbath schools and secular instruction). Standardized periodical
literature guided faith, and set procedures were provided for study
in ordered sequence—by, for example, Jehovah's Witnesses and
Christian Scientists, as well as by Seventh-day Adventists.[13]
Mormon ward and stake organization participated in the same
thrust towards rational organization, planning, and future provision.[14] The adoption of such arrangements set the new sects on a
course of development in which, sooner or later, they would face
the accumulated cost of pitting efficiency against spirituality.

[12] Compliance with religious prescripts is necessarily a normative form of
compliance, motivated by an appeal to shared and ultimate *values*. In other work
organizations, compliance may be elicited by remuneration, where the motivation is
by an appeal to the accommodation of (shared and/or conflicting) *interests*. It
follows that the fundamental assumptions about human action proceed from quite
different, and at times mutually contradictory, premises in these two situations. For
a discussion of the nature of compliance, see A. Etzioni, *A Comparative Analysis of
Complex Organizations* (New York: Free Press of Glencoe, 1961).

[13] For a fuller discussion, see Ch. 7 below.

[14] On this aspect of Mormonism, see J. Heinerman and A. Shupe, *The Mormon
Corporate Empire* (Boston, Mass.: Beacon Press, 1985).

System, routine, and economies of scale evolved, in the twentieth century, into the rigidities of instrumentalism—a hardening of the organizational arteries. The new efficient methods of one period became identified as the faceless, impersonal, alienating bureaucracy of the next. The new procedures lacked the sanctifying legitimation of antiquity: their sheer instrumentalism was in itself an invitation to condemnation whenever a reappraisal of spiritual values occurred as in most movements from time to time it does. The paradox occurs of conservative leaders defending rational procedures against progressives who campaign against them in the name of inspiration, spontaneity, and the need to mobilize and motivate believers and to quicken the life of the spirit. Such dispositions spring not only—perhaps not even mainly—from endogenous currents within religious movements. They are also acquired from the wider society in which 'de-structuration' has become fashionable as a response to the over-rationalized social system. Political demonstrations, radical protests, ecological concern, and campaigns for the control of science (particularly in the field of medical ethics) are comparable with the contemporary challenges to church order and clerical authority. House fellowships and the underground church—both widespread in Europe—reject formal procedures and institutional contexts. Even the electronic church—concealing its own dependence on highly rational techniques and organization—challenges the set and systematic arrangements of the past. All of them are an aspect of contemporary patterns that reject the capacity of instrumental values in the service of organizing man's religious dispositions, and those churches which adopted well-organized structural forms are those which, with the onset of these reactions, have probably suffered most.

The Matter of Denominational Distinctiveness

An important facet of a sect's shift towards denominationalism is the steady relinquishment of the pristine rigour of its theology and ideology. As the self-conception of collectivity changes from asserting the uniqueness and indispensability of its truth, and moves towards claiming parity of status with other denominations in a culturally pluralist tradition, so the emphasis on distinctiveness diminishes. Unions are proposed as Christians perceive that, faced with the overwhelming secularity of the wider society, different

denominations have much in common. Ecumenism, which churchmen tend to see as a response to spiritual forces, may be no more
than the reaction of weak organizations to a declining market in
which secular agencies compete more effectively for the time,
energy, and money of individuals. As sects mature, they tend to
surrender even those concerns espoused in their original charter.
Thus, in Britain Baptists, who once upon a time believed—
necessarily to be called Baptists—in adult baptism, began between
the wars to amalgamate locally with Congregationalists, who
did not. Congregationalists, so-called by virtue of their congregational polity, have united with Presbyterians, and have accepted
their system of synodical government. The Primitive Methodists,
who wanted in the nineteenth century to get back to early
revivalist tactics, rejoined in the twentieth the Wesleyans whom they
had earlier abandoned. The Free Church of Scotland, which left
the established Church in 1843 because its members held that the
established Church had not sufficiently protected the principle
of establishment, began, as early as 1863, talks with the United
Presbyterians, who rejected the establishment principle altogether;
and the two churches united, regardless of this fundamental
distinction, just over three decades later. In more recent times, the
Presbyterians, who do not believe in bishops, voted for a union
with Anglicans, who do.

Thus ecclesiastical principles, once thought to be virtually
indispensable for the true church and for obedience to God's will,
are abandoned, and their legitimations forgotten. Time—and it
may be said, distance, where distance relates to the mission field—
erodes the circumstances in which certain truths were hard fought
for: the fight for them ceases, and they are no longer seen as
necessary truths at all. What applies to teachings and organization
also applies to practice. Charismatic manifestations in Pentecostal
churches have steadily diminished in enthusiasm and even in spontaneity as those churches have become more socially respectable,
while the Charismatic Renewal movement introduced glossolalia
to main-line denominations—Episcopalian, Roman, Presbyterian,
and Methodist—which some fifty or sixty years before had been
eager to condemn the self-same practices among Pentecostals. Even
better-insulated bodies manifest the same pattern. Thus, at one time
Seventh-day Adventists might well have considered that only
sabbath-keepers would qualify for salvation: today they are less

disposed to think so. Indeed, in the last thirty years or so, the movement's literature, beginning in 1957 with an official work *Seventh-day Adventists Answer Questions on Doctrine*, has increasingly come to reduce the emphasis on denominational distinctiveness. The trend became even more pronounced in the early 1970s in *So Much In Common*, a joint production with the World Council of Churches, whilst an alternative approach towards the same end is evident in a work by one of the movement's theologians, in which most of the vigorously held Adventist beliefs are traced directly to some of the English Puritans.[15]

In the pattern of church growth, distinctiveness becomes relativized. Yesterday's essentials become today's optionals, lingering as badges of identity which connote a denominational culture, the primary strengths of which may have come to be group association, kinship networks, insulating devices, and separate institutional support systems. And even the last-named may do little to support the faith ideologically. In Belgium, all institutions have ideological affiliations, so that, as a Catholic, the individual goes to a Catholic school and a Catholic university, he joins a Catholic trade union, insures through a Catholic insurance agency, buys his house through a Catholic building soiciety, travels through a Catholic travel agency. The Socialists and the Liberals each have their own parallel systems, and sociologists call this arrangement pillar structures. Recently, Belgian Catholic sociologists have asked: 'What is Catholic about a Catholic hospital or a Catholic university?' Their answer is: 'Little, very little indeed.'[16] Professional, not Catholic norms regulate personnel, and secular techniques prevail. There is no denominational distinctiveness, nor even much religious distinctiveness—only a lingering image of something supposedly different. It is in the fact of institutional support, not in any reinforcement of specifically denominational values, that the present-day utility of

[15] See B. B. Beach and L. Vischer, *So Much in Common* (Geneva: World Council of Churches, 1973); and B. W. Ball, *The English Connection: The Puritan Roots of Seventh-day Adventist Belief* (Cambridge: James Clark, 1981).

[16] See J. Billiet, 'Secularization and Compartmentalization in the Belgian Educational System', *Social Compass*, 20/4 (1973), 569–91; K. Dobbelaere, 'Professionalization and Secularization in the Belgian Catholic Pillar', *Japanese Journal of Religious Studies*, 6/1–2 (1979), 39–64; K. Dobbelaere, J. Billiet, and R. Creyf, 'Secularization and Pillarization: A Social Problem Approach', *Annual Review of the Social Sciences of Religion*, 2 (1978), 97–124; K. Dobbelaere, M. Ghesquiere-Waelkens, and J. Lauwers, *La dimension chrétienne d'une institution hospitalière* (Brussels: Editions Hospitalia, 1975).

these agencies lies, and clearly such support might easily be organized on other bases—political allegiance, locality, professional association, or through purely utilitarian mutual help associations. Ancillary institutions may be agencies of preservation for collectivities which claim a religious *raison d'être*, but the circumstances in which denominational preoccupations grew have changed. Commitment may persist as much to the collectivity as to specific denominational values, and indeed those values themselves may have become less clear and less compelling for many who remain attached to the collectivity itself.

Growth and the Effects of Secularization

Secularization is the process in which religion loses its social significance, and the pattern of growth of every denomination has been affected by this long-term social process. Just how secularization affects each movement varies according to the sect's specific teachings and the extent to which these have been liberalized and the sect denominationalized. It varies also from one society to another and within the same society for each context or region. Thus, in the United Kingdom secularization has been apparent in the decline in church membership and attendance: in the United States attendances have been much less affected, and the process has worked primarily to produce an internal transformation of the churches and a diminution in the religious context of their activities. Generally, in the cities religious attendance and belief has declined more rapidly than in rural areas: there tends to be lower church membership density in areas where there is higher population density. Further, peripheral or rural areas often sustain a more vigorous and stricter adherence to religious beliefs and contingent moral practices, and resist the liberal and libertarian tendencies of the cities.[17] Thus, in Scotland it was the remote islands and highlands which objected to the late nineteenth-century liberalism of the Free Church, which eventually led to their separation as the so-called 'Wee Frees'.[18] There are parallel cases elsewhere. Rural areas remain, at least for a time, more attached to

---

[17] The differential incidence of religious practice between peripheral and cosmopolitan areas is an issue explored by D. Martin, *A General Theory of Secularization* (Oxford: Blackwell, 1978).

[18] *History of the Free Presbyterian Church of Scotland* (Inverness, n.d.).

the remnants of an older social order which in the urban metropolis is already in decay. The importance of religion to the social system diminishes more rapidly in the city than in the village, where major institutions (economy, politics, law, education, health, etc.) are mediated still by interpersonal relationships and not by bureaucratic agencies. Of course, the countryside is steadily urbanized, and the secularizing influences at work in urban life gradually, and increasingly quickly, penetrate rural areas too.

A powerful factor affecting secularization is the mobility of population, both vicinally and socially. Movement causes the weakening of personal affiliations, and, of all social institutions, religion is the one most dependent on personal relationships. Geographic mobility, in weakening personal ties, indirectly affects religious commitment. Main-line denominations are familiar with the problem of 'transfers' and the leakage which attends them. When members move from centres of denominational strength to areas of weakness, they may forge new social ties with people who do not belong to their own denomination, and who, indeed, may not belong to any. The process has been documented in the expansion of Methodism in Britain.[19] As Methodists moved to the suburbs, they often found the nearest church more convenient than the nearest Methodist church, or, if that church was far away, found no church at all. In areas of strength, a denomination invests capital, builds facilities. It then becomes committed to service this investment, pay off its debts, maintain its properties, and all of this limits its ability to embark on new investment in other areas. Financial obligations impose rigidities on the organization which may not be perceived by its members as they move away from centres of denominational strength. In doing so they both weaken the centres and make it more difficult for the denomination to serve both the membership which remains and the new districts to which the migrant members have dispersed.

Social mobility also affects the growth of a movement. The pattern is familiar. Relatively poor, underprivileged groups have often formed the constituency of sects. Sectarians, by religiously prescribed asceticism, a work ethic, industry, sobriety, discipline, methodical application, and the avoidance of luxury and extravagance, accumulate wealth and so rise in the social scale. The

---

[19] See R. Currie, *Methodism Divided* (London: Faber and Faber, 1968).

temptation they face is that they will associate increasingly with outsiders of similar social status. The more they do so, the more incongruous become their religious beliefs and the dispositions acquired with them in conditions of poverty. If sect allegiance and status become utterly incongruous, they leave. Alternatively, sectarian rigour may be gradually relaxed, particularly where sects become denominationalized, one aspect of which process is increased association with outsiders. Yet, it is unlikely that members will do much to promote religious outreach to their status peers, whilst, at the same time, they have become increasingly detached from the disadvantaged classes which constituted the movement's original intake. If the underprivileged are still recruited, they are likely to find it difficult to adapt to life in a movement many of whose members have acquired greater wealth and perhaps even higher social status.

The external constituency of a religious movement is, at any one time, normally a homogeneous unit, as MacGavran has suggested, but social mobility leads to divergences of status between members and the constituency which remains outside.[20] Cultural incongruities develop, so cutting a movement off from its original social base without it finding a new one. When a church recruits heterogeneous populations, brought together through migration or in spite of differential social mobility, tensions arise. Middle-class converts to Charismatic Renewal did not easily or frequently join classical Pentecostal sects. The experience of Seventh-day Adventism in Britain of the induction of West Indian immigrants into a previously entirely white denomination provides a variant example. Polish Catholics were not readily assimilated into churches dominated by the Irish and the Italians in the United States, and there was evident persisting tension between the largely middle- and upper-class recusant Catholics in England, and the lower-class Irish who have provided the church with most of its priests. The conversion of unaccommodated Catholic Puerto Rican migrants to New York to Pentecostalism is another illustration.

Obviously, the effects of mobility may be mitigated in a movement which retains distinctiveness of doctrine, ethic, and practice. As Dean Kelley has observed, 'strong organizations are strict', and strictness implies a coherent policy and consistent

[20] D. A. McGavran, *Understanding Church Growth* (Grand Rapids, Mich.: Eerdmans, 1970).

attitudes in the face of such secularizing phenomena as social mobility.[21] Strictness is not only a matter of maintaining high standards of admission—indeed, admission may not be much at issue for movements experiencing the pressure of social mobility—but of maintaining rigour in commitment, in morality, in reinforcing insulating devices and members' consciousness of kind. Once the criteria by which a movement is differentiated from the wider society, or even from the generality of Christendom, become obscure, that movement loses a large part of its *raison d'être*. Without such distinctive commitments, members cease to take their primary sense of identity from their religion. Indeed, their religious allegiance becomes merely one among a number of attributes and affiliations, such as marital status and kinship relations; occupation; education; residence; business links; voluntary organizations, and the like, by which social identity is located. Further, without these distinctive commitments, a movement may itself become transmogrified, and, as a consequence of secularization, some issues once incidental may acquire a more central place as the essentially religious and moral concerns of members diminish. Thus, the Quakers losing their distinctive beliefs became largely a peace movement. The Salvation Army has steadily become identified with good works for down-and-outs. The Student Christian Movement has become a forum for all kinds of political and libertarian causes that are quite incidental to the core doctrines of Christianity.[22] The Seventh-day Adventist Church has not yet moved so far down the secularizing path. The distinctive doctrines—which I take to be those relating to the Advent, the sabbath, the Sanctuary, and mortalism, with the dietetic observances as a supportive institution[23] —remain, and they sustain the denomination against the forces which have acted as a solvent on other Christian churches.

As society grows more secular, the distinctive norms of the Christian sect may become subject to increased strain: they are harder to promulgate to the members, and harder to defend to a less biblical and more sceptical outside world. The more a

[21] D. Kelley, *Why Conservative Churches are Growing* (New York: Harper and Row, 1972), 95.
[22] S. Bruce, *Firm in the Faith* (Aldershot: Gower, 1984), 65–94.
[23] Here I follow G. Maxwell, 'The Distinctive Mission of the Seventh-day Adventist Church', in V. Carner and G. Stanhiser (comps.), *The Stature of Christ: Essays in Honor of Edward Heppenstall* (Loma Linda, Calif.: privately printed, 1970), 89–98.

movement has persisted in its sectarian orientation, the stronger it is likely to be: its membership is inured to its exacting distinctive norms and beliefs, which are still seen as vital issues of faith. The cost is that the movement is increasingly at odds with the wider society. Liberal elements within the movement will find this situation uncongenial, and may want to make common cause with secular advocates of positions similar to their own on various social, political, and ethical issues, and may indeed very much want the denomination to appear more 'normal'. In general, this posture, like that of Catholic priests who dispute their Church's attitude to celibacy of the priesthood, is often a half-way house for those who will sooner or later abandon active allegiance. Paradoxically, it is the distinctive, uncommon characteristics of a movement's teachings and practices, rather than the generally shared tenets of mainstream denominations, that are the principal bulwark against absorption into the secular world.

The currents of secularization in society make all churches and sects more marginal to society's functioning. Their significance in the social system becomes bracketed with recreational pursuits, activities in the free zone of choice. An increasingly sharp contrast occurs between the self-interpretation of religious bodies and the actual importance accorded to them. Although they take themselves with immense seriousness, they are increasingly disregarded both by the agencies of the social system and by the public at large. The climate is such that it becomes more difficult for any movement to find an external constituency of sympathetic potential converts. Such sympathizers would themselves risk becoming more marginal in the wider society, and yet would have no claim on the supportive community life of the movement itself. If such sympathizers do convert, then they are less likely to be replaced within this external constituency of sympathizers by other members of the general public.[24] So, movements which retain distinctive sectarian elements, and which stand in this sense apart, find that in the contemporary scene they become even more isolated. At the same time, newly converted outsiders are unlikely to be wholly assimilated until they reinforce their commitment with friendship and kinship ties—until then they remain volatile. There is some slight compensation,

[24] My argument follows that advanced by R. Currie, A. Gilbert, and L. Horsley, *Churches and Churchgoers: Patterns of Church in the British Isles since 1700* (Oxford: Clarendon Press, 1977), 120.

however, for movements which are recruiting few outsiders. They avoid high losses, since the children of existing members are retained better than are converts. Movements in this stage of growth thus come to rely more and more on internal recruitment, and enjoy lower turnover rates. Losses by slow attrition there may be, but long-existing sects and denominations become dependent on birth-rates. Thus, in the context of secularization, it is common for a religious movement that has existed for some decades to gain perhaps three-quarters of its membership from internal recruitment.[25] Where the proportion is smaller, then we must expect to find high rates of turnover, as among Jehovah's Witnesses. When a movement relies on internal recruits, then it reaches a plateau—a plateau which becomes almost a segregated enclave, a marginal phenomenon in the secularized society of our times.

The social context affects religious minorities in a variety of other ways, unconsidered here: for example, in the effect of incidence of war (particularly, but by no means exclusively, on those sects which object to taking up arms); or even in such apparently innocent matters as the compulsory provision of social welfare for sects which reject all dependence on the state.[26] But among external factors, secularization must be seen as the most pervasive influence shaping, together with a movement's own internal characteristics, the course of its development.

[25] This is just about the estimate of internal growth made about 10 years ago for the Seventh-day Adventist Church in North America by G. Oosterwal, *Mission: Possible* (Nashville, Tenn.: Southern Publishing Association, 1972).

[26] For a discussion of the influence of war in general terms, see Robert Currie *et al.*, *Churches and Churchgoers*, pp. 113–15; for a particular case study, see B. R. Wilson, 'Apparition et persistance des Sectes', *Archives de sociologie des religions*, 5 (1958), 140–50. Some Mennonites have migrated from country to country to escape involvement with the secular state. Those who had settled in Mexico migrated to Belize (then British Honduras) at least partly because of the Mexican government's declared intention of incorporating them into its social security system in 1955: H. L. Sawatzky, *They Sought A Country: Mennonite Colonization in Mexico* (Berkeley and Los Angeles: University of California Press, 1971), 331–2.

7

American Sects:
Their Impact on Europe

NOT all sects evolve within the continuity of one society; many of them increasingly, and increasingly effectively, mission overseas, and their development reflects the diversity of the societies into which they spread. Religious diffusion does not, of course, for long proceed from only one centre, and in recent centuries there has been a reversal of the balance of religious trade between countries from that which prevailed in earlier centuries. Leaving aside those patterns of migration that have seen Muslim and Hindu, Sikh and Buddhist communities establish themselves in Europe and America, and the Westernized off-shoot new religious movements that claim association with these exotic traditions, Christian sectarianism has also displayed a proclivity, either by dint of migrating votaries or of local conversions, to become disseminated throughout the Christianized world, and even beyond.

There is a marked contrast between the European sects which migrated to the United States and those which, originating there, have spread their influence in Europe. Quite apart from the larger dissenting denominations, Congregationalists, Baptists, Presbyterians, and subsequently Methodists, most of the European groups which settled in America went not only seeking refuge, but also to withdraw from an oppressive social order. Many of them were pietists, introversionist groups who found in America the opportunity (or sometimes experienced the necessity) to establish vicinally segregated communitarian organizations, and to perpetuate cultural traits which, though distinctly European in style, were paradoxically more easily maintained in the New World than in the Old. Such were the Mennonites (and particularly the Amish), the Hutterians, the Ephrata Community, the Zoarites, Rappites, the Amana Society, and the Shakers.[1] These groups have excercised very little

---

[1] For an account of some of these and similar movements, see J. A. Hostetler, *Amish Society* (Baltimore: Johns Hopkins University Press, 1963); id., *Hutterian Society* (Baltimore: Johns Hopkins University Press, 1974); J. W. Bennett, *Hutterian*

return influence on Europe, with the exception perhaps of the larger and more denominationally organized divisions of the Mennonites (although some, in search of less sullied social contexts, have diffused their influence to underdeveloped parts of the world, and this is particularly true of the stricter groups of Mennonites, who have established colonies in Mexico, Paraguay, Java, and Belize.[2]

The American sects that have most influenced Europe have been those that originated in the United States, and which have absorbed particularly American styles of religiosity. The lack of a 'return' from the migrating groups (excepting again the major denominations) is to be explained by the fact that those European sects that migrated to America were seeking refuge, and were therefore not themselves disposed to seek large numbers of new converts; some indeed were distinctly 'ethnic' in style, and maintained an almost ethnic barrier to admission. It is indigenous American groups that manifested the ethos of expansionism; optimism (in respect of recruitment if not in their ideology); pragmatism in their organizational goals and sometimes in their religious perspectives; and a capacity for rationalization and routinization of religious activities, and certainly of their organizational procedures. Some of these characteristics have also marked the influence of the American wings of major denominations on their European, and particularly on their British, counterparts, as instanced by the long-term export of revivalistic religion from the United States to the rest of the world. Revivalism affected, in greater or lesser degree, most of the major Protestant denominations in Europe, and particularly the evangelical wing of the Church of England, Lutheranism, Methodism, and even the originally doctrinally less receptive Church of Scotland.[3] Among sects, the extent of this particular influence has

Brethren: The Agricultural Economy and Social Organization of a Communal People (Stanford: Stanford University Press, 1967); K. J. R. Arndt, *Georg Rapp's Harmony Society 1785–1847* (Philadelphia: University of Pennsylvania Press, 1965); G. L. Gollin, *Moravians in Two Worlds* (New York: Columbia University Press, 1967); C Nordhoff, *The Communistic Societies of the United States* (New York: Schocken, 1965; 1st edn. 1875); R. S. Fogarty, *Dictionary of American Communal and Utopian History* (Westport, Conn.: Greenwood Press, 1980).

[2] The story of the Mennonites in Mexico is in H. L. Sawatzky, *They Sought a Country: Mennonite Colonization in Mexico* (Berkeley and Los Angeles: University of California Press, 1971); J. W. Fretz, *Pilgrims in Paraguay* (Scottsdale, Pa.: Herald Press, 1953); F. Kliewer, 'Die Mennoniten in Brasilien', *Stadenjahrbuch*, 5 (São Paulo, 1957), 233–46.

[3] A detailed discussion is provided in J. Wesley White, 'The Influence of North

varied, being most marked in those that have the closest connection with evangelical Protestant denominations—sects that have been labelled 'conversionist' because of their emphasis on the necessity of a conversion experience (and sometimes also on subsequent emotional experiences in enlargement or reaffirmation of the experience of conversion).[4] But all the American sects that have really exerted influence abroad have shared an aggressive concern for recruitment; a diminution of the distinction between laymen and professionals (and the elimination of sacerdotalism); a strong tendency towards the centralization of organization and the replacement of local community structures by a more conscious establishment of 'local branches'; and the use of mass media (the mass distribution of cheap, or even free, literature; radio; and television).

Clearly, not all of these tendencies are equally evident in all movements. Variations in period and circumstances of origin, in ideological stance, and in the extent to which there has been an accretion of subsidiary concerns, all influence the measure in which these general attributes are characteristic. But the broad ethos of American culture and society is as evident in American sectarianism as it is in the major American denominations. American sects have less 'sense of the sacred', less sense of the profound distinction between sacred and profane, and less reverence, in religious devotions as in personal styles, than was traditionally the case with religion in Europe.[5]

Several American sects or groups of sects have been influential in Europe. The movements that have exerted more controlled and specific influence widely in Europe are Jehovah's Witnesses, Seventh-day Adventists, Christian Scientists, and Mormons.[6] (For

American Evangelism in Great Britain between 1830 and 1914 on the Origin and Development of the Ecumenical Movement', (University of Oxford D.Phil. thesis, 1963). For a brief account, see B. Wilson, 'American Religion: Its Impact on Britain', in A. J. N. den Hollander (ed.), *Contagious Conflict: The Impact of American Dissent on European Life* (Leiden: Brill, 1973), 233–63.

[4] For a discussion of this term, see B. Wilson, *Religious Sects* (London: Wiedenfeld and Nicholson, 1970), 41–2.

[5] This point is developed in B. R. Wilson, 'Religion and the Churches in Contemporary America', in W. G. McLoughlin and R. N. Bellah (eds.), *Religion in America* (Boston: Houghton Mifflin, 1968), 73–110.

[6] There is an extensive literature on each of these sects, particularly so on the Mormons. For an excellent overview, see T. O'Dea, *The Mormons* (Chicago: University of Chicago Press, 1957); also K. J. Hansen, *Mormonism and the*

comparative figures see Table 1.) Of less influence, but very active in Europe, has been the Worldwide Church of God (formerly the Radio Church of God), the organization founded by the late Herbert W. Armstrong. The most diffuse influence has been that of the Pentecostalists (a generic designation for a very large number of sects which differ on many details of theology and ecclesiology, and, more incidentally, in style, sophistication, and social composition, but all of which share doctrinal commitment to the continuing operation in the present age of those 'gifts of the Spirit' described in the New Testament, and in particular to the significance of 'speaking in tongues').[7] Pentecostalism followed, reinforced, and carried further the influence of the even more diffuse Holiness movement which spread its evangelical ideas of sanctification to Europe in the last half of the nineteenth century. The separated sectarian groups preaching Holiness (as distinct from the undenominational revivalists who made by far the greater impact) established a number of fellowships, especially in Britain and Germany. New Thought, the movement for metaphysical mind-healing, has had some rather diffuse importance through several separate organizations which have their own membership and organized meetings (the Unity movement is one of the largest), but also as a cult among people who belong to other fellowships, or among those who belong to no organized movement.[8] Several other religious bodies which originated

American Experience (Chicago: University of Chicago Press, 1981); L. J. Arrington and D. Bitton, *The Mormon Experience: A History of the Latter-day Saints* (London: Allen and Unwin, 1979). On Jehovah's Witnesses, see T. White, *A People for His Name* (New York: Vantage Press, 1967); J. A. Beckford, *The Trumpet of Prophecy* (Oxford: Blackwell, 1975); M. J. Penton, *Apocalypse Delayed* (Toronto: University of Toronto Press, 1985). On Christian Science, there is no one wholly satisfactory study, but see H. A. Studdert-Kennedy, *Mrs Eddy: Her Life, Her Work, Her Place in History* (San Francisco: Fairallon Press, 1947); and Charles S. Braden, *Christian Science Today* (Dallas: Southern Methodist University Press, 1958). For a sociological account of Christian Science in Britain, see B. R. Wilson, *Sects and Society* (London: Heinemann, 1961). On the Seventh-day Adventists, see, for historical origins, R. L. Numbers and J. M. Butler, (eds.), *The Disappointed: Millerites and Millenarians in the Nineteenth Century* (Bloomington, Ind.: Indiana University Press, 1987); D. L. Rowe, *Thunder and Trumpets: Millerites and Dissenting Religion in Upstate New York, 1800–1850* (Chico, Calif.: Scholars Press, 1985); M. Bull and K. Lockhart, *Seeking a Sanctuary: Seventh-day Adventism and the American Dream* (San Francisco: Harper and Row, 1989).

[7] For a general history of Pentecostalism, see N. Bloch-Hoell, *The Pentecostal Movement* (London: Allen and Unwin, 1964), and for Pentecostalism in various countries, W. J. Hollenweger, *The Pentecostals* (London, SCM Press, 1972).

[8] The only comprehensive treatment of the dispersed and diffuse New Thought current in western religion is the old but unsuperseded work of C. S. Braden, *Spirits*

TABLE 1. *The Western European membership of American sects (compared with membership in the United States)*

Country	Population (000,000s) 1986	Jehovah's Witnesses		Seventh-day Adventists		Mormons	
		1972	1986	1968	1986	1972	1986
USA	242.5	431,179	717,565	404,511	672,253	2,133,758	3,863,598
Austria	7.5	10,077	16,185	2,614	2,877		3,100
Belgium	9.8	15,224	21,343	1,207	1,607		7,300
Denmark	5.1	13,760	14,796	3,988[b]	3,331[b]		2,400
Finland	4.9	11,340	16,012	5,222	6,249		4,000
France	55.5	45,012	89,785	5,010	8,715		16,500
Greece	9.7	16,158	22,815	268	279		250
Italy	57.2	25,810	134,677	3,311	4,929		12,000
Netherlands	14.6	21,769	28,367	3,228	3,986		6,600
Norway	4.1	6,106	7,929	5,416	5,466		3,700
Portugal	9.7	9,841	29,617	3,579	6,711		7,100
Spain	38.8	16,672	63,453	2,612	5,313		11,600
Sweden	8.3	13,052	20,350	3,787	3,312		6,800
Switzerland	6.5	8,326	13,373	3,846	4,087		5,600
West Germany[a]	61.1	95,975[a]	116,152[a]	26,245[a]	24,956[a]		29,900
Great Britain	55.3	65,693	101,863	11,741[c]	16,611[c]	71,415	124,600

[a] Includes W. Berlin.

[b] Includes very small no. in the Faroe Islands.

[c] Includes the Republic of Ireland.

Note: Seventh-day Adventist Church also reports a considerable following in Eastern Europe. In 1986 there were members in the following countries: Bulgaria, 3,259; Czechoslovakia, 7,780; E. Germany, 9,425; Hungary, 3,598; Poland, 4,605; Romania, 56,557; Yugoslavia, 10,206.

in America—for instance, Moral Re-Armament and the Charismatic Renewal movement—cannot properly be described as sectarian, but are more aptly seen as cults within other denominations, and they are therefore left aside in this discussion. Finally, the Church of Scientology, in so far as it may be said to be sectarian, has, in the last four decades, become a widespread psycho-therapeutic movement which has ministered to hundreds of thousands of people who have undertaken courses of instruction or undergone therapy from Scientology 'auditors'.[9]

Several of these movements regard their local assemblies more as 'branches' than as autonomous churches, and the procedures in the branches are uniform throughout the world. Thus, the Christian Scientists, whose central organization—a board of directors—is at the Mother Church in Boston, Massachusetts, follow a Sunday service in which the 'lesson-sermon', composed of scriptural citations to be read alternately with extracts from the Christian Science textbook, *Science and Health*, is everywhere the same. The form of the service is identical: only the hymns and local announcements differ. Jehovah's Witnesses use the *Watchtower* as a catechistical source in their meetings, and their literature ensures uniform and practically simultaneous coverage of doctrines in all their local Kingdom Halls. Even the Seventh-day Adventists, whose services have much more local variation, not only in content but also in style—some being much more 'churchy' than others—use a quarterly compilation of lessons for their Sunday morning Sabbath school meetings which, although local ministers are free to invite their own speakers, follow at least a common theme, and this is the core of Sabbath school activity.

Thus, although the point does not hold for all American movements, there is among the influences of sectarianism a significant development of unified religious practice, made possible by the use of printed guides to teaching. It has helped to ensure a measure not only of doctrinal unity but also of simultaneous

in Rebellion: The Rise and Development of New Thought (Dallas: Southern Methodist University Press, 1963).

[9] A thorough study of the early development and organization of Scientology is found in R. Wallis, *The Road to Total Freedom: A Sociological Analysis of Scientology* (London: Heinemann, 1976). For an inclusive discussion of the organizational proclivities of Scientology (and a comparison with the Christian Science Church) see R. Wallis, *Salvation and Protest: Studies of Social and Religious Movements* (London: Frances Pinter, 1979), 25–43.

concern with particular issues at the local level of each of these various world-wide movements. It functions, too, to maintain the ideal of corporate unity in groups which are, in fact, very much larger than the term 'sect' suggests, and which, without such devices, might be faced with dissimilar patterns of development in different cultures and among different status groups. All the sects that use detailed pre-arranged programmes of worship, and which attach importance to uniform procedures, are groups which emphasize that doctrine must be true in every detail. In such movements, ideological control from the centre is a protection against schism and centrifugal diversification.

Different as are Christian Scientists, Jehovah's Witnesses, and Seventh-day Adventists in other respects, these three movements rely to a considerable extent on the dissemination of literature as a means of winning new recruits. The late nineteenth century, the time at which all of them were founded, was the age of the new mass reading public, and until the turn of the century a very large proportion of all published books and periodicals were religious: these movements emerged in that period of burgeoning religious literature, and adopted the printed word as a major agency of propaganda. All three movements have used door-to-door canvassing, although Christian Science abandoned this method of disseminating Mrs Eddy's writings at an early date, preferring to maintain reading rooms (every Christian Science church is required to support one) in which a proper atmosphere of reverent study is created, and in which there is no suggestion of a commercial concern with 'sales'. All Mrs Eddy's published works, the movement's periodicals, and the small number of authorized works (most of them biographies of Mrs Eddy rather than expositions of doctrine) are available—to be read on the premises, borrowed, or bought. The colporteur has remained prominent in the Seventh-day Adventist movement. For Jehovah's Witnesses door-to-door canvassing is the vital means of assuring the movement's growth. Mormon missionary work, too, depends on similar activity, and whilst a smaller proportion of Mormons are engaged in this work, the young American canvassers who serve for two years in the mission field are familiar figures throughout Western Europe (and elsewhere in the world).

The literature of the Christian Scientists is written and printed in the United States for distribution throughout the world. The

Adventists and the Witnesses operate presses in other countries, but the bulk of their material originates in America, and the American style of presentation is as evident in their literature as it is in that of Christian Science. The extent to which congregational life follows American patterns differs in the three movements. The Adventists have always favoured a higher degree of local autonomy, and have indeed encouraged their membership in different countries to maintain a sense of national culture and identity. In consequence, the atmosphere of Adventist churches differs from one country or context to another. Adventists also rely somewhat less on their own literature for the content of their services, which follow devotional styles that are closer to the conventional pattern of older Protestant denominations, even though their congregations tend to be the focus of a somewhat separate community life.

Neither the Witnesses nor the Christian Scientists permit local initiative in the content or order of their services, or in the life-style of congregations. In effect, a highly programmed and routinized procedure is followed which bears the strong imprint of impersonal corporate activity. The communal element of congregational life is not stressed, and individual participation is required to conform to prescribed times and procedures. Although Mrs Eddy herself occasionally manifested some degree of national and ancestral pride, she also emphasized the objective and timeless quality of her teachings which transcended all earthly associations, leaving little room in Christian Science for personal, local, or national styles. The Witnesses reject all local and national allegiances, and see themselves as already a people prepared for the Kingdom of Jehovah soon to be manifested on earth. Their teachings owe less than does Christian Science to distinctively American influences, much as the movement's organization and procedures bear their imprint.

Sects for which literature is central to evangelistic effort frequently produce additional material that is of only semi-religious interest. Clearly there may be a variety of reasons for this development: as a more subtle strategy for presenting their distinctive message; as a way of providing their converted following with a wider span of approved interests and of extending the area of control over them; as a method of keeping large printing houses busy and so reducing overheads by the diversification of products which the faithful should buy and (in the case of the Adventists and

Witnesses) canvass. Mrs Eddy, in deciding to publish the *Christian Science Monitor*, which soon became the best-known and most respected periodical of sectarian provenance, had in mind a newspaper that, whilst reporting the news, would also conform to the precepts of Christian Science, avoiding undue emphasis on human tragedy, sin, disease, and death, the reality of all of which Christian Science denies. (This policy led the newspaper's war reporters into some curious circumlocutions when reporting casualties in the First World War.) Undoubtedly, Mrs Eddy wished her newspaper to influence the wider secular society as well as providing her followers with a source of secular information which would not in itself corrupt their world-view. Whether she saw the *Monitor* as in itself an agency for recruitment to Christian Science is less clear: the newspaper carries only one relatively short article on Christian Science metaphysics each day. Nor is it clear how the *Plain Truth* fits into the conception entertained by Herbert W. Armstrong of the mission of his Worldwide Church of God, a sect that has used literature and, radio, and later television from Luxembourg and in America, almost to the exclusion of all other techniques in the recruitment of members.[10] For some time, the *Plain Truth* (which is published in several European languages and which is sent free to anyone who requests it) carried vivid descriptions of the events that the movement believed were to occur with the outworking of prophecy. Later, policy changed and the journal became to all appearance a secular magazine preoccupied with social, scientific, and especially environmental issues. For some years, the fact that this journal was published by a religious organization was virtually concealed, but that policy was later abandoned.

Awake is a fortnightly periodical of Jehovah's Witnesses which is much less explicitly concerned with doctrinal matters than is the *Watchtower*, the official and essentially doctrinal organ of the movement. Whilst it is always made clear that *Awake* is a vehicle for Witness ideology, drawing out the implications of Witness teaching and prophecy in many spheres of social and civic activity,

---

[10] The troubled history of the Worldwide Church of God has not been recorded in full. Useful information is contained in a work which does not purport to be a strictly sociological analysis: see J. Hopkins, *The Armstrong Empire: A Look at the Worldwide Church of God* (Grand Rapids, Mich.: William B. Eerdmans, 1974).

this publication endeavours to be a periodical of general interest in serious affairs with appeal to those who are not Witnesses.

The Seventh-day Adventists are perhaps the sect with the largest and most diversified literary output. Its scope reflects the many-sidedness of Adventism, and the wider degree of regional and local autonomy which the organization tolerates. There are, apart from strictly doctrinal magazines which circulate little beyond the confines of the movement, a number of periodicals devoted to quite specific concerns, in particular to health. Those devoted to prophetic exegesis, to religious liberty, and to education reveal the strong imprint of the movement's stance on these issues, but some of the health publications appear more general in their concern to disseminate dietetic (and often vegetarian) principles, hygiene, standards of wholesome living, and abstinence from tobacco and alcohol. A wide range of literature is carried by Seventh-day Adventist colporteurs, workers for whom this is a full-time job.

Different in the foregoing respects as are these three movements (Witnesses, Adventists, and Christian Scientists), all can be said to represent relatively intellectual styles in religion, in the sense that knowledge of teachings, promoted through the printed word, is indispensable for any who seek membership. All of them emphasize, albeit in different ways, practicality. Pragmatism is a substantive value for Christian Science; it is the key to the organizational techniques of the Witnesses; and even among the Adventists there is strong concern with practical matters, systematic organization, and highly routinized annual collections of funds for a variety of denominational causes, in which the leaders claim to 'make the Seventh-day Adventist dollar the hardest working dollar in the world'. Christian Science claims to be as demonstrable as mathematics and thoroughly practical. Proper application of the knowledge of God is believed to lead to real benefit in this world, in health, wealth, longevity, intelligence, pleasure, and happiness. The Witnesses have developed highly systematic and efficient methods of organizational deployment of personnel for the dissemination of their literature. Mainly by well co-ordinated door-to-door canvassing and the use of thoroughly rehearsed techniques, contacts are made and those interested are offered courses of Bible study. Although the ultimate goals of the Witnesses are substantive—preparedness for God's coming kingdom—their interim activities are highly instrumental and rational. The Christian Scientists manifest a similar value-orientation less in their recruitment techniques than in their actual doctrine. 'Christian Science works' is a slogan which would not make sense applied to the faith of the Witnesses or the Adventists. Yet, different as is the role of doctrine and its legitimations in these movements, both Adventists and Witnesses manifest a highly pragmatic attitude in their affairs.

In many ways, Christian Science represents the first important *organized* attempt to harness religious ideology rationally and systematically to the service of secular goals. Extreme as is the formulation of the values of pragmatism, instrumentalism, and optimism in New Thought groups generally, this orientation was also a growing element in American religiosity in the major denominations in the late nineteenth and early twentieth centuries. The established churches in Europe have been less ready to proclaim that religion is an aid in the attainment of quite specific 'success goals' in the lifetime of an individual, but in the popular inspirational writings of Bruce Barton, Norman Vincent Peale, Bishop Sheen, Ralph Trine, and various other American spiritual writers, these ideas became the staple religious diet of millions of people in the United States.[11] They manifest a degree of calculation, the conscious rational use of religious means for secular ends, and egocentricism, which stand in some contrast to the predominant preoccupation of traditional European Christianity with social control, moral constraint, guilt and penance, and the maintenance, through religious agencies, of a framework of social order.

Success goals, although widely represented in the major American religious denominations, have perhaps never been dominant even there, and their appeal to Europeans of the same denominational persuasions has been slight. In the teachings of New Thought and Christian Science, however, this pragmatic, instrumental orientation to religion has been widely disseminated in Europe, particularly in Protestant countries. The significance of New Thought is not easily assessed, although its votaries have been active throughout Western Europe, particularly in Britain, France, and Germany. The organizational weakness of New Thought bodies and the lack of emphasis on traditional conceptions of membership, worship, and congregational assembly have perhaps reduced the effectiveness and

[11] The themes of secular success and well-being as goals of religious practice in America are explored in L. Schneider and S. M. Dornbusch, *Popular Religion: Inspirational Books in America* (Chicago: University of Chicago Press, 1958).

durability of their influence. Of movements in this general tradition, only Christian Science has successfully adopted the traditional model of religious involvement and church commitment. From its first introduction in the 1890s, Christian Science flourished in Britain, especially between the two World Wars, winning the adherence of a considerable number of middle-class adherents and some influential public figures among the aristocracy, a few MPs, and some high-ranking military, naval, and diplomatic figures. It was never so successful in continental Europe, except in Germany, where it continued to grow well after the Second World War (at a time when its growth had ceased in Britain). The movement has published no membership figures for Europe, but it is doubtful if, even at its peak, there were as many as 30,000 members in Britain, or more than 10,000 in West Germany, the countries in which its success was greatest. Its adherents in other European countries appear to have included a more than representative number from the middle and upper classes.

Although emerging in Britain much later, Scientology may be considered in this context as representing a positive and optimistic faith with some features in common with the earlier New Thought bodies. When, in the 1960s, this body moved its main centre of operations to Britain, hundreds of young people (in their 20s and 30s) were recruited in Britain and from the rest of Western Europe to take courses in Sussex and Edinburgh. The Scientologists have never made public the total numbers enrolling in their programmes or seeking affiliation with their Church, but certainly many thousands of Europeans have been involved in the movement, even if many of them have not sustained their involvement. Scientology has appealed to people mostly under 40 years of age, and in this stands in marked contrast with Christian Science and the earlier New Thought cults, the votaries of which have always been middle-aged and elderly, with a considerable preponderance of women among them. Whereas the earlier movements were preoccupied with bodily healing, Scientology's concern is much more with mental health, and exercises to improve the intelligence, and this perhaps explains the age constituency of each of these different movements.

Scientology, Christian Science, and the New Thought bodies present the sharpest contrast with traditional European styles of religious thinking. All the other major American sects shared doctrinal perspectives with their European predecessors or contemporaries. The adventist sects (principally, Jehovah's Witnesses, Seventh-day Adventists, the Worldwide Church of God, and the Christadelphians—the last-named today numbering about 16,000 in Europe, most of them in Britain) share certain broad features of pre-millennial prophetic exegesis with some fundamentalists within the major Protestant denominations. Throughout the nineteenth century, there were within Protestantism sects and fellowships which entertained apocalyptic expectations that, at least from the perspective of the outsider, were not dissimilar. Following the mortalist views held by some seventeenth-century Puritans (Milton conspicuously among them), these groups rejected (or modified) the notion of man's possession of an immortal soul, and from the diverse possibilities within Christian eschatological and soteriological traditions, have concentrated on the resurrection of the body to occur at a time associated with the second coming.[12] Important as they were for the cohesion of particular groups and their maintenance of a sense of separate identity, these doctrinal issues cannot be said to have had any very significant *social* consequence, however. But certain currents of thought have been reinforced by the infusion of these various streams of sectarian teaching, sustained by financial resources drawn from the United States, and borne by the new techniques of evangelism pioneered there.

Of course, sects do not remain unchanged over long periods of time. The Witnesses have considerably and consciously amended their pattern of activities, moderating the aggressive style which earned them widespread opprobrium in the 1930s. They and the Adventists have had to come to terms with the size and dispersion of their membership: the idea of a sect counting its following in millions was not part of a nineteenth-century conception of things. All these movements have needed at times to reinforce their sense of apartness from the world and to evolve techniques for the maintenance of commitment. The Seventh-day Adventists, more than the others, have gradually accepted a less intensely sectarian stance, and in some respects have come closer to a denominational position, but such a process is hindered by their distinctive

[12] The inheritance by the Seventh-day Adventists of various doctrines from the Puritans has been traced by B. W. Ball, *The English Connection: The Puritan Roots of Seventh-day Adventist Beliefs* (Cambridge: James Clarke, 1981).

teachings that mark their members off from others—the keeping of the seventh-day Sabbath and the dietetic demands of the Old Testament. [13]

Perhaps the most important general social influence of these adventist sects has been their determined position as conscientious objectors to military service. The Adventists are generally prepared to serve as non-combatants, usually in medical corps, but Witnesses and Christadelphians who, in one or other of the World Wars, were eligible for conscription to military service, have been almost completely uncompromising in their response. This has given these movements considerable—and in wartime, unfavourable—publicity. It may, however, have done something to promote the rights of conscientious objection and, gradually, to have made recognition of those rights more acceptable to a wider public, even for those whose objection has not been lodged on specifically religious grounds. Slowly, in one European country after another, even in Catholic countries like Spain and Portugal, conscientious claims for exemption from military service have been granted, and these sects have undoubtedly contributed to that process.

In other social matters, the influence of these three groups differs. Neither Witnesses nor Christadelphians are teetotallers, although they are non-smokers. The Adventists have used their resources to combat the use of both alcohol and tobacco among the wider public. From time to time they have made common cause with other fundamentalists in forming pressure groups against the liberalization of laws relating to alcohol, and in an attempt to persuade governments to publicize the dangers of smoking and drinking. An Adventist five-day cure for smokers has been used by many outsiders, some of whom, in consequence, have become interested in the movement. Christian Scientists and Mormons prohibit tobacco and alcohol (and, like Adventists, tea and coffee, although this particular injunction has had no evident social consequence, and appears to be not infrequently ignored even by loyal members of these sects). The presence of Christian Scientists in legislative bodies in Britain, as in America, has occasionally been

[13] For some time, the Seventh-day Adventists have maintained observer status at the World Council of Churches, but the items referred to together with their 'sanctuary doctrine' and the thesis of an 'investigative judgement' are significant differences from the doctrines of orthodox Protestant denominations. For some discussion, see B. B. Beach and L. Vischer, *So Much in Common* (Geneva: World Council of Churches, 1973).

useful to pressure groups concerned with tobacco and alcohol (and at times for those seeking protection for unorthodox therapies), but sectarians of adventist persuasions have not been disposed—and in the case of Witnesses and Christadelphians are firmly opposed—to participation in political processes or public service.

Displaying considerable contrast with the rationalizing tendencies of sects discussed above are movements which belong to an entirely different strand of American sectarianism—the Holiness-Pentecostal tradition.[14] Although some of the sects within this stream have very large followings (the Church of the Nazarene is the largest Holiness sect, and the Assemblies of God and Church of God, Cleveland, are among the largest American Pentecostal sects) and hold together many church communities in denominational unity, the emphasis in all of these movements is on personal experience in the local congregation. Ideologically, they are committed to conversion as the central Christian experience, and to subsequent sanctification experiences. In the case of Pentecostal sects, there are vital further blessings for the believer in the 'baptism of the Holy Spirit' and the exercise of the Spirit gifts (as described in 1 Corinthians 12) which they, in contrast to other Christians, believe were not confined to the apostolic age but are operative today.[15] The subjectivism of these movements and their commitment to emotionally stirring religious experience limit the extent to which routinization of organization and activities is possible. The more expressive Pentecostal groups have had far greater influence in Europe than have Holiness sects, although the early revivalists in the Holiness tradition exerted considerable attraction for evangelicals within Protestant, including Anglican, churches. Pentecostalism provides opportunities for feelingful religion, for enhanced spontaneity, freer expression, and the indulgence of the emotions at a level unknown, and indeed unsought, in the more restrained, intellectual styles of sectarianism discussed above, in which emphasis is on doctrine

---

[14] The Holiness Revival of the 1860s to 1880s is treated in T. L. Smith, *Called Unto Holiness. The Story of the Nazarenes: The Formative Years* (Kansas City: Nazarene Publishing House, 1963). For the development of Pentecostalism and its relation to the earlier Holiness tradition, see R. Mapes Anderson, *Vision of the Disinherited* (Oxford: Oxford University Press, 1979).

[15] There is now an extensive literature on glossolalia, but see for two contrasting approaches, F. D. Goodman, *Speaking in Tongues: A Cross-Cultural study of Glossolalia* (Chicago: University of Chicago Press, 1972); and C. G Williams, *Tongues of the Spirit* (Cardiff: University of Wales Press, 1981).

rather than experience. Pentecostal sects have, over time, become more restrained than they were at their beginning, but even where a somewhat denominational (as distinct from sectarian) structure has evolved, it is the free, vigorous, and at times even ecstatic utterance in the local congregation which really distinguishes Pentecostal religion.

American Pentecostalism owed a good deal to the emotional freedom of traditional Negro Christianity, and Negroes were prominent among the early leaders and converts. Emotionalism, invocations, noisy outbursts, and sustained choruses characterized early Pentecostal meetings. Sermons were often crude and un-grammatical, and the music was drawn directly from Negro jazz. The decorum and dignity associated with religious devotion in Europe was either abandoned or unknown, and the contemplative tradition of Christianity was totally alien. Only a few years after its beginnings in Kansas in 1900, Pentecostalism was brought to Europe, first to Norway and then swiftly to other countries in northern Europe. Although in Europe, Pentecostalism was more pastorally controlled than had orginally been the case in America, it remained a more vigorous and enthusiastic style of religion than— revivals apart—was ever common even in the conversion-oriented Protestant denominations in Europe. Recruits were drawn almost entirely from the less well-educated working classes, and, at least until after the Second World War, overwhelmingly in Protestant countries.[16] Using revival techniques and campaigns of 'divine healing' (rather than dissemination of literature) as their means of recruitment, Pentecostalism often drew in a volatile public with an unstable commitment. Its social impact was slight, although Pentecostals often joined, and indeed stimulated, other evangelical Christians in the promotion. of interdenominational campaigns. They provided the main manpower for a variety of public causes, such as campaigns supporting temperance, Sunday observance, and moral crusades like the Festival of Light, as well as in demonstrating opposition to Roman Catholicism. Although some Pentecostalists were conscientious objectors in the Second World War, the mass of the rank and file were never persuaded to adopt this position. These

[16] Detailed accounts of European (and other) Pentecostal churches are provided in W. J. Hollenweger (ed.), *Die Pfingstkirchen: Selbstdarstellungen, Dokumente, Kommentare* (Stuttgart: Evangelisches Verlagswerk, 1971). For a detailed account of one British movement, see Wilson, *Sects and Society*, pp. 15–118.

sects tended to ignore political affairs and, although they have generally supported conventional social norms and civic order, in typical evangelical fashion they have regarded individual conversion as a better basis for social improvement than programmes of social and institutional reform or the provision of social welfare. The social and political orientations of Pentecostalists (although they have never been given party political expression) are, in common with those of most other fundamentalists, conservative. Innovation in devotional procedures is accompanied by profound distrust of political and social change. This particular combination of attitudes may be related to the fact that Pentecostal religion draws heavily on styles and themes of religion as presented to children in Sunday schools: simple images, free expression, facile dichotomization of right and wrong, rhythmic music (accompanied by hand gestures and repetitive choruses), all serve to evoke childlike responses. 'Old time religion', the religion which Pentecostals usually canvass, is often the religion of childhood reawakened by activities that rekindle old emotions. The literalism, enthusiasm, emotionality, and social conservatism are linked by their common inheritance from the individual's past.

In this conservative orientation, sectarian Pentecostalism differs from the apparent orientations of the neo-pentecostalists of the Charismatic Renewal movement—in which the gifts of the Spirit (and particularly 'speaking in tongues') have been demonstrated, since about 1958, among Catholics and Protestants of various denominations. This movement, since it is not sectarian, is not our concern here, although it is an American influence on European religious thought and practice, and harnesses Pentecostal styles to meet the widespread demand for authenticity, immediacy, and radical spontaneity as a protest against the over-institutionalization of modern life. The attitudinal correlates of the charismatic movement are, as one might expect, quite different from those of 'classical' sectarian Pentecostalism.[17]

Although there is a strong puritanical element in American sectarian religion, this orientation is by no means uniformly adopted by all American sects. The millennial sects—the Adventists, Witnesses, Christadelphians, and Worldwide Church of God—

[17] For an account of Charismatic Renewal, see R. Quebedeaux, *The New Charismatics* (New York: Doubleday, 1976), and for an up-dated revision, id., *The New Charismatics II* (New York: Harper and Row, 1982).

share with fundamentalist groups such as the Holiness and Pentecostal sects, a somewhat restrictive attitude towards involvement in the affairs of the world. Social control of individuals is evident in all of these movements, and although the outsiders' stereotype of sectarianism as joyless, narrow, oppressive, and censorious, is almost always in error, all of these movements are anti-hedonistic. Members must gain their joy (which is usually extolled either as a present reality or at least as an anticipation of what is to be experienced in the next world) in prescribed ways. But the content of prescription varies considerably, and from an outside point of view there is a clear distinction between the millennial and Pentecostal sects on the one hand, and movements such as Christian Science and Scientology, and also Mormonism, on the other. Christian Science does maintain a certain control over its adherents through its particular type of mental discipline, but apart from the restrictions on tobacco, alcohol, drugs, and recourse to medicine, Christian Scientists are, within the bounds of conventional morality, generally free to enjoy the world, and their ideology emphasizes the happiness which adherents should experience. The focal point of control is less the adherent's activities in the world than his commitment to truth as prescribed by the movement. Scientology also tends to leave its members free to participate in the world in their own ways, with an emphasis on the enhanced enjoyment of life which scientological training itself is said to confer. In this movement, too, there is an attempt to control the individual through the redefinition of his situation and by the inculcation of specific mental orientations. There is evidence that, within the inner organization of Scientology, a rigorous code of discipline is maintained in respect of the performance of staff members in their work to recruit new members. Those who fail to reach their targets may suffer social ostracism and degradation, but this scarcely affects 'lay' Scientologists. Their social and moral behaviour is of no concern to the Church of Scientology, although at times in the past individual members have been disciplined for associating with apostates ('suppressive persons') who were critical of scientological therapeutic practice.

Mormonism—no less distinctively American in style than Christian Science—rejects conventional puritanism. Its teaching is optimistic and universalistic—virtually all men may expect to enjoy eternal life. 'As man is, God once was; as God is, man may become' and

'Men are that they might have joy' are Mormon dicta that summarize the movement's soteriological position. Recreation, including sport, dancing, and entertainment, are not only tolerated but have always been actively encouraged. Salt Lake City had a theatre before it had a temple. Despite the strong social and communal character of their Church, Mormons are free to engage in secular business, politics, and social affairs. The Mormon rejection of Protestantism's traditional puritan inheritance may be an important element in the movement's contemporary appeal. Mormon recruitment in Europe, particularly in Britain, Scandinavia, and Germany was, from as early as the 1840s, considerable, but because of the early policy of inducing converts to migrate to Utah the long-term influence of Mormonism in Europe has been rather less than it might have been.[18] In the early years, the almost pan-American and nationalistic implications of Mormon doctrine reinforced dispositions towards emigration to America: only since the Second World War has Mormonism sunk sizable roots again in

[18]   It is this fact of Mormon migration that accounts for the brevity of allusion to them in this discussion of the influence of American sects in Europe. The initial success of Mormon missionaries in Britain and Scandinavia is well known: within three years of the start of missionary work in the 1830s there were 1,600 Mormons in Britain; by 1842 there were 7,500, and by 1851, they numbered 33,000: P. A. M. Taylor, *Expectations Westward* (Edinburgh: Oliver and Boyd, 1965), 19–20. Thereafter, the policy of inducing converts to emigrate and the scandal caused by Brigham Young's pronouncement regarding polygamy served to diminish the popularity of Mormonism in Britain. Over 55,000 emigrated from Britain. To Mormonism, at that time, migration was vital, and Mormon publications virtually canvassed emigration to America. The *Millennial Star*, a Mormon publication published in Liverpool, was 'devoted to American interests, providing an indoctrination far broader than its Mormon base': W. Mulder, *Homeward to Zion: The Mormon Migration from Scandinavia* (Minneapolis: 1957), 80. The editorial of a German-language Mormon periodical asked in 1860, 'Why have you so many Saints who have not yet emigrated . . . Those who do not gather [in Zion, i.e. in Utah] can make no claims on His protection': G. Scharffs, *Mormonism in Germany* (Salt Lake City: 1970), 66. European Mormons who failed to emigrate apparently tended to leave the Church, and those who did survive over the long run tended to assimilate in style and church practice to patterns of European indigenous dissenting religion. Once Mormon mission activity in Europe revived, in the decades following the Second World War, Mormons of long standing did not always readily accept the importance which Americans attached to temple rituals—so long had they been accustomed to Mormonism without access to a temple. (The Mormon temple in Surrey was built in 1957–8, at a time when the Mormon Church authorities, in a change of policy, began to build temples for local congregations outside America in many parts of the world.) D. J. Davies, 'Mormons at Merthyr Tydfil' (University of Oxford B.Litt. thesis, 1972).

Europe, and although it has enjoyed considerable growth it cannot yet be said to have had any very marked social influence.

Sectarianism is always necessarily a minority phenomenon. Over the long term, the balance of denominational trade weighs heavily in favour of European exports to America. The return flow of religion of American origin to Europe has been modest in comparison, and the movements themselves, although by no means unimportant in their influence, have been small. The significance of American sects, always allowing that their impact has been in no sense unified, has been greater than the figures for membership might suggest. Sectarian religion is more intense than church religion, and sectarians are more committed and socially more conspicuous. Whereas religion as represented in the dominant churches, Catholic and Protestant, tends to decline in its influence, sects, in contrast, continue to exert a considerable hold over their members, and at the same time to sustain remarkable figures for membership growth. In most European countries during recent decades both the Witnesses and the Mormons have been experiencing increase greater than the rate of population growth, and all this whilst attendance in the dominant churches has in many parts of Europe been declining. The Mormons have had particular success in Britain, and during the 1960s and 1970s, the Pentecostalists expanded considerably in Italy and even in Portugal.

Protestant Europe has provided the most congenial climate for American sects. Catholic countries were for a long time successfully able to resist the emergence of sects, either through restrictive legislation or as a consequence of the Church's attitude towards deviant forms of religion. The inroads made by Pentecostalists in Italy (and particularly among the poorer classes in the South) have occurred largely through the agency of returning immigrants who have brought to relatives at home the faith that they have adopted in the United States or in Brazil. The success of Pentecostalism in Italy begins to parallel the early impact that it had in Sweden, where, until recent immigration by Catholic workers from southern Europe, it was the largest denomination after the state-supported Lutheran Church. The licence for greater emotional freedom which sectarian Pentecostalism provides has had its greatest appeal among the least sophisticated sections of the population. The Scandinavian Pentecostals are now long established and have acquired respectability, and it may be the case that Pentecostalism in Sweden is today less sectarian than the newly formed assemblies in Italy. The half-century lag between the movement's impact in the two countries reflects not only the resistance of the Catholic Church in Italy, but also something of the lag in social development between Sweden and the Italian south.

All sects represent some measure of protest againt the cultural life-style of their contemporaries, and constitute a comment— whether conscious or unconscious—on the inadequacy of prevailing moral norms or social facilities and opportunities. In that they appeal to rather different social classes, they address themselves to rather different perceived deficiencies. Thus, whereas most sects appeal to less educated sections of the population, Christian Science, New Thought, and perhaps also Scientology, have had more impact on the middle classes. They are less ascetic and offer wider intellectual opportunities for their recruits. They share with some others, as we have noted, the practicality, rationality of procedure, and the sense of purposive commitment. They are perhaps less implicitly egalitarian than the more radical adventist groups, even though all sects offer channels for social mobility through their own organization. New opportunities to take leadership roles, and to acquire status within the sectarian society are offered in all these movements. Sects make a strong reassertion of certain abiding human values, and all of them provide specific grounds for hope in an uncertain world, offer the occasion for service and self-expression (even if within a very circumscribed framework) in a cause which offers total, absolute, and final meaning for the individual's life and the course of contemporary society and its future.

8

Jehovah's Witnesses in a Catholic Country:

A Survey of Nine Belgian Congregations

(WITH K. DOBBELAERE)

SINCE the Second World War, three sectarian movements have achieved considerable growth in continental Europe. Of these, Jehovah's Witnesses have received perhaps most attention from scholars,[1] and it has become apparent that this movement has acquired a following even in countries in which Protestantism has never been particularly successful. In Belgium, a country with a population that is about 85 to 90 per cent Catholic, the Witnesses today number about 20,000 people. Of this number about 14 per cent have been recruited from among immigrants to Belgium, the majority of these converts being Italians. Our enquiry sought to identify Witnesses in conventional sociological terms, and paid particular attention to the participation in the movement of immigrants. This chapter is divided into a short section on the history of the Witnesses in Belgium; an indication of research procedures; a subdivided presentation of the principal findings from analysis of questionnaires; and concluding comments on the recruitment, involvement, and social integration of Jehovah's Witnesses.

The Message and the Organization

The movement today known generally as Jehovah's Witnesses, and more officially as the Watchtower Bible and Tract Society, dates from the 1870s, and is the most forthright exponent of biblical prophecy in the adventist tradition. The central teachings of

---

[1] The other movements are the Mormons and the Pentecostalists: see Ch. 7 above. On the Witnesses in Europe, see J. A. Beckford, *The Trumpet of Prophecy* (Oxford: Blackwell, 1975); M. Gebhard, *Die Zeugen Jehova's: Eine Dokumentation über die Wachtturmgesellschaft* (Schwerte (Ruhr): Freistühler Verlag, 1971); Q. J. Munters, 'Recruitment as a Vocation: The Case of Jehovah's Witnesses', *Sociologica Neerlandica* 7 (1971), 71–82; and Ch. 9 below.

Jehovah's Witnesses aver that the end of this dispensation is at hand; that God's Kingdom is soon to be instituted on earth; and that it is the duty of Jehovah's Witnesses to proclaim this message and to bring it to the attention of all mankind. The complete establishment of God's Kingdom will be preceded by Armageddon, in which death and destruction will occur on a wide scale, but thereafter the survivors of Armageddon will, together with the resurrected dead, inherit a peaceful and blissful life on earth, in preparation for a final testing before the end of the millennium.[2]

The Watchtower Society in Brooklyn, New York, publishes literature to make people aware of this divine scheme of things. Those who accept the duty of 'publishing' the news of God's Kingdom (hence 'publishers') call themselves Jehovah's Witnesses, and they are organized in congregations at local assembly halls, each of which is known as Kingdom Hall. Witnesses meet usually three times a week: two of these occasions are each divided into two separate meetings of an hour's duration each. The remaining meeting is intended for Bible study held privately in the home of a member. The meetings provide opportunities for instruction in the Bible, in methods of expounding its teaching, and in techniques of public speaking, engaging others in conversation, and, generally of 'witnessing' to the Truth. Biblical exhortations concerning moral comportment are also expounded, and the ethical principles on which life is to be lived are the subject of talks and, sometimes, of question and answer sessions based on articles in the *Watchtower*.

A publisher (as an ordinary member of the movement is called) is expected to spend whatever time he can in 'preaching work'—that is in door-to-door canvassing. Some members become pioneers, in which case the expectation is that they will undertake this work for ninety hours a month. Pioneers often take part-time jobs and live on smaller incomes in order to engage in this work of witnessing. Auxiliary or temporary pioneers may work for shorter periods in which they undertake to do sixty hours of canvassing a month. Full-time agents for the Society, known as Special Pioneers, live on very small incomes and devote 140 hours a month usually to work

---

[2] For a fuller account of the teachings and organization of the movement, see Beckford, *Trumpet of Prophecy*; M. J. Penton, *Apocalypse Delayed* (Toronto: University of Toronto Press, 1985). For historical aspects of the movement's teachings, see T. White, *A People For His Name* (New York: Vantage Press, 1967), and the useful, if somewhat less neutral, study by A. T. Rogerson, *Millions Now Living Will Never Die* (London: Constable, 1969).

of this kind (unless they have special assignments in mission fields or in the branch offices of the organization). Local congregation leaders are elders (who rotate in office), and they, sometimes called congregation servants, divide among themselves on a uniform and instituted basis, the work of maintaining and supervising the congregation and its meetings, and organizing the systematic publishing work in their assigned territory. These servants have (usually younger) assistants. All congregational roles are confined to men, but women undertake witnessing work, and may become pioneers or special pioneers.

History of the Movement in Belgium

Although Pastor Charles Taze Russell, founder of the Watchtower movement, visited Belgium in 1891, regular preaching of the Watchtower message began in Belgium, in Charleroi, only in 1901. Growth was initially slow but by 1912 seven small study classes existed, all of them in the Liège and Charleroi areas, with a total attendance of about seventy people. The First World War decimated the movement: five members remained in 1918. Ten years later, twenty-eight publishers were at work, and a branch of the movement opened in Brussels in 1929. The movement was strongest in Liège and among miners in Limburg: by 1932, there were sixty-four publishers in Belgium, of whom twenty-two were pioneers. By 1935, there were thirteen congregations, of which, notably, three were Polish-speaking. The appeal of the movement to immigrants was evident, then as now.

The movement encountered various difficulties: the Minister of Justice expelled one member of Polish origin in 1934; the Ministry of Economic Affairs for a time asserted that a door-to-door canvasser needed a colporteur's licence; in 1938 the movement experienced some hostility from the Catholic Church—perhaps because Witnesses were at that time refusing to undertake military service; and in March 1940 the movement's literature was banned. Under the Nazis, Witnesses were persecuted. Several were sent to concentration camps, and at least one was executed: but mimeographed magazines were circulated, and the members even succeeded in getting 6,000 copies of their publication, *Enfants*, printed by Erasme de Bruxelles. The movement grew in the war years, and in 1945 there were 747 publishers in Belgium.

The police surveillance continued until 1952, and the government expelled more members in the early 1950s, but growth continued: 3,000 publishers in 1952, and 7,000 by 1960. In 1976, there were 277 congregations (118 French-speaking; 114 Dutch-speaking; 28 Italian-speaking; 8 Greek; 7 Spanish; 2 English; and Hungarian, Portuguese, and Turkish groups in Brussels). The growth of immigrant groups induced the movement to start a teaching programme: Italian and Greek immigrants were taught either French or Dutch, although this proved difficult for older people. To discover how many Italian publishers there were, the movement organized a special assembly in Italian in Charleroi in 1965, and found that there were so many that separate Italian-speaking congregations were then formed. Subsequently, the Society had to face a different problem: the children of immigrants were, by the mid 1970s, learning Dutch or French, and were often unable to follow meetings in their mother tongue, which was the only language in which their parents could follow. In consequence, some congregations organized schools for Greek children to learn Greek, and encouraged the parents of Italian and Spanish children to teach their children at home, with books provided by the Society, so that parents and children should not be separated in attending Kingdom Hall meetings. In general, the Society has been pleased by the result of these language-teaching policies, and some young people have since become public speakers in the language that they have learned.[3]

Procedure

It is not normally possible to study the members of a small religious movement by standard techniques of random sampling. As a matter of expediency, to establish our credentials and good faith, it was necessary in our study of Witnesses in Belgium to seek introductions to congregations that were willing to allow us to distribute questionnaires and conduct interviews. Seven congregations were selected and two others were added subsequently, and all of them were willing to co-operate in our research once our purpose had been explained. The congregations constituted four Belgian con-

[3] The historical information on the growth of the movement in Belgium was provided by M. Gillet of the Belgian branch of the Watch Tower and Bible Tract Society.

gregations (three Dutch-speaking and one French-speaking); three Italian immigrant congregations (all Italian-speaking); and two congregations of Belgians and foreigners (one using the Dutch language, and the other French). The overall response rate to our questionnaire was 47 per cent of the total number of publishers. However, we deliberately excluded those below the age of 15 years, and were this age-group excluded from the total number of publishers our response rate would be somewhat higher. (See Table 2.)

The study was undertaken in Leuven-Wilsele, Kraainem-Stockel-Saint-Gilles-Brussels, and Genk-Waterschei. The three areas represent different ecological contexts: Leuven-Wilsele is a small city and adjacent rural area; Kraainem-Stockel-Saint-Gilles-Brussels is a largely suburban and city area; Genk-Waterschei is an industrial district into which Italians had migrated in the early post-war years. The Italian congregations in Brussels had been founded by immigrants who had originally settled in the Genk-Waterschei

TABLE 2. *Response rate*

Congregations	No. of questionnaires returned		No. of publishers (1976)
	No.	%	
Belgian congregations	126	41	305
Dutch-speaking (Flemings)	95	45	210
Kraainem (Brussels)	32	43	75
Leuven (Louvain)	35	43	82
Wilsele (Louvain area)	28	53	53
French-speaking	31	33	95
Stockel (Brussels)	31	33	95
Mixed congregations	116	57	203
Dutch-speaking (Flemings)			
Waterschei (Limburg)	63	55	115
French-speaking			
St Gilles (Brussels)	53	60	88
Italian congregations	125	45	279
Genk (Limburg)	38	46	83
Bruxelles Midi			
(Brussels South)	45	54	84
Bruxelles Nord			
(Brussels North)	42	38	112
Total	367	47	787

district. The response rate differed among congregations, being the lowest in Stockel, the congregation based around the headquarters of Witnesses in Belgium, which was approached through the officials of that branch office, and in Brussels North, which was approached through the good offices of members in Brussels South. Elsewhere our purposes were always explained directly to groups of elders in each congregations. Once this contact had been made, questionnaires were distributed after regular meetings, and were collected at later dates. During the meetings, volunteers among the congregation were interviewed by the researchers, and by students who participated in the Leuven-Wilsele area.[4]

Despite the high incidence of immigrants in our sample, the Witnesses proved to be a generally settled section of the population. The mean number of years of residence in the community in which they were then living was fourteen to fifteen years, with 31 per cent having been there for less than six years, and about 40 per cent longer than fifteen years. Of the Witnesses whom we studied, 93 per cent lived in industrial districts, and on the basis of Van Naeltens's (1970) index of urbanization,[5] more than 50 per cent came from considerably urbanized places, but the remainder lived in less urbanized or rural districts. Belgium is, of course, a highly urbanized country, and we cannot, from our arbitrary choice of congregations, indicate to what extent our sample is representative, although there is reason to believe, from other evidence, that there are few Witnesses in rural districts.

The Belgian Witnesses who responded to our questionnaire are younger than the general population of the districts in which they live: 84 per cent of the Witnesses were under 55 years of age, compared to 68 per cent of the general population. The same tendency was also evident among the Italians (for whom the dividing age of 45 is used): 83 per cent of·the sample were below this age, compared with 70 per cent of the Italian population in Belgium as a whole. The Italian population of Witnesses in the study was younger than that of the Belgian Witnesses, but this finding might be accounted for by other factors, namely, the

[4] Grateful acknowledgement is made for the assistance of P. Anaf, E. Palmans, F. Schoovaerts, M. Schuurmans, I. Stouffs, and C. Vanduffel, for help in coding and tabulating of G. Verscheuren, and for advice during analysis of Dr J. Billiet.

[5] M. Van Naelten, *The Degrees of Urbanity: A Factor Analytical Approach as Applied to Belgium* (Leuven: Interfakultair Institut voor Stedebouw en Ruimtelijke Orending, 1970).

difficulty—perhaps including a measure of illiteracy—experienced by older Italians in answering questionnaires.

The sex distribution of the respondents confirmed the visual impressions gained by attendance at congregational meetings: 54 per cent of the respondents were women compared to the general population in which 52 per cent are women. This relatively representative balance of the sexes among Witnesses contrasts strikingly with the considerable over-representation of women attending mass in the Catholic Church in Belgium.[6]

Of the Witnesses we studied, 76 per cent were married, 16 per cent unmarried, 5 per cent widowed, and 3 per cent divorced or separated. The mean number of children among the sample was 1.94, a figure that is influenced by the mean number of children among the Italian couples, which is 2.33.

The common assumption that those attracted to sectarian groups are likely to be less well-educated than the general population was not borne out among the Witnesses in our sample. Generally speaking, the Witnesses went to school to a later age than the general population in the same districts. (See Table 3.) In part, this might be explained by the fact that they are younger than the general population, but certainly it cannot be contended that in this case sectarianism is associated with inferior education. At the age-level of post-secondary education, the difference entirely disappears. But at this point another factor sometimes supervenes. Some Witnesses abandon higher education in favour of undertaking a part-time job or a job which will leave them more time to engage in door-to-door missionary work. There was at least one

TABLE 3. *Age at leaving school (%)*

Age	Brabant		Limburg	
	General population	Witnesses	General population	Witnesses
14 years and under	53	43	56	42
15–18 years	33	43	33	48
19 years and over	14	14	11	10
Total	100	100	100	100

[6] L. Voyé, *Sociologie du geste religieux. De l'analyse de la pratique doménicale en Belgique à l'interprétation théorétique* (Brussels: Editions Vie Ouvrière, 1973).

such case in our sample, and there may have been others: but other members of the group had received full-time higher education and one was a university student, and these had not abandoned education for pioneering work. Despite the tendency for Witnesses to devaluate higher education, some 29 per cent of the sample had received further education, beyond that of the normal school curriculum. More than 80 per cent of these had had vocational training of some kind, most commonly in professional education or in modern languages.

From a comparison of professional status at the time of the research with status at the time when they became Witnesses, we see—although the differences are not great—that, for those in our sample, becoming a Witness did not appear to induce downward social mobility. (Table 4 shows professional status after conversion.) The upward mobility of Italian Witnesses was greater than that of the Belgians, but this is an expectable pattern for immigrants. This finding, must however, qualify the view, sometimes expressed, that joining a sect with a strong adventist and millennial ideology is an indication of hopelessness in this world, and is associated with the abandonment of normal social and economic aspirations in everyday working life. Even though Witnesses do sometimes give up well-paid positions in order to take up 'pioneering', there is no evidence of a significant effect of such decisions in the data that we gathered.

TABLE 4. *Professional status distribution of sample*

Professional status	% distribution
Unskilled workers	6
Specialized workers	12
Skilled workers	10
Merchants, farmers	5
Clerical	12
Managerial (junior)	2
Professional	0
Students	4
Jobless	4
Retired	14
Housewives	27
No answer	4
Total	100 (367)

Assimilating profession (or former profession) and education, we are able to distribute our respondents to appropriate social and occupational classes. From this evidence, it appears that two out of three Witnesses in our sample belong to the working classes. When the results are compared with the social and occupational class composition of Belgian society provided by census data,[7] we see that the working class is distinctly over-represented among members of the movement (see Table 5).

TABLE 5. *Social class in Belgium compared to social class among Jehovah's Witnesses in existing sample*

	Witnesses	Witnesses	Census
Working class		65	47
(lower working class: unskilled and semi-skilled)	43		
(upper working class: skilled workers)	22		
Clerical		18	26
Middle class (merchants, farmers)		8	14
Managerial		2	6
(junior managerial)	2		
(senior managerial)	0		
Professionals (academics, etc.)		0	4
Unclassified		7	4
Total %		100	100
Total no.		367	3,524,538

We may take it that all Witnesses manifest a very high level of commitment to their religion, and comparing their class distribution with what we know of the involvement of different social classes in the Catholic Church in Belgium, a clear contrast emerges. In the Catholic Church, active involvement is positively associated with higher status. Workers are less likely to be practising Catholics than are middle-class people, and a large proportion of the Belgian working class are no more than marginal Catholics, who attend

[7] Census data: Nationaal Instituut voor de Statistiek, *Volkstelling 31 December 1970*, pt. 8. *Beroepsbevolking*: A. Rijk, *Provincies, Arrondisementen en Taalgebieden* (Brussels, 1975), 113, table 33.

church only for rites of passage. The middle classes are only partially involved, and although they have a higher level of practice, engaging in more than the rites of passage, in general they do not attend church regularly. The groups most involved in the Catholic Church in Belgium are clerks, managers, and professionals.[8]

Among our respondents, 21 per cent had always been Witnesses, which is to say they were either inborn or were the children of parents who joined the movement before they, the children, reached the years of discretion. About 5 per cent of the sample had no religion before they became Witnesses. Of the 274 who had previously belonged to another religion, 92 per cent had been Catholics, 3 per cent had been Protestants, 3 per cent had been of some other religion, and 2 per cent did not answer the question.

Of those who had been Catholics, 27 per cent had been devout; and a further 33 per cent had practised at least irregularly. Thus, it is clear that not only lapsed Catholics were attracted to the Watchtower movement: indeed, it appears, from what we know generally about church involvement in Belgium, that the Witnesses have recruited randomly from the general Catholic population, taking more or less proportionally from among devout, irregular, and non-practising Catholics. Compare the evidence provided in Table 6 for involvement in the Catholic Church.[9]

Recruitment

Whatever may be the convergence of sects and the needs of those who become sectarians, as hypothesized, for example, in the relative deprivation thesis, there remains a lacuna in all such theories: namely, how a sect is made available to its potentially recruitable public. Whatever the characteristics of those who join a movement may be, and whatever the needs which a movement satisfies, the actual process by which a movement makes people aware, not only of its existence as a movement, but of its claims and attractions, is one that stands in need of examination, and in our

    [8] J. Billiet and K. Dobbelaere, *Godsdienst in Vlaanderen. Van kerks katholicisme naar sociaal-kulturele kirstenheid* (Leuven: Davidsfonds, 1976), 33.
    [9] Information on Flemish dioceses is from K. Dobbelaere, 'The Secularization of Flanders (Belgium)' in *The Acts of the 15th Conference on the Sociology of Religion* (Lille: CISR, 1979), 271–91; and on the Archdiocese of Mechelen-Brussels, from Billiet and Dobbelaere, *Godsdienst in Vlaanderen.*

TABLE 6. *Involvement in the Catholic Church in the Flemish dioceses[a] and the archdiocese of Mechelen-Brussels compared to former involvement in the Catholic Church of sampled Witnesses (%)*

Religion	Flemish dioceses (1976)	Archdiocese of Mechelen-Brussels (1976)	Witnesses[b]
Catholics			
Devout	37	23	27
More than rites of passage	± 50	± 60	33
Rites of passage			27
No practice			
Other religion	2–3	3–5	5
No religion	8–10	10–12	6
No answer			2

[a] Limburg and Louvain area included.
[b] Those born in the Watchtower organization excluded.

study we devoted our attention to what people could tell us of their first contact with the Witnesses.

From our data, it was immediately apparent that the house-call was the most effective single technique of recruitment. This was especially so with the French-speaking women and the Italian men in our sample. Almost as effective as the house-call was the influence of parents: almost as many Witnesses had come into the movement because of parental influence as through the effect of a house-call. That parents should exert such an influence is clearly expectable in any long-persisting sect. The Witnesses in Belgium are in a stage of relatively rapid growth, however, and in such a phase recruitment from exogenous sources is always likely to exceed endogenous recruitment.[10] The Witnesses in Belgium include a high proportion of first-generation members, amounting to 74 per cent of the total of our sample.

In spite of this proportion, when to parental influence is added the influence of other family members, then kinship becomes easily the most important agency of recruitment. The influence is more powerful with women than with men. The importance of personal

[10] For a sophisticated model of the pattern of recruitment to religious movements generally, see Robert Currie *et al.*, *Churches and Churchgoers: Patterns of Church Growth in the British Isles* (Oxford: Clarendon Press, 1977).

influence is sustained by the fact that the third most effective medium is the category of friends and acquaintances, who are more influential with men than with women. We observe that Italian women were mostly recruited through the family, and that this was even more powerfully the case with the Dutch-speaking Witnesses, among whom the men were as likely to have been influenced by friends and acquaintances as by a house-call. Housewives (as a subcategory among the women) were not more likely to have been recruited through house-calls than were others.

If we exclude those who became Witnesses before the age of 15, the impact of the parents understandably falls, from 26 per cent to 8 per cent of the total sample. Of the schoolchildren in the sample, some 76 per cent had been recruited by their parents. Adults are thus mostly recruited by house-call (about 35 per cent) or family members (26 per cent). If we control the sample for their involvement in their previous religion, the Catholic Church, we discover that there is a difference between those Witnesses who had been devout Church members, and those who had been less involved, or not at all involved, in the Church. Within each linguistic community, those who had been devout Catholics were predominantly recruited solely by house-calls. Those who had been less integrated in the Church, or completely outside it, had typically become Witnesses either through house-calls or through the influence of family members. Clearly, as time passes, a movement must normally expect to rely increasingly on the recruitment of the second (and subsequent) generations of members. The Witnesses in Belgium have only recently been in a position to recruit second-generation members on any scale, and we asked those respondents who had children to inform us about the proportions of their offspring who had become Witnesses, and we sought to uncover the influence of different variables in producing this result. (See Table 7.)

It is apparent that sex itself does not greatly affect the success rate in recruiting the next generation, but age appears to do so. The older the children, the fewer are Witnesses. Age has a stronger effect on female children than on males. Understandably, where only one parent is a Witness the influence is, at all ages, lower. However, as shown in Table 8, when the parents are divided in their religion, the influence on children appears to be greater when the father is a Witness in either case; however, girls in divided

TABLE 7. *% of children who are Witnesses at the time of our study according to age, sex, and parental religion*

Age	Sex				Parents Witnesses?				Total	
	Male		Female		Both		One			
15–19	78	(23)	97	(30)	97	(29)	83	(24)	91	(53)
20–24	57	(29)	76	(22)	72	(29)	59	(22)	66	(51)
25 and over	44	(46)	49	(54)	59	(60)	41	(40)	52	(100)
Total	62	(98)	68	(106)	72	(118)	56	(86)	65	(204)

TABLE 8. *% of children of divided parents who are Witnesses according to sex and the religious status of father and mother*

Sex				Which parent is a Witness?			
Male		Female		Father		Mother	
41	(39)	65	(47)	66	(41)	43	(45)

families are more likely to be Witnesses than are boys. Of course, in such an analysis there is a concealed element. We can assess the differences in the retention of children at different ages, but we have done so at one point in time. Clearly, as children themselves grow older, there may be an effect of their growing independence of their parents, but there may also be an effect that arises from the passage of time itself, and from the extent to which children were 'brought up in the truth'.

To some extent light can be thrown on this problem by taking into account the age of the children at the time at which the parents first began a Bible study with the Witnesses, and by controlling for age. What then appears, from Table 9 that is,

(1) (reading from the bottom figure of each column), the older the children were when the parents began their Bible study, the less influence parents had on their children (following from 100 per cent at age 15 to 19 years, to 88 per cent in the 20 to 24-year-old group, and so to 58 per cent of those who were 25 or more);

(2) (reading the top row) the influence of parents diminished as the children grew older: this confirms Table 7.

TABLE 9. *% of children who are now Witnesses according to their actual age and the age when their parents started Bible study*

Age when their parents started Bible study	Actual age			Total	
	15–19	20–24	25 and over		
Under 10	86 (37)	59 (34)	58 (28)	68	(59)
10–14	100 (12)	66 (5)	100 (7)	92	(24)
15–19	100 (4)	100 (4)	69 (13)	81	(21)
20–24	—	88 (8)	33 (6)	64	(14)
25 and over	—	—	58 (40)	38	(40)
Total	91 (53)	66 (51)	52 (51)	66	(198)

Social status appears to make no difference in the influence of parents on their children. But when the extent of the involvement in their congregations of parents is taken into account, a difference does arise (see Table 10). The more involved the parents are, the more likely it is that their children will be Witnesses, even though this influence diminishes with the increased age of the children (as is the case with the sample in general).

TABLE 10. *% of children who are Witnesses according to their age and the involvement of their parents in the congregations*

Age of the children	Parents are:			Total	
	Member	Auxiliary pioneer or servant	Elder or pioneer		
15–19	81 (21)	100 (9)	100 (15)	91	(45)
20–24	50 (28)	75 (8)	100 (15)	61	(41)
25 and over	43 (47)	52 (21)	57 (7)	47	(75)
Total	53 (96)	68 (38)	89 (27)	63	(161)

Thus, in sum, the influence of parents on children is greater when parents are very involved in the congregation; when the children are young, and especially so with females; and when the parents are united in their belief. In divided families the influence of the father is more significant. Influence diminishes as children get older, and with children of 25 years of age or more, about half are Witnesses.

We have already seen that family members have an impact on the recruitment of individuals. We may expect then that, in comparison with some sects which tend to recruit isolated individuals, the Witnesses will show evidence of clusters of kinsfolk in membership. We sought to discover the kinship range in membership, including family-in-law. The Italian Witnesses proved to have an average of 8.2 kinsfolk who were Witnesses, and the Belgian an average of 5.2: those of mixed marriages had an average of 4.9. The general distribution of kinsfolk is shown in Table 11. Very few Dutch-speaking Witnesses have no kin in the congregations. The Italians attain a very high proportion with ten or more kinsfolk in the movement.

In Table 12 we may see that nearly half the entire sample had immediate kin (father, mother, brothers, and sisters) in the

TABLE 11. *Distribution of kinsfolk who are Jehovah's Witnesses (%)*

No. of kin	Italian	French-speaking	Dutch-speaking	Total
0	12	19	6	11
1	18	19	21	20
2	17	15	18	17
3–4	16	13	23	14
5–6	8	18	16	14
7–9	5	4	14	9
10 and more	18	2	8	9
No information	6	10	4	6

TABLE 12. *Which kinsmen are Jehovah's Witnesses? (%)*

Nuclear family of origin	49 (343)
Father, mother, and brother(s) and sister(s)	21 (343)
Father and brother(s) and sister(s)	1 (343)
Mother and brother(s) and sister(s)	9 (343)
Father and mother	5 (343)
Brothers and sisters	9 (343)
Father	2 (343)
Mother	2 (343)
Ascendants	40 (343)
Grandfather	5 (343)
Grandmother	9 (343)
Father	29 (343)
Mother	38 (343)
Affines	
Brother(s) and sister(s)	41 (343)
Aunts and uncles	18 (343)
Nephews, nieces, and cousins	29 (343)

movement. The religious association with grandparents is very small, but this arises from the recency of the development of Jehovah's Witnesses in Belgium. (We cannot, of course, assume that influence necessarily passes from older to younger persons, since grandparents may have been introduced to the movement by their children or grandchildren). In at least 40 per cent of cases, the Witnesses in our sample had at least one ascendant in the faith, and among these almost always the mother. The extent of affiliation of affines indicates the extent to which, on the evidence of this sample, the Watchtower movement, even though it has a relatively recently recruited following, is a family faith, in which kinship ties reinforce the distinctive culture of the movement.

This impression is reinforced by the evidence concerning the family-in-law. Of married Witnesses in our sample 43 per cent had at least one kinsman-in-law—a parent, brother, sister, or ascendant—in the faith. Combining data on the family of procreation and the family-in-law, we see from Table 13 that over and above the 60 per cent who counted at least one close kinsman or kinsman-in-law as a Witness, of whom half have them on both sides, a further 30 per cent had at least one distant relative or relative-in-law in the faith. Given this picture, we see the importance of relatives in the recruitment of new Witnesses.

TABLE 13. *% of types of family members of which they have at least one in the faith*

Nuclear family on both sides	22
Nuclear family and ascendants on both sides	8
Nuclear family on one side	25
Nuclear family and ascendants on one side	5
Distant relative(s) or relative(s) in law	30
None	10

Obviously, no modern movement consists only of consolidated families, and 34 (10 per cent) of our respondents were the only members of their families who were Witnesses. Some 50 per cent of these individuals were married; 26 per cent were single; 9 per cent were widowed; and 15 per cent were divorced or separated. One in three of these people was extremely isolated, and more than 50 per cent of these people considered themselves to be discriminated against. Two out of three were women; they were older than the average of our respondents, and two out of three of them were from the lowest social status. House-calls accounted for 60 per cent of them becoming Witnesses, and 50 per cent of them record that they were attracted to the movement by the friendship, warmth, love, and unity of the Witness congregation. Thus, all in all, with respect both to the wider society and to the family situation, those in this group were relatively isolated and of lower social status. This was especially true of French-speaking people: among whom 60 per cent of this class were isolated individuals (as against 40 per cent among the Italian- and Dutch-speaking groups) and one of two was older than 65 years. In this they stand out rather sharply since, in general, the French-speaking Witnesses were better integrated into the total society than were the Dutch- and Italian-speaking groups. We must allow that our French-speaking congregations were from Brussels or its suburbs, and this particular milieu may of course produce a higher proportion of isolated individuals than is found in other parts of the country or in other congregations.

One consideration that may be hypothesized as an important aspect of joining a religious movement is the possibility of discontent with one's previous religious affiliation. We asked our respondents what, apart from the actual teachings of the Witnesses, attracted them to the movement, and from that open-ended question we elicited nine types of response in which the respondent registered discontent with his or her previous religious affiliation. Of the 250 who had changed their religion to become Witnesses we obtained several answers to our question and we record the first three reasons given. (See Table 14.)

Discontent with Catholic doctrine is the reason most frequently mentioned—by about 40 per cent of respondents. Unmarried people were more likely to register this complaint than were married individuals, while those from divided families mentioned less than others the contradiction between doctrine and practice. When these various reasons for leaving their former faith were compared with the respondents' own assessments of their attachment to their earlier religion, we found that 42 per cent of devout Catholics mentioned discontent with doctrine; some 64 per cent of irregular practising Catholics, and around 54 per cent of non-practising Catholics. This was the only ground which revealed any difference among these three types of ex-Catholics. Of course, we

TABLE 14. *Reasons given for leaving former Church (%)*

Reasons	Mentioned			Total
	First	Second	Third	
Discontent with priests	16	1	0	17
Absence of love and fellowship	4	0	0	4
Contradiction between doctrine and practice	12	3	0	15
Discontent with doctrine	28	9	1	38
Discontent with liturgy	4	6	1	11
Low ethical performance of laity	1	2	0	3
Disposition of Church towards the world	4	5	3	12
Attitude of the Church towards believers (differences in class, etc.)	7	4	2	13
Discontent with attitude of the Church towards money	2	3	1	6
Other reasons	5	2	1	8
No answer, or no second or third reason	17	65	90	17
Total %	100	100	100	(^{a})
Total no.	(250)	(250)	(250)	(250)

^{a} Does not add up to 100 since some respondents gave more than one reason.

must acknowledge that comments of this kind are made retro-spectively and it is not possible on this evidence to assess just how keenly this discontent was felt before the individuals left the Church. On the other hand, they did leave and must have had reason for doing so, whether these reasons were specifically religious discontents or considerations of a more social character.

Turning to the positive attraction of becoming a Witness, apart from the attraction of 'the Truth' itself, respondents again sometimes mentioned more than one characteristic. As we have said, warmth, friendliness, love, and unity were the most regular mentioned items, but honesty, and personal comportment in 'acting out biblical principles' were also qualities that Witnesses cherished.

There were, broadly, three types of familial situations into which our respondents might be divided: united families in which man and wife were both members of the Watchtower organization; divided families, when only one spouse was a Witness; and single persons, i.e. unmarried, widowed, divorced, or separated people. Of our respondents, 63 per cent were spouses in united families; 14 per cent were spouses in religiously divided families; and 23 per cent were single persons.

Expectably, single persons were younger than others, reflecting the proportion among them of the as yet unmarried: 55 per cent were less than 25 years old, as against only 14 per cent of married persons. The spouses of religiously divided families were older than those from united families—80 per cent of the partners from religiously divided families were 35 years or older, as against 40 per cent of the partners from a united family. Correspondingly, more of the spouses from religiously divided families were jobless, perhaps mainly retired people.

Spouses from a united family had an average of 6.7 members of their family in the Watchtower organization. For spouses from religiously divided families the mean was 4, and for single persons the average was 5.4 members. In 62 per cent of religiously divided households, the wife was the Witness.

Where both partners became Witnesses after marriage, the modal difference between the time of baptism of man and wife was one to two years, although they were mostly baptized at the same time. When either husband or wife was baptized first, no typical pattern emerged. Before baptism, an intending publisher must study the Bible. For 251 people we acquired data on the interval between beginning the Bible study and baptism. For 49 per cent it took one year; 12 per cent needed less than one year, and altogether 77 per cent were baptized within two years of commencing their Bible study. Those needing more than two years of Bible study were usually labourers, people in lower social classes, and those with only primary school education. Of those needing less than one year of study, men outstripped women by two to one: conversely, of those needing more than two years three out of five were women.

Involvement

The conventional wisdom about sects is that there is a strong expectation of equal and total commitment among the membership. Certainly, in comparison with the division of labour that prevails within a church organization (as, to mention only the crudest distinction, between laity, secular priests, religious, and third orders) the formal impression conveyed by a sect is of a consistent standard of very high involvement. But even among sectarians there are differences in the degree of even formal involvement among the members. These *may* reflect differences in the sense of personal commitment, but they may also merely reflect differences in the life circumstances of individuals. Our evidence tells us about formal involvement, in terms of service which individuals undertake within the movement; it does not, of course, measure differences in actual commitment, nor does it indicate the extent (sometimes limited) in the opportunities to take up positions of service.

Of our sample, 71 per cent did not indicate that they undertook any specific service for the movement (although, since all were 'publishers' all were committed to undertaking door-to-door witnessing). The rest had undertaken (or were undertaking) some particular service: 17 per cent of the sample were or had been temporary pioneers; 9 per cent of the entire sample were or had been pioneers or elders, and 4 per cent were or had been special pioneers (that is to say individuals who give up other work to act as full-time missionaries for the movement).

In other religious bodies, for example in the Catholic Church in Belgium, social class and level of education are positively correlated with involvement in the organization. Correlations of this kind were not in evidence in our sample of the Jehovah's Witnesses. Age, however, was associated with involvement. Special pioneers were predominantly at the younger end of middle age—60 per cent of them being in the age category 25–34 years. Three out of four pioneers, former pioneers, and elders were 35 years of age or older. Only one out of five people younger than 25 years undertook any special service, and these were mostly temporary pioneers or assistants to one of the congregation servants. Sex also affects involvement, but this is a consequence of the movement's Bible-derived prohibition on the participation of women in congregational life: pioneering is the only service position open to women. It must be stressed, however, that all Witnesses are encouraged to serve by publishing, and in this sense the typical Witness does much more active religious work than do members of the churches.

To become a special pioneer or elder demands not only willingness to serve, but recognition of one's abilities and one's thorough socialization in the teachings and life-style of the movement. Almost all of those holding these positions had been baptized for five or more years (see Table 15). Moreover, 75 per cent of special pioneers had never had another religion and were second-generation Witnesses: one of the three others had been a non-believer, and the other two had been Catholics. The standing

TABLE 15. *Involvement and number of years since baptism (%)*

Baptized	Special pioneers	Pioneers or elders	Other members
2 years and less	—	—	29
3–4 years	—	12	17
5 years and more	100	88	54
Total %	100	100	100
Total no.	(12)	(34)	(321)

in their former religion (mostly Roman Catholicism) of those elders and pioneers who were converts was of no consequence for their standing as Witnesses, even though of the Witnesses who were or who had been pioneers or elders 42 per cent had been devout Catholics previously, compared with 20 per cent of other members. Their standing in the Watchtower organization had a slight influence on their legitimation of their discontent with their former religion: the more involved they were in the Watchtower organization, the more they mentioned the contradiction between doctrine and practice in their former church (15 per cent of the regular members; 21 per cent of the part-time pioneers, servants, or assistants; 32 per cent of the elders or pioneers), and the more they rejected the disposition of their former church towards the world (9 per cent of the regular members, and 29 per cent of those more involved).

Conversely, these more involved individuals were more likely to legitimate their acceptance of Watchtower teachings by reference to the fact that Witnesses comport themselves in accordance with biblical principles. This particular element of what attracted them to the movement was offered by 16 per cent of the regular members; 20 per cent of the part-time pioneers and assistants; 25 per cent of the elders and pioneers; and 50 per cent of the special pioneers. Clearly, those who were more involved, which usually meant that they undertook more extensive hours in the preaching work of witnessing, were more likely to be aware of those forms of argument used in presenting the Watchtower case to Catholic laymen who were approached as possible converts.

The involvement of Witnesses in their organization is a function of their standing in the movement. Social factors have no impact at all on their standing: quite the contrary, Witnesses in general are not integrated in the wider society, and those least integrated of all with the outside world are the special pioneers. Table 16 indicates that some 70 per cent of the Witnesses were somewhat isolated socially, in the sense that they were not involved in the activities of the general public, as based on membership of social organizations, newspaper-reading, listening to the radio, watching television, or engaging in hobbies that involve social contact. Some 40 per cent of the special pioneers were strongly isolated, as measured by these indicators, in comparison with 10 per cent of other Witnesses. It appears, therefore, that there is a rough balance—greater involvement in the movement implies more isolation from the wider society. Witnesses themselves would, of course, expect to find just such a balance, and although they do not eschew all the activities in which other people engage, they tend, the more involved they are in the Watchtower organization, to wish to associate less and less with outsiders except for the contacts entailed in their own preaching work.

TABLE 16. *Standing in the Watchtower organization and integration in the wider society (%)*

Degree of social integration	Special pioneer	Pioneer or elder	Auxiliary pioneer	Regular member	Total
Extremely isolated	—	—	—	—	—
Strongly isolated	42	12	15	12	13
Isolated	25	50	47	61	56
Integrated	33	29	28	21	24
Strongly integrated	—	6	10	4	5
Very strongly integrated	—	3	—	1	1
Total %	100	100	100	100	100
Total no.	(12)	(34)	(58)	(259)	(363)

Social Integration

Involvement in the Watchtower organization appears, then, to determine the extent of the Witness's social integration in the wider society. We measured social integration by the criteria referred to above, and we summarized the information by awarding scores to the responses. The respondent could score from 0 to 5 points on a scale measuring integration with the wider society.

TABLE 17. *Integration in the wider society by type of congregation (%)*

Degree of social integration	Italian Congregation	French-speaking	Flemish-speaking	Total
Extremely isolated	—	1	—	—
Strongly isolated	17	8	13	13
Isolated	68	48	51	56
Integrated	10	37	27	24
Strongly integrated	2	5	6	5
Very strongly integrated	3	0	1	1
No answer	—	1	2	1
Total %	100	100	100	100
Total no.	(125)	(84)	(158)	(367)

Table 17 indicates the differences for our three types of congregation.

It is clear that Witnesses in general insulate themselves from the wider society. The Italian-speaking congregations are more insulated than are the Dutch- and French-speaking Witnesses (85 per cent as against 57 per cent and 64 per cent).

Almost all Witnesses reported that they had a radio (94 per cent), and 84 per cent had a television set: thus, detachment from the wider society may be said to start with abstention from reading newspapers, avoiding hobbies that entail social contacts, and remaining aloof from social organizations. Of our respondents, 25 per cent read a newspaper: 30 per cent of the Belgians, and 14 per cent of the Italians. This may be compared with Colson's finding that 79 per cent of the Flemish population read newspapers.[11] Two out of three Witnesses had a hobby, but for only one in five of those who pursued a hobby, did that hobby involve them in wider social contacts. Most of the hobbies in which Witnesses were engaged were individual activities, such as reading, listening to music, and photography.

Witnesses clearly make the choice to retreat from the social world into the community of the faithful, and that choice involves change in their outside activities. Respondents were asked about membership in social organizations before they became Witnesses and afterwards. Before becoming Witnesses, 22 per cent had

[11] F. Colson, *Leesgedrag en lectuurvoorziening* (Leuven: Sociologisch Onderzoeksinstituut, 1972), pt. I, p. 86.

belonged to various social organizations; at the time of the survey, only 9 per cent held such memberships. Of these, most were memberships in trades unions, accounting for 74 per cent of those who were members of outside social organizations. At the time respondents became Witnesses, trades unions had accounted for only 41 per cent of all memberships. Of course, for economic reasons, it is more difficult to give up membership of a union than of other types of organization. Very few Witnesses sustained memberships in cultural associations (two in our whole sample, compared to twenty-one in the days before they became Witnesses) or sporting associations (three compared to eighteen in earlier days).

Not only as measured by formal membership, but also as indicated by friendships, can it be maintained that Witnesses have limited contacts with people outside the movement. As we see from Table 18, 54 per cent of the Witnesses who responded to our enquiry reported that they had no friends outside the movement, while more than two out of three Witnesses count the majority of their friends to be Witnesses.

TABLE 18. *% of Witnesses who have friends outside the Watchtower organization*

Friends outside Watchtower organization		Belgians	Italians	Total
None		48	65	54
Minority	20 ⎫			
Half of them	2 ⎬	41	25	35
Majority	7 ⎪			
All	12 ⎭			
No answer		11	10	11
Total %		100	100	100
Total no.		(242)	(125)	(367)

Perhaps not surprisingly, given their separation from the world, some Witnesses considered themselves to be discriminated against by people in the outside world. Of our respondents, 31 per cent asserted that they had had reason to feel that they had experienced discrimination from others. This had been experienced principally in their work situation and from members of their families.

However, some 48 per cent reported that they had experienced no discrimination, and 21 per cent could give no answer. In Table 19, for those who reported discrimination, we indicate its sources.

TABLE 19. *Circumstances in which Witnesses who reported discrimination experienced it (%)*

In what situation or by whom	%
Work situation	34
By family members	23
By neighbours and acquaintances	16
At school	12
In other places	11
Not specified	12
Total %	108[a]
Total no.	(113)

[a] Some respondents reported discrimination in more than one situation.

Conclusion

Our study of this sample of Jehovah's Witnesses in Belgium had indicated something about the way in which a distinctive self-isolating but growing social group recruits members and sustains its way of life. Such a movement is clearly always likely to be attractive to people who are in some measure already isolated from the wider society, as the success of the movement among immigrants (Polish workers in the 1930s and Italians and others in more recent times) suggests. Our interview material, to present samples of which lack of space precludes, indicates that others, besides immigrants, were relatively isolated people before becoming Witnesses—people with few friends, or people who had recently moved from their original places of residence into strange communities, for example. Obviously, this was not true for all or even for a majority of members of the movement, but it was undoubtedly one source of recruits.

On the other hand, although we have used the word 'isolated', it must be clear that once someone is a Witness, isolation is a distinctly relative matter. If Witnesses are 'isolated' from the wider society, they are certainly no longer isolated as individuals. Indeed, becoming a Witness is for some perhaps a way of overcoming isolation. Again and again, Witnesses said that they 'did not know what friendship meant until I became a Witness', or 'before I had no one, but now I have brothers and sisters everywhere'. In some respects, Witnesses are perhaps much less isolated than are many people whose lives are integrated into the normal patterns of social life in the wider society, in which, however, they have relatively few really close ties, and, in modern conditions, perhaps no sense of communal belonging. The friendliness of the Witnesses was repeatedly mentioned by people who spoke of what, in addition to 'the truth', they had found attractive about the movement, and some contrasted it with the distance of fellow church-goers in their previous religious involvements, and also with the remoteness and indifference of priests. We have used the concept of insulation from the wider society which perhaps better represents the style of social involvement which Witnesses maintain.

A movement so preoccupied with publishing its message as the Witnesses makes recruitment a very strong focus. A study such as our own throws no light on the turn-over of personnel within this rapidly growing sect, the very rates of growth of which may conceal a considerable incidence of 'leakage'. One of the elders in the Genk congregation said to us: 'If all who had been in contact had stayed, there would be ten times more Witnesses than there are today.' That, of course, is an off-the-cuff impression and may well be a much exaggerated estimate. None the less, many people who have been in the movement for some time recognized that the retention of members is a problem.

All adventist movements have the endemic problem of the continued delay of the events expected at the end of the present dispensation. The Witnesses have withstood an unexpectedly long period of waiting better than some other sects, and they have become cautious about the exact time when the new kingdom is to appear.[12] Yet, if a movement recruits rapidly, the sense of disappointment may itself be somewhat allayed since newer members have not waited so long, and since each new recruit experiences initial exhilaration, and must subsequently settle into the stable life patterns of witnessing before he becomes really exposed to the possibility of feeling disappointed. Each recruit, too, provides a new focus of interest, restoring buoyancy and zest to

---

[12] A brief discussion of the most recent disappointment and its effect on Witnesses is provided in B. Wilson, 'When Prophecy Failed', *New Society*, 26 Jan. 1978; see also Penton, *Apocalypse Delayed*.

older members, so that a strong recruitment orientation functions in these two ways to insulate an adventist sect from the expectable effects of the delay in the fulfilment of prophecy.[13]

Older members need such re-invigoration if commitment is to be sustained. The movement, by its own conception of the Truth and of its own mission, can permit no diversions, nor any relaxation of its demands. The question and answer sessions from the *Watchtower* must continue, week after week; the relatively routinized procedures for training members in public-speaking and in active canvassing permit of little variation; and even the international assemblies held every summer and the Circuit assemblies held more often, are essentially standardized events, predictable in terms of content and style, year by year, and quarter by quarter. But these are the only excitements which the movement admits. Waiting for anything and in any circumstances can be boring, and routine procedures do little to reduce ennui once it sets in: it is the conviction of having a priceless Truth and the certainty that one is right, together with the prospect of a blissful reward in the future, that sustain the commitment of Witnesses. As one intelligent interviewee said, when asked about the difficulties he had experienced in becoming a Witness:

I was struck by how simple it all was—I would even like it a bit deeper. It is always the same at meetings, but on the other hand you have to see it is necessary: there are people here who have been in the Truth longer than I have, and they are still only beginners, and they need a simple message . . . There are things you don't understand immediately, but later you do. That is why we go on repeating, and repeating.

---

[13] More generally, for this effect in respect of early Christianity, see J. G. Gager, *Kingdom and Community* (Englewood Cliffs, NJ: Prentice Hall, 1975).

9

Becoming a Sectarian:
Motivation and Commitment

DURING the period of their emergence and growth, sects are generally discussed in terms of opprobrium, perhaps because most of those who have written about them have been people not only of other theological persuasions, but often people with vested professional interests in sustaining their own theology against that of others, or, occasionally, they have been men of decidedly rationalistic temper, eager to condemn all religion by reference to what they take to be the latest and most patent religious outrage to common sense. By the time a sect becomes a historical phenomenon it is likely that those still interested in it will discuss it with a measure of detached objectivity: for contemporary sects, only sociologists are likely to espouse the same canons of ethical neutrality and objectivity that are, perhaps so much more easily, endorsed by historians in their treatment of things past.

Objective as he may be, the historian knows that much of his source material about sectarianism in the past is likely, in the nature of its provenance, to be biased. With such sources, it becomes difficult to make judgements about sectarian motivation. Sectarians themselves have not usually been men capable of putting down the considerations that entered into their decision to adopt a particular religious persuasion: and when they have done so, their comments have often been regarded as too slanted or fanatical to merit serious attention. Commonly, sectarian converts have been more concerned to set out the proofs of their principles, almost in rejection of the idea that a right-thinking man, specifically a member of his own sect, could have any motives at all but that of discovery and acceptance of the truth. Much of the internal written source material on sects has come from leaders, but even these sources have sometimes been subject to editing, censorship, or restriction of access by their faithful followers: so it was with the papers of Mary Baker Eddy, such has been the practice of the

Mormons, the Exclusive Brethren, and in some measure the Jehovah's Witnesses.

For historical sects, then, neither the writings of the sectarians themselves, nor the evidence of commentators (including apostates, whose motives for writing, let alone the substance of what they write, must always occasion suspicion), can take us far towards an understanding of motivation and commitment. Nineteenth-century sects, however, sometimes offered us another resource: they sometimes produced a periodical literature entirely for internal consumption, which not infrequently dealt with issues in which differences, policies, and strategies were at stake, and from which something could be gleaned about motives and the mechanisms for eliciting commitment. In the twentieth century, even this source has deteriorated in quality if not in quantity: much of the sectarian literature of recent years has been written with the consciousness that the world is leaning over the writer's shoulder. As sects have grown, and particularly where they have acquired hierarchic and even bureaucratic centralized administrative structures, internal differences tend to be glossed over, controversy muted, or presented in a form in which only those thoroughly conversant with the context can read between the lines to discover just what issues are really at stake. As sects have become large international movements, so their literature has become, in consequence, impersonal, official, and remote from the rank-and-file believer and his motivations. In an inflationary age, even smaller sects that are unaffected by bureaucratic impersonalism can no longer put their concerns so readily into print as they could in the nineteenth century, and for them the less durable cyclostyled sheet, the newsletter, ignored by libraries (even when not positively rejected by librarians), comprise the ephemera in which, if anywhere, revelations are made about individuals, about motives, procedures, and disputes.

In contrast with these disadvantages which the study of historical sects presents, research into contemporary sects offers distinct and perhaps unique advantages. Ideally without any theological *parti pris* (although there are some prominent exceptions), the sociologist may do what the historian cannot do—involve himself in the life of a sectarian movement. Tactfully approached, some sects, even the most intense and rigorous such as Witnesses and the Children of God, may admit a neutral observer into their religious and communal life. He may not only observe and participate, but he may ask direct questions of the people whom he is studying. The method is time-consuming and may induce considerable emotional stress, and the information that is gained is often incommensurate with the time expended, but as information it is of a high order of authenticity. These procedures suffer from drawbacks of their own, but they do yield direct information, and information that is much less seriously subject to selectivity and premeditated secondary elaboration than is normally the case with the written word, whether in the form of published articles, or diaries and letters (which, among sectarians, are in any case rare commodities). The interviewer or the participant may always seek additional elucidation. He may double-check his impressions or his records. He may seek a clarification of ambiguities. He may question the relationship of one statement to another. And he may elicit important information about the background and context of the evidence that he is given. In some circumstances he may be able to interview two or more members of the same family and get two or more versions of particular events and experiences.

The advantages of studying sects accrue not merely from the opportunities for enquiry afforded by sociological methods, but also from some of the intrinsic qualities of the sect itself. Sects offer a unique field of enquiry in a variety of respects, but of particular importance for an understanding of religious motivation is the fact that within those groups that we designate as sects religious commitment is a value that utterly transcends all other obligations and relationships. If a man is an Anglican or a Methodist, this is but one among many of his attributes—he is also a lathe-turner, a pigeon-fancier, a trade-unionist, a harmonica-player, and so on. If a man is one of Jehovah's Witnesses, a Seventh-day Adventist, or even a committed Pentecostalist, this is the single most significant fact about him. His religious commitment is supposed, by him, by his co-religionists, and even by his workmates, kinsfolk, and acquaintances, to influence in very high degree, not only his attitudes but the choice and quality of performance of all his social roles, and perhaps even to determine them.[1] It follows, that if

---

[1] It is difficult to agree with William James when he wrote, 'Converted men as a class are indistinguishable from natural men; some natural men even excel some converted men in their fruits . . .': *The Varieties of Religious Experience* (New York: New American Library of World Literature edn., 1958), 192. Sectarians generally

religious motivation is so much superordinate to all other motivations, so the motivation for becoming religious in this way must
have been unusually powerful and distinctive. Here we have a
conundrum: were the primary motives that led an individual to
become religiously committed and that led him to espouse religious
motivations for the conduct of his life in themselves essentially non-
religious? Or are we to presuppose a religious disposition in the first
place, which at some point simply found powerful and distinctive
expression?

Sectarian commitment is of course, from the perspective of the
wider society, deviant in both kind and degree, with respect to
beliefs, practices, and social comportment. The sect establishes an
alternative *Lebenswelt* for its adherents, both in their intellectual
apprehensions of reality and in their social relationships. The sect is
exclusive, tolerating no dual allegiances, no compromise with its
principles, no defections from the standards of conduct that it
endorses, and no infringement of the taboos that it maintains. It is a
bounded community, ideally allowing no ambiguity, and in
actuality allowing very little, with respect to the status of adherents,
its claim to a monopoly of truth, and an exclusive warrant for its
practice. Above all it claims the transcendent allegiance of all those
who belong, and it does so on the basis of its own supernatural
legitimation.

Undoubtedly sects have attracted investigation because they are
deviant minorities, but in its assertion of totality and in its emphasis
on distinctive boundaries a sect approximates the anthropologist's
tribe. It is a culture, or at least a subculture in itself, but in this lies a
difficulty for those interested in religious motivation. The very
totalism of the sect induces a high degree of conformity in which
individual motivation is often subsumed in corporate purposes.
Thus, although in sectarians we have people who are profoundly
motivated by religious considerations, we have the difficulty that
their common religious commitment is supposed to motivate them
in much the same way. Once in the movement, the individual's
motivations are supposed to be those of the ideal member. There is
a premium on conformity and there are standard tests—of social
behaviour; of performance in recruitment service; of volubility in

are readily distinguishable from 'natural men', although that is more usually and
completely the case of those who belong to sects where conversion is (as it was in the
cases to which James principally referred) a sudden experience.

prayer or in speaking in tongues; of being able to pursue a line of doctrinal exegesis; of abstinences, and so on—by which conformity is measured and in accordance with which behaviour is regulated. In particular, any unauthorized exercise of spirituality (such as being a vegetarian among Christian Scientists, or being a teetotaller among Christadelphians, or practising meditation among Jehovah's Witnesses) would meet at least with surprise and vague disapproval, as an implicit intimation that the individual concerned regarded the sect's own behavioural directives as in some way less than adequate. Divergences do exist among members of the same sect, of course, but with respect to so basic a matter as motivations, the differences are difficult to discern, and might be most fully visible at the point at which individuals become sectarians.

Why, then, does an individual join a sect? What induces him to abandon an existing pattern of life, and an existing state of belief or unbelief (however vague it may be) for a commitment that is so totally at variance with that of the generality of men in his society, and which in some measure must set him over against other men, at least as a man apart, if not as a man at odds with the wider society? One is asking, then, not merely about religious motivations and religious commitment, but about how such strongly religious dispositions were first summoned.

In putting this question, one may note in passing that although almost all sects insist on the individual's personal and voluntary decision to seek fellowship, and insist on the maintenance of rigorous standards, none the less, a distinction may be made between those who enter the sect as the children of parents who are already members and the first-generation converts. Although formally all enter on the same terms, and all are subject to the same continuing tests of eligibility and the same sanctions for misconduct, the individual who comes to the sect without having had what might be called a 'sectarian upbringing' experiences a much more radical reorientation of values. We might ask, then, of these people—the converts—what exactly induced them not merely to abandon, but also to renounce their former way of life, and to accept religious considerations as the determinants of all actions and decisions in all other departments of life.

To ask converts why they were attracted to the sect to which they now belong is, initially, to get a response that validates the decision by reference to the ideological terms in which the sect as a collectivity seeks legitimation. Such legitimations may be primarily intellectual, primarily experiential (in the sense of emotional experience); they may (and in the Christian world they usually do) include direct reference to scripture as a source of knowledge, and sometimes as a source of specific prophecy that forecasted the events of recent history and in particular the emergence of the sect itself. 'The Truth', as sectarians of many kinds commonly refer to the message of their own particular movement, is a self-evident and sufficient reason for their allegiance. But why, behind the slogans and the stereotypes, do sectarians take the message of their movement as the sufficient and convincing 'truth', which not only explains life, the world, and the purposes of God in history, but which also established principles in the light of which to organize their own lives? The answers to questions about what attracted them to the movement, the elicited statements about their lives, reveal, understandably, a wide variety of personal circumstances. Motivation is not completely and clearly uncovered even by protracted interview, but a sample of responses (in this case from a number of Jehovah's Witnesses in a congregation in the south of England) provide statements of conscious motives, and indicate some background circumstances and perhaps some unconscious predispositions.[2]

Case no. 1 is that of a married bricklayer's labourer of 19, of no previous religion, who had been introduced to the movement by his father-in-law. He said of his conversion:

I became interested in the Truth through my father-in-law. When he came to the Kingdom Hall and asked for a [Bible] Study for himself, I thought he was mad, and when the two Witnesses used to come to their house, I was often there. I was impressed, and I began sitting in on the Study, and I developed a conscience. I got to thinking that smoking was wrong, and I stopped, and from there on I progressed. My father-in-law was just coming into the Truth himself, and it was seeing what a change it made in him that impressed me, because he used to be a bad person the same as myself. I told my father about it and I told my probation officer. They told me a lot about Jehovah's Witnesses—they were lies. I asked why do people tell these lies, and this stimulated my interest. My probation officer told me that they had

---

[2] These responses were elicited by asking people to relate, in the course of recounting how they came to join the movement, 'What, apart from the Truth itself [the movement's teachings], first attracted you to Jehovah's Witnesses?'; 'Have you experienced any blessings?; 'Did you have any difficulties in becoming a Witness?'; and 'Has being a Witness occasioned any changes in your life?'.

sex within their families, and he professed to be a Christian, though he used to swear and smoke himself . . . My friends were surprised—they couldn't believe it and didn't think it was going to last. One of my friends actually came into the Truth himself, and he married my wife's sister, which astonished my friends a lot more. I still like to see them, and regard them as good friends, and I think that they respect me a bit because of my conduct. My mother herself said, if it weren't for being in the Truth, I'd be in prison. That is all finished now. I've never been in trouble since I've been in the Truth. My conscience wouldn't allow it. I've got a happy marriage: it wouldn't have been as good as it is if I hadn't been in the Truth. My wife thinks that but for the Truth we wouldn't be together, because of the way I used to act before—because we came into the Truth together . . . I stole a car and lots of other things. I was in court for actual bodily harm, for threatening behaviour, driving without insurance and without passing a test, theft—all different cases—drinking under age, lots of other things, and lots of things I got away with. All of this is a thing of the past. I've given up getting drunk. This makes it clear why my mother [who is not a Witness] thinks it a good thing, because she was a bag of nerves when I went out—and this was why she recommended to my father that the younger brothers should come to Kingdom Hall (but my father doesn't see it).

It is perhaps not appropriate here to subject a statement of this kind to extended analysis, and ultimately the idiosyncracies of individual cases are of less interest than general patterns, but we may note the underlying themes: pride in having acquired a conscience; the possible stimulation arising from the opposition of his father (with whom his relations have always been bad) and his probation officer; the pleasure in having become a celebrity as a bad character reformed. In the background is the importance of the reinforcement of family ties with the family into which he is marrying—a family which itself is at that moment undergoing conversion and a reintegration of values.

Case no. 2 is that of the father-in-law of the young man in the preceding case: a married semi-skilled manual worker, who had been a Roman Catholic. He had become for a time one of Jehovah's Witnesses while in the forces, and after refusing to wear his uniform had then been put in prison: after his release, and on getting married, he 'fell away', but after twenty years he returned to his sectarian faith. Recounting his experience, he said:

I'd been wondering about things and wondering if there was a God. Suddenly the world situation became tense—with the Arab oil business, and things were getting worse, and suddenly I could see it. So I came to Kingdom Hall and asked for a Bible Study. I was unhappy. My marriage was dodgy. I was chasing women, leading a worldly life, everything others would do, terrible things—encouraged by TV. You become detestable to yourself. You look at society and ask where is it going to go. I feel a lot better for looking forward to a new system of things. I'm motivated to do things. I did things out of selfishness before: now there's no greed. It doesn't worry me any more . . . the money will be worth nothing. I've always wondered why we are here. You see people dying. Why are we here? They are told—Evolution, but if they examine it carefully, and the teachings of religion, when I studied with Jehovah's Witnesses, I could see for myself. God has a purpose. You are being used at present. If you lead a nice life at present—you've got to work nine hours a day. What is there? Too much materialism. Man is bogged down with factories and cars and is not really free.

. . . I'm really grateful to have come back, because if Armageddon had come in the twenty years I was out of the Truth, I'd have been gone. When I returned I was really depressed, and wept—and the TV showing starving children, and I've wept. I can't understand why man does this to man— there must be something driving man on. Now I realize what the Bible says is true, about Satan being the God of this system.

. . . Now I consider everything a blessing—earning a living. I've been self-employed—car-dealing. My conscience wouldn't let me repair cars as I used to do. I owed taxes. I earn more money than anyone in the factory—I earn big bonuses. I keep working. It upsets some men in the factory. They smoke and say 'Why keep on?' They want all that goes in society except the work that goes with it. I consider my family coming in the Truth as a blessing. My two girls were going out with two notorious characters— trouble-makers, in the police courts. Today, it's all changed. One was notorious—he's changed and still changing . . . I had difficulties: the opposite sex. You have to watch your eyes, your thinking, and what you read: you don't have to go for girlie magazines. These things give me a bad conscience and a bad life. I can't turn that away, but the Scriptures tell me how to be forgiven providing I don't persist in them . . .[But people] don't want to change their ways. If you've found the easy way of making money, you don't want to change. You can understand people not wanting to know. I feel sorry for people who've been deceived [by different religions]. They'll die at Armageddon—we've got to get out and save them. I'm doing no more than I should. I feel so motivated, I've got to tell people what is true. Eventually they may pick up a seed . . . people have had enough of the system. Things still trouble me. I even feel I'm not worthy, though one shouldn't feel that way. I'm getting a clean conscience, and I've got to guard it. Jehovah has given me that conscience—and I'll not do the wrong things that I was doing. I've got to make sure and come to meetings and think about others instead of myself. I must think of fellow man first. I've always worked pretty hard. I've become honest. Before I took things I considered perks. I've got a better marriage: I'm not deceiving my wife as I used to. I used to have inferiority complex (or guilt). I no longer suffer embarrassment when talking to people like you. I feel a better person than I was—no violent temper, which I had. I'm not me no more.

The theme of conscience occurs again, which is not entirely usual as an expressed emphasis in this way among Jehovah's Witnesses, whose religion does not dwell on guilt, and indeed this convert said that he ought not to feel unworthy, which is in accordance with the movement's teachings. In this case, and we shall notice it in others, and perhaps it is more appropriate for a middle-aged man than for his young son-in-law, there is despair about the state of the world. There is the emphasis on new beginnings, and there is the process of externalizing one's rottenness. The insistence on the need to act to save others is perhaps a justification of one's own decision and certainly a reinforcement of newly chosen values.

Case no. 3 is that of a once divorced remarried man of 37, working as a radio and TV service manager, who had formerly been an agnostic. He said:

I had just come out of prison as a conscientious objector on humanitarian grounds, during National Service. I was classed as anti-religious and therefore I went to prison. I had a three months' sentence. The Jehovah's Witnesses called on me about a week after my release. I said, 'Don't talk to me about religion', and he said, 'Many of us have been in prison, too' . . . The Jehovah's Witnesses did not interest me, but my mother became interested. [We may suppose that this was about 1958 or 1959.] In 1971, I started to study [the Witnesses' literature]. Originally, I was interested because it seemed a good thing for myself and my fiancée, but she said don't do anything about it. After ten years she went off with my best mate and my 3-year-old daughter, who I discovered wasn't even mine. The Witnesses had called in this period, but she wouldn't listen. I didn't want what they said to become a crutch for me. It took a lot [of thought] to make me accept. [This appears to have been after his wife had left him.] I met my present wife at the meetings here in Kingdom Hall.

[What attracted me was] the harmony among the congregation—and their unitedness throughout the world. How can God be partial to some and not to others?

I used to lose my temper a lot and swear. I used to chuck the [radio and TV] sets about a bit: my temper is better now. I used to have quite a problem with masturbation—this is now totally controlled. I used to tell bad jokes, but this is now completely controlled.

The message of the Witnesses and the benefits of social involvement in their well-integrated group life became available for this respondent (after some early acquaintance and attraction) just at a time of personal crisis. The individual accepts the sect, as he was tempted to do before his first marriage, when that marriage has broken down. There is a measure of self-awareness in not wanting 'what they said to become a crutch for me'.

Case no. 4 is of a married woman of 48, working as a part-time home-help, herself the mother of four sons, the youngest dead from drowning, and with a husband much opposed to her membership of Jehovah's Witnesses. She said:

I was attracted by their answering Bible questions that I couldn't get any answer to [elsewhere] . . . When they came to the door they were able to answer my questions. My husband was amenable at first, till he found they were Jehovah's Witnesses: then he wouldn't let them come again. So I went to them. The more I studied, the more it made sense. One saw why there was suffering in the world. I couldn't find out what I'd done to deserve so much suffering—and I saw it wasn't from God. It became clear that whereas some people have all the good fortune and others none—why if God was love should there be a difference? It looked as if there wasn't a God, but I couldn't accept evolution. When I came to realize that it was Adam who wrote the first five chapters of Genesis, it began to make sense—that was the simplicity, honesty, and truth of the whole thing. I had questioned vicars and priests who said I had to believe and one said that it wasn't for the likes of me to know. The Witnesses could answer the questions.

My husband had made me feel incompetent and unable to be a proper mother and I developed an inferiority complex. We were not allowed to have friends to the house unless they were people he knew. He had been a sergeant-major and he expected them [the children] to be men before they were boys. I could never see the end of it. There was a gap between the boys [of about fifteen years] and I prayed for strength to stay with him till all the boys were old enough. None of the boys are at home now—the two middle ones were turned out at 16: the youngest was made such a fuss of till he died. I am still living with my husband, and the two oldest boys are now married.

At first I wasn't allowed to mix [with Witnesses] and sometimes I used to come when he was at work. When I did come, it felt as if I was coming home, and everyone was so friendly. This feeling of belonging and everyone in the same boat, and understanding the purpose of life—giving a purpose to life. It is everything about it [that attracts me]—knowing the whys and wherefores. I can't imagine what life would be without it. I had tried suicide before coming into the Truth. I thought it would be better if I was out of the way. It was a help when my son died: I knew he had only gone to sleep. He was drowned, and three weeks before they found the body. It was a help even to my husband: he asked a Jehovah's Witness to conduct the service, although he had nothing good to say of them before or since. But the blessing is that I know I shall see Tony again.

I now have a wide range of friends that I never had before, and a purpose. I never feel alone, helpless, or useless. I feel that I can do something. It has given me life . . . My husband does object—he's locked me out and hit me at times. But no matter, I still come. He is away today, but when he is at home I go to the Central [a more conveniently timed meeting] so I can be home the rest of the day with him.

For this woman, the Witnesses provided an alternative *Lebenswelt*, gave her purpose and restored self-confidence in an apparently scarcely tolerable marriage situation. There is an intellectual emphasis in the initial attraction that the movement exerted, and both emotional and intellectual elements in the factors that sustained her commitment.

Case no. 5 is that of 35-year-old married driver-salesman, formerly a lapsed Anglican, with a wife who was not one of Jehovah's Witnesses. He said:

I was going to emigrate to Australia. I had done National Service abroad and I was restless. I wondered a lot about life and death, and I wanted to emigrate to do something with my life. I went to Perth, Western Australia in 1970. I had a few problems—I didn't have my car—it was held up in the dock strike. Having no car, two jobs proved inconvenient, and I went to work close by, at some seedling nurseries. There I came in contact with the Truth: I was labouring at the nurseries and there was a young pioneer working there. He refused to touch the blood and bone manure for the plants.[3] Everyone laughed. I didn't: I asked him why. He told me about the Bible. He witnessed to me, and placed the Truth book with me. With the many problems I had—we had no car and things were not going right—I used to read the Truth book, and it was like giving a donkey strawberries: it was like dragging me from darkness to light . . . There was a terrific friendship among the Witnesses. There were no barriers. The man who gave me the Bible Study was the top architect in Perth, and there was no side—the hours he would spend, all free of charge of course. It surprised

---

[3] Jehovah's Witnesses consider that the Bible proscribes the ingestion of blood.

me to see so many walks of life with no barriers, myself being just ordinary educated. And there were Italians and Yugoslavs, and you would go round to their homes with no barriers at all. I came back at the beginning of 1973 for the sole reason to get my family to listen. I'd tried with letters. If your Mum and Dad's life are in danger, you'd come back. It cost a lot—£4,000 at least—a mortgage to try to get the family to listen. It hasn't worked yet—not even with my wife. She is friendly with Jehovah's Witnesses but there is no desire [on her part to join]. She didn't want to come back from Australia, but being head of the family I made the decision. I've known Italians go back from Australia for the same reason. Many people have said, 'You didn't like it in Australia', but I've said that if I thought there were many years left for this system, I would go back.

[The Truth is] an answer to life. I've always had the feeling there was something greater than man. Many times I'd think, 'You will die one day'. I could never understand: a vicar once went abroad and while he was away his family were killed: that was puzzling. I'd think of things like that. Death used to shake me a lot. The wife's father died suddenly: it disturbed me a lot. I saw my two sons born in the room. [The Truth] was the answer to life. It was not so much that the system was coming to an end: it was the answers in the Truth book. Biggest thing now is why the wife and I divide on this . . . She has no desire and that worries me a lot. After four and a half years in the ministry, once a week speaking to all walks of life from doctors to dustmen, and all different religions, I've not come against anything to show me that we don't have the Truth. I changed my ways of thinking a lot. I was 34 years of age: I'd done all the bad things. I had to put on a new personality. I've got reason for living, and hope for the future. World events and problems don't get me down any more. Death doesn't worry me any more . . . I have the free feeling. I've come out of a dark tunnel.

Clearly, the sect has a strong intellectual appeal for this man: the sect answers questions. It also breaks down barriers: the eradication of differences in social status is clearly of some importance to this respondent.

Case no. 6 is that of a married woman of 44 with five children, formerly Anglican, and the wife of a disabled skilled manual worker. She said:

[Apart from the Truth itself, I was attracted by] the friendliness and genuineness of the Jehovah's Witnesses who came to the house, and the welcome that I received at Kingdom Hall. I used to feel terribly shy, but the Witnesses did not make me feel small or laugh at me. I used to be serious and deep. The Truth really brought me out. They are genuine friends. I have never wanted for anything, although I have had many trials. The children have plenty of clothes: we help one another. I have a real hope for the future: I don't seek to associate frequently with worldly people.

Poverty and difficult circumstances lie in the background for this respondent who is impressed by the friendship of the Witnesses and by her own acquisition of confidence from being among them. Case no. 7 is that of another married woman, the wife of a carpenter, with four sons, the youngest of whom was spastic: she and her husband had both been Witnesses since 1952. She said:

One Sunday morning a Witness called. I was in the middle of cooking and very angry. I questioned her, 'Why do you keep calling when we want nothing to do with you?' She was little and quiet, and she shamed me. They called back by arrangement. My husband said, 'Anyone but them': he carried on working [when they came] and made a lot of noise. After he said, 'I deliberately made the noise, but what you've said in this last half hour made more sense than I've ever heard from the Methodists—may I come in and listen?'

[I was attracted by] the meekness of the Witness who called on me—she was only eighteen. I was so rude to her. The Witnesses' attitude was marvellous. They said, 'The reason why we come round is because we love our neighbours'. It took us about two years to really get the message. Previously, I had been awkward—no one could get on with me. I used to beat my children—but it changed. The house became happy and full of laughter—a greater unity. The children began to respect us and show love. [What is impressive is] the love. We can go and pop in, and they are really glad to see you—the love is absolutely marvellous.

When I had my youngest son [the spastic], the doctor said, 'This should never have happened'. The sister in charge hated Witnesses. Nobody came when the baby was born, although I rang and rang—and the child's brain was damaged because of no oxygen. My treatment was not good in hospital, even the doctor recognized that the treatment was bad. However, I left a marvellous witness behind me. I am always being praised at the way in which I bring up and manage to help raise him [the spastic child].

The husband of this woman also asserted, in a separate interview, that the love experienced in associating with Witnesses was something that 'you couldn't get outside'. In this case again, there is evidence of both the communal support gained from the movement and the appeal of the attitudes and dispositions which the movement encourages. In this case, the serious trauma comes much later, long after the respondent became a Witness, but being Witnesses is clearly important for them during this trial, allowing them to reinterpret events and to remain contented despite family misfortune.

In Case no. 8, family tragedy appears to be a much more significant element in prompting conversion. This case is that of a married woman, the wife of a press reader and the mother of four children, and formerly a Methodist Sunday School teacher, whose husband was not one of Jehovah's Witnesses. She said:

My husband had contracted polio; mother had died; and at this time the Belgian Congo problems had arisen which really broke my heart, because of the situation of the children. I asked the minister about it but he said, 'They don't know any different', which was surprising because the Methodists were doing what they could. Then came the house-call [by Jehovah's Witnesses]. I was very rude to the Witnesses. One of them returned the following week, and I asked why they were called 'Jehovah's Witnesses'. She quoted the Bible, Matthew 6, and I asked about the Belgian Congo. The [account of the] Kingdom was the first thing that made an impact on me.

When my husband became completely paralysed, the Methodist minister asked his congregation of seven hundred and fifty if anyone would offer to fetch him from hospital for the weekend: only one volunteered. He had been attached to the church since the age of nine, and was a scoutmaster, and was known to all the congregation. This surprised me.

When I had been studying with the Jehovah's Witnesses for about a year, I became very ill with malignant cancer, and had a breast, womb, and ovaries removed. This Kingdom Hall had a rota to visit my house and did all the house-work, etc., and at this time I was not even baptized. They really practised what they preached. This also impressed my husband. [One blessing is] peace of mind—against all the odds, with my husband still in a wheelchair and four children to look after. My husband now comes to the Sunday meeting—although he was very anti. He had actively worked against my becoming a Jehovah's Witness. He [now] says, 'If everyone behaved as they do the world would be a wonderful place.' My husband and [our] friends can see a difference between those sons who are and those who are not Witnesses.

This already religiously committed woman apparently changed her religious allegiance and accepted her sectarian faith following personal tragedies and in a period of concern about world affairs—towards all of which her own church had shown indifference.

But not all conversions occur in circumstances of severe personal upset. Thus, in Case 9, that of a married roofing contractor of 29 with two young children, who had been a nominal member of the

Church of Scotland, there are no such traumatic events to relate. He said:

[Apart from the Truth itself] at the very first meeting, the friendliness of the members impressed me most. An elderly gentleman [had] called and offered literature. The day was wet and I was feeling down in the dumps. I couldn't afford the book, so I took the magazines. He arranged to call back and see me for my opinion—but I wasn't in. When I came home, mother told me that he had called and kept the appointment. He had left an invitation to a public talk. That day I attended my first public meeting, and I've been going ever since. This happened in Glasgow. I joined the book study and have attended regularly ever since. I met my wife here on holiday at the Kingdom Hall. A week later, I came down here to live. The person who originally showed interest [presumably in conducting a Bible Study] was disabled—that she had time to visit me was very attractive.

I am happily married and I think a lot of this, because I have generally a fiery temper, but knowledge of the Truth quells this feeling. Many things I avoid: friends in Glasgow are in all sorts of trouble, but the Truth helps me to avoid this and protects me. To be able to bring my children up as Jehovah's Witnesses helps me to protect them also. My mother and father—my mother, although she at first encouraged me—raised objections. She accosted one brother and sister [that is, sect brother and sister, Jehovah's Witnesses] on the bus and on the street: these were the people who were studying with me. My parents argued and raved, but the brother and sister said, 'Don't let that stand in your way'. It made no difference to their attitude. About three months afterwards, I managed to get my mother to come to the Kingdom Hall, and the first person who spoke to my mother was the Jehovah's Witness she had shouted at . . . It has made me a lot more placid, helped me to understand other people's feelings and given me a greater interest in all other men—makes me more outgoing. I feel I am raising my children properly. I have a reasonably nice home, a good business, and this I put down to Jehovah.

The easy and unproblematic acceptance of a radically different religious position—at least as recounted by this respondent, stands in sharp contrast to the stories of bereavement, a criminal past, and the striving for intellectual certainty recounted by others. He is impressed by the people, their concern and conscientiousness, as if this were his first acquaintance with a consciously moral community, association with which has added a dimension of moral control to his own life.

Case no. 10 is that of 36-year-old married driver-salesman with four children; he had formerly been a Roman Catholic, but had lapsed about three years before becoming interested in the Witnesses. He said:

I've always believed in God. When the Witnesses called, I said to my wife, 'Get rid of them', but she talked to them. My inclination was to go and tell them what was right (from my Roman Catholic upbringing). I chatted about an hour. They told me things the church had never told me: the new system on earth, and they showed me Scriptures. I said I'd have to look into it. It aroused my interest, and having a neighbour who was a Witness, I went to talk to her. My wife was expecting, and I thought that if there was going to be destruction [at Armageddon], I had to look into it from their point of view. The neighbour came often to chat, and she gave me the Bible Study. It took her two years to convince me. I stopped completely in 1968. I realized I had to do something positive. I had a spell in which to think, and we were unsettled by not doing anything. After a year, I came back again to the meetings, to the Ministry Service and so on. I was very reserved, and I wouldn't read aloud. I was nervous of doing things that you had to do to be one of Jehovah's Witnesses. Once you realized that they were not there to pick holes, it became different. The main thing [that attracted me] was their friendliness, and the open way of going on with each other. In church you didn't know anyone, you didn't know the priest. There was the association [among Witnesses], and once I started coming here everyone was friendly, and this made it more social—we hadn't had that at church. Because I was reserved, I needed someone to come to me because I wouldn't have made the approach to them. In a little time there was nothing that they wouldn't do for you. I would sooner ask Jehovah's Witnesses than my parents, although my parents would do anything for me.

Life is a lot more peaceful now. I don't have problems. I've not had a lot of experiences. Life has run smoothly, and what I've prayed about has been answered in one way or another. Presenting material in public [giving short talks] was the biggest problem [in becoming a Witness]. It was put to me gradually and in a nice way [that I ought to do this]. If it had been said at the beginning, all I'd have to do, it would have frightened the life out of me. You feel you are not qualified till you learn slowly. They put me in charge of the accounts and this was frightening and a worry, but I've done it for a year now. They do have a good system which is virtually foolproof. I do it in my head now—I've given up the calculator.

One becomes more law-abiding. Before I'd adhere to the thirty mile an hour limit only when the police were there—now you keep it. God can see what you're doing, and so there is no point in trying to deceive anyone. Certainly, the Scripture helps a lot with the children. When correcting them, you can align Scripture with your correction: they appreciate that Jehovah is in a close relation.

Before, at work, there were underhand things going on, which I wouldn't tolerate once I started studying [the Truth]. Drawing stock from stores, and they thought you were soft for not picking up trivial items in a dishonest way. The organization makes you aware that there is no difference between taking a packet of paperclips and a £5 note. What isn't yours, isn't yours.

The benefits of a warm, supportive community is evident, in this case not only providing moral regulation and the satisfactions of assured rectitude, but also providing the encouragement to learn new skills. Diffidence and embarrassment are overcome—'I do it in my head now—I've given up the calculator.'

The ten accounts provided above differ in expectable ways from one another, although there are recurrent elements and shared assumptions and emphases. They indicate what the respondents *now* consider were the motives that brought them to a specific religious commitment, and the subsequent experiences that reinforced it. There is an evident tendency in these accounts to indicate the functions of religious commitment. Perhaps the questions themselves may have stimulated certain types of response, yet in none of these responses, nor in any of the others that I have collected, is there from anyone a denial of the positive functions of believing. No one has said: 'I realized that it was the truth and that therefore I must believe it, although I experienced only suffering from doing so, and realize that it would be much better for me were I not to believe it, or were it to be shown untrue.' Perhaps such a response defies too explicitly the logic that all (sane) men assume to be operative in their decisions. Yet it is clear that for those for whom religious motivation is transcendent, there is the implicit and apparently unvarying assumption that what is true will also be good, that what one believes to be true will also be beneficial. Some of the functions of believing are evident and manifest to the respondents themselves: the sense of intellectual certainty; the acquisition of a sense of purpose; the benefits of mutual help within a segregated and totally committed group; the attainment of self-confidence; the development of certain talents; the prospects of a better future; unequivocally stated moral standards. Others may be only implicit, or hypothesized by the external observer: the opportunity to acquire status; compensation for misfortune; even social support for socially inadequate people.

The functional benefits of sect adherence become apparent to converts only slowly, however, and even though becoming a

Jehovah's Witness is itself a slow process, without any dramatic or sudden change of heart, thus allowing the convert to gradually develop an awareness of the benefits of adherence, none the less, functions cannot bear the whole weight of explanation of conversion, particularly if we are concerned with the initial attraction of religious commitment. Nor can the entire burden of explanation be shifted to a more general and abstract level, although this is the level at which sociologists, no doubt in contrast to historians, have often sought to make their contribution. The two most frequently invoked general theses about the causes of sect emergence, and thus implicitly about collective dispositions to accept religious commitment, are offered with different degrees of refinement. The first such general theory, if it can be flattered by the description, is that of anomie: sects are said to arise in social conditions in which there is uncertainty about mores, norms, and values, and the groups most prone to religious solutions are, correspondingly, said to be those that are particularly exposed to the disrupting process of social change. I propose to say little about anomie: in so far as it is true it is also trite, and as a thesis it is too ill-defined to lend itself to adequate empirical specification.

The second thesis demands more attention because it has acquired wider acceptance, and because in some respects it has been given greater specificity. This thesis is that of relative deprivation. Perhaps it is an indication of the lack of specificity of each of these theses—both anomie and relative deprivation, that they are not set forth with the rigour that makes it apparent at what points they might contradict each other (which, if they were properly grounded theories, they would certainly do). Nor do they—although I leave this point until later—seem to me to address the central question of determining just who in a given population will become religiously committed, who, in the case we have under review, will become sectarians.

Relative deprivation refers 'to any and all of the ways in which an individual or group may be, or feel disadvantaged in comparison either to other individuals or groups or to an internalized set of standards'.[4] The thesis is a modification of older assumptions, not always graced by the term 'relative deprivation', that sects began

[4] C. Y. Glock, 'The Role of Deprivation in the Origin and Evolution of Religious Groups', in R. Lee and M. E. Marty (eds.), *Religion and Social Conflict* (New York: Oxford University Press, 1964), 27.

with individuals who suffered economic disadvantage. In Glock's formulation, deprivation is not regarded as necessarily economic in origin, and Aberle provides additional comparative reference for present deprivation, by extending it to include not only other groups, but also the past conditions (real or imagined) of particular individuals, and the legitimate expectations that they might have entertained about the present.[5] In practice the formulation that is employed is that of 'felt deprivation', which is intended to indicate that the sense of deprivation may or may not be objectly warranted, and further that even where the sense of deprivation is objectively justified its causes may not be perceived. Initially Glock sought to use the concept in explanation of the origins of new movements, both religious and secular: subsequently he came to suggest that the concept explained not only new movements but all religious dispositions: religious commitment was itself a response to a sense of deprivation.[6] People became religious because in some way they felt deprived and were unable to perceive the real causes of their condition, or, if perceiving these causes, were unable by rational action to affect them. Religion then became an agency of compensation. Thus, the implication is that religious motivation and commitment stem from the lack either of information or of intellectual capacity; from frustration because the causes of deprivation are not perceived or cannot be eradicated; or from delusions. Religion is in effect reduced to an irrational response. It becomes an agency by which a change is produced in the way in which deprivation is regarded and its causes understood: only in very limited cases is a shift to a religious commitment in any sense an adequate response to the feelings of relative deprivation (and these, as I view the matter, are the cases in which the concept of 'deprivation' is least appropriately used).

It is unnecessary here to discuss the refinement that Glock has introduced into the concept of deprivation, extending it from essentially economic causes to social, organismic, ethical, and psychic causes of deprivation, or to consider the type of collective agencies that he believes arise in response to each of these. Nor

[5] D. F. Aberle, 'A Note on Relative Deprivation as Applied to Millenarian and Other Cult Movements', in S. L. Thrupp (ed.), *Millennial Dreams in Action*, Comparative Studies in Society and History, Supplement 2 (The Hague: Mouton, 1962) 209–14.

[6] This later formulation is to be found in C. Y. Glock and R. Stark, *Religion and Society in Tension* (Chicago: Rand McNally, 1965), 242–59.

need we consider in any detail the research in which he sought to demonstrate that among a representative sample of the membership of the Episcopal Church in the United States, those who, as measured by objective indices, might be described as more deprived were precisely those whose church commitment was greatest.[7] We need only note that with respect to conversion to religion, the thesis indicates some general probabilities about what sorts of people might be 'at risk'. But we may also observe that the subjective element in the deprivation thesis seriously impairs its rigour. Just which people will *feel* deprived, and just which of these will seek religious compensation? Some, whose· objective circumstances would warrant feelings of deprivation, may not entertain them, or doing so may not seek or accept religious solace for those feelings. Why, we may ask, do some people not feel deprived when, by all objective criteria, they are deprived, and why, even of those who feel deprived, do only a proportion become absorbed by religious groups? Do none of the undeprived become religious? Here, then, we have an important intervening variable: the religiosity, or the openness to religion, of those who are converted. Perhaps implicitly the relative deprivation thesis assumes that with the increase of cause-and-effect thinking and of rational action, men who are objectively deprived will, more and more, take appropriate, empirically justified, steps to eliminate the causes of their deprivation—or will have such action taken for them by the welfare state.

Were that the case, then, only the relentless problems of personal anguish, the need to cope with the untoward, and the search for ultimate meanings, would operate as sources for religious dispositions. The idea of relative deprivation as such might be seen as an iconoclastic challenge to pure religious motivation. Yet, at least in Christianity, the appeal to the deprived is quite explicit: religion is offered as a compensation. 'Come unto me, all ye that labour and are heavy laden, and I will give you rest' (Matt. 2. 28). Compensation and reassurance are the rewards of faith, and the deprived in this world may take further pleasure, relatively, in the idea that the rich man will hardly enter the kingdom of heaven. In Christianity, if not in all the higher religions, compensatory benefits are an explicit part of religious ideology, offered as a distinct stimulus to faith, sometimes as an almost crude exchange principle.

[7] C. Y. Glock, B. B. Ringer, and E. R. Babbie, *To Comfort and to Challenge* (Berkeley and Los Angeles: University of California Press, 1967).

Let us, then, not cavil at the relative deprivation thesis on the grounds that it seeks to uncover unworthy motives for religious commitment. We may, however, aver that there is no evidence that only those who feel relatively deprived become religious, unless we cause that conclusion to follow from our definitions or unless we posit a general condition of relative deprivation for mankind.

We may keep in mind the postulation of relative deprivation, and of the social conditions of moral uncertainty that is called anomie, when seeking to uncover the mechanisms of religious conversion. From our life-histories we can obtain some idea of those mechanisms, and we can augment this information by taking account of the range and availability of religious solutions that are proffered to meet men's needs. We must ask just what types of sect exist. Men choose among sects in some respects, and neither the concept of anomie nor the relative deprivation thesis, even after Glock's distinction of types of deprivation, provide cogent evidence about just which individuals will respond to particular sectarian solutions to their daily life problems. Becoming a sectarian is a voluntary choice: it implies exposure to sect ideology and practice; some sort of conscious decision or set of decisions; and a subsequent process of socialization that leads the individual to express his needs, and to meet his needs, in ways different from those of the majority of men.

At best, we may hope to uncover recurrent patterns, the incidence of which may differ with different age-groups, sexes, social classes, ecological contexts, cultures, and historical periods. Just possibly they may differ with different basic personality types, but evidence of psychological differences that is independent of, for example, allegiance to the sect itself, is perhaps impossible to collect on any significant scale. (Perhaps, too, there is in such an approach an implicit assumption, which I should regard as gratuitous, that deviant religious movements necessarily mobilize people who suffer big personality disorders.) If we remain at what might be called the emergent level of the social, we need perhaps to take into account the fact that divergent patterns of religious commitment are to a considerable degree institutionalized in Western societies. If we take sects alone, we have already a wide choice of patterns of organization of religious life. The cases that we have examined are drawn from only one sect, and we should expect to find different ways of accounting for the conversion process, and indeed different processes, were we to examine converts to other persuasions. I do not wish here to propose a typology of patterns of sectarian commitment, but we should need to distinguish, to complete our task, at least those sects, such as Jehovah's Witnesses, the rationale of which is intellectual, from sects that are emotionally oriented, expressive, and consummatory.[8] We might construct other variables: sects concerned with recruitment explicitly contrasted with those preoccupied with the in-group's own sanctity; rationalistic sects and those essentially therapeutic, subjective, and mystic; sects that are world-renouncing and those that are world-embracing. In these various groups, the language of religious commitment and the experience of induction would be variable phenomena. Sects are differentially available, and each mobilizes its following by a unique set of recruiting techniques which vary from the house-canvass of the Witnesses to the revival meetings of the Pentecostals, and the social programme of the Mormons. Each creates its own context in seeking to awaken men to their discontents or in providing an articulation for discontents already felt. All have their own arrangements and procedures for the incorporation of the individual and for his socialization to group mores, norms, and values. All of them, with varying degrees of emphasis, offer new meanings for life, whether couched in primarily intellectual or emotional terms.

Clearly, there is no one pattern of conversion, or of awakening in an individual a superordinate sense of religious motivation. The profound change of values (implicit or explicit) may occur from a variety of circumstances and according to various procedures. Thus, if we were to generalize from what we know already of sects, we might, for instance, characterize Jehovah's Witnesses as an authoritarian movement, in which dogmatic certainty is a cardinal value. It is ideologically and intellectually well insulated from the wider society, emphasizing formal learning procedures of socialization, and a predominantly intellectual, if literal, commitment. It demands a high degree of clearly specified participation in sect activities, and the purposes that become part of God's new world order. It offers a minimum of ritual, emotional involvement, and worship. The sect is a community of work.

[8] For a typology, albeit not specifically directed towards the problem of religious motivation, see B. R. Wilson, *Religious Sects* (London: Weidenfeld and Nicolson, 1970).

Were we to consider Christian Scientists, by way of comparison, we should again see an intellectual, but in this case a highly abstract, orientation. The sect provides a metaphysical philosophy to which a votary must become intellectually committed for his own advantage rather than as a participating member of a group with collective purposes. The advantage is his own rather than that of the group or of the wider society. Communal involvement is low, and insulation from evil is operative only at a mental level for each individual. There is little demand for participation, and there is scarcely any opportunity, and then of a very formalized kind, for individual initiative within the religious context. There is no real community, only an association of those seeking and employing a particular regime of mental hygiene and therapy.

With Pentecostals, we should in general find very low intellectual commitment and an emphasis on the experiential, with much less effective insulation from the wider society except for the actual time demanded by participation in the meetings. Emotional intensity in a pattern of ritualized spontaneity would be the chief evidence of participation. Initiative within a given framework of expressive activity is encouraged in the repetitive creation of a community of love.

For these and many other groups there is no one pattern of conversion, no one way of articulating the manner in which religious motivation has been summoned. Whatever may be the differences in background circumstances, in patterns of deprivation, if we accept that proposition (and sectarians themselves, in telling of the benefits of their new faith, often imply that there has been deprivation), we should certainly find differences in accounting for the acquisition of present compensations. Thus, a Jehovah's Witness would tell, as we have seen, a story of gradual intellectual conviction about the meaning of contemporary world events. He would emphasize the acquisition of a coherent authoritative intellectual comprehension acquired by study. As Beckford has said, there is a sense in which he might be claiming to have achieved his own salvation.[9] There is little discussion of faith, and

---

[9] J. A. Beckford, 'Accounting for Conversion', *British Journal of Sociology*, 29/2 (1978), 249–62. For a critique of the relative deprivation thesis in accounting for conversion among Jehovah's Witnesses, see id., *The Trumpet of Prophecy: A Sociological Study of Jehovah's Witnesses* (Oxford: Blackwell, 1975), 154–8. For an incisive critique of the thesis in general, see R. Wallis, *Salvation and Protest: Studies of Social and Religious Movements* (London: Frances Pinter, 1979) 3–7.

not much of guilt, which indeed is in some respects what converts must overcome to be Witnesses. The process is slow not sudden, and sudden conversion would be, for Witnesses, a matter for suspicion. For them there is a rational account of a cumulative process revealing a better life and better social relationships which are themselves an earnest of the better things of the new world order that is to come.

The Christian Scientist would also emphasize gradual intellectual attainment, but with a much less specific application to the contemporary scene. The acquisition of abstract metaphysical principles has a more egocentric, therapeutic, and manipulative significance, even though it claims to stand on universal and objective premises. Salvation is a highly individuated phenomenon, a progressive, this-worldly experience. The pace may not be forced, even though the process is sustained by study. People 'come when they are ready', and make their demonstrations progressively. There is no emphasis on faith, nor on guilt, but only on understanding. Salvation is an expression of independence, it is 'ours by right', with physical and material benefits serving as proofs of advanced spiritual thinking.

For the Pentecostals, conversion is sudden and radical, a 'heart experience', in which the individual is 'born again'. It occurs usually in an emotionally charged atmosphere, with emphasis on sin and guilt, grace and faith: salvation is individual but as one of a body of sinners. The event is recalled, recounted, re-enacted, and relived in the routines of the meeting, as guilt and sin are recurrently transformed, at least in recollection, and in the conversion of newcomers into 'saved' people. The emotional relation with Jesus is paramount, and dependence and gratitude are the appropriate responses. The experience is intense; it often defies verbal articulation and is to be communicated only emotionally.

Each sect has its own conception of conversion and of religious motivation: each specifies the terms in which experience must be understood and recounted (although they differ in the importance that they attach to the activity of recounting their own histories).[10]

[10] Thus, while Christian Scientists are encouraged to offer 'testimonies' both in their regular meetings and in their journals (usually of specific experiences of healing), and while Pentecostalists have ample opportunity to recount their own conversion experiences, Jehovah's Witnesses have no such institutional provision. Some of those whom I interviewed told me that they had never before recounted their own experience of joining the sect.

In a sense, sectarians learn of their own motives subsequently, or at least they learn subsequently how to articulate them in an appropriate way—in a way satisfactory both to themselves and their fellow religionists. They bring their reasons for conversion into conformity with group expectations, gradually eliminating idiosyncratic elements and reiterating in-group justifications. There may be, for many, predisposing events—bereavements, illness, intellectual or emotional confusion—but the sect has to find those who are thus afflicted, and, finding them, to convince them of its offer to make all things new by the transformation of values that it proposes. For those it reaches, some find the sect rekindles old dispositions, learned perhaps in Sunday school, for others it awakens hidden doubts, or challenges unexamined propositions about life and the world. It offers a context of concern and fellowship for people who, once experiencing life in the sect, become conscious that formerly there was something missing in their lives. Just as recounting conversion experience involves learning a language, so undergoing conversion is itself a process of learning (and unlearning). Individuals are socialized to conversion, and subsequently they learn how to express, in appropriate language, just what has happened. If this leaves us in some doubt about the motivations that have prompted men to accept a sectarian commitment, that is perhaps because we do not accept entirely at their face value the explanations which sectarians themselves offer us or the language and the concepts in which these explanations are uttered. Perhaps the most that we can hope to do is to note certain patterns of background experience and certain sequences of experience and decision. Such patterns may be of varying incidence from one sect to another, since in each sect men will learn to organize mentally and verbally their recollection of their own experience.

Part III

Modern Minorities:
The New Religious Movements

10

New Religious Movements:
Some Preliminary Considerations

THE very concept of 'new religious movements' presents its own distinctive difficulties for sociology. New movements have been a recurrent phenomenon in the context of Christian cultures in the West. Most of them—ridiculed, persecuted, or suppressed—were destined, in a relatively short time, to disappear: some, however, persisted until they ceased to be 'new'. Thus, in England, the early divisions of Protestantism—the Congregationalists, Presbyterians, and Baptists, the new movement of their day—gradually came to be known as 'historical dissenters'. In Japan, some of what are today referred to as 'new religions' began as long ago as the mid-nineteenth century, and writers have distinguished these from later movements chronologically—old new religions as against newer ones.[1] The paradox of the idea of 'old new religions' makes abundantly apparent the difficulty of using chronology as the point of departure for a sociology of religious movements: but what other points of departure might we use?

Sociologists look for broad explanatory schemes that summarize in general and abstract terms the typical patterns of relationship and the probable courses of actual empirical change. Yet it is clear that there must be limits to the utility of encapsulating in abstract general terms intrinsically and empirically diverse cultural, social, and spiritual phenomena and processes. The sociological task is to embrace, in analytical formulations of wide application, diverse cultural contents—and the unstated, but implicit assumption of sociologists is that their concepts, like those of natural scientists, should be of universal applicability. Despite these high aspirations in the study of religious movements both in the West and in Japan, we have, none the less, had to resort to such weak descriptive terms as 'new' and have had to qualify 'new' with such apparently

---

[1] See the distinctions discussed in the chapter 'New Religious Movements' in Ichiro Hori *et al.* (eds.), *Japanese Religion: A Survey by the Agency of Cultural Affairs* (Tokyo and Palo Alto: Kodansha International, 1972), 92–4.

contradictory terms as 'old new': and this indicates just how far we are from possessing a real sociology of religious movements. Has the time then come to recognize the impossibility—in any terms that are not unduly vague— of any *general* theory of new movements? Certainly, we should not seek, as sociologists have sometimes been wont to do, to produce a theory that seeks to be outside time and space, even though we wish our concepts to apply outside and beyond the confines of any one culture or historical epoch.[2] If sociology is not to abandon the real world for purely theoretical artifice, then, we are always likely to be in some degree captive to the empirical circumstances of given cultures, of geography, and of history.

New religious movements are phenomena that tax our existing conceptual apparatus. The concept of 'the sect'—widely used, not only with specific meaning by sociologists, but also more loosely by laymen—does not meet the diverse demands made upon it. To have any rigour, the concept requires specification, but such specification is all too likely to carry the imprint of a particular culture and particular theological tradition.[3] Nor is the term cult, which Wallis has usefully redefined to indicate a movement that breaches the exclusivism normal in the Christian tradition, adequate to cope with the different assumptions of non-Christian cultures.[4] In other

---

[2] Max Weber wrote, 'The more comprehensive the validity—or scope—of a term, the more it leads us away from the richness of reality since in order to include the common elements of the largest number of phenomena, it must necessarily be as abstract as possible and hence *devoid* of content. In the cultural sciences, the knowledge of the universal or general is never valuable in itself': *The Methodology of the Social Sciences*, trans. E. Shils and H. A. Finch (Glencoe, Ill.: Free Press, 1949), 80.

[3] For a fuller discussion, see B. R. Wilson, *Magic and the Millennium* (London: Heinemann, 1973), 9–18.

[4] See R. Wallis, 'The Cult and its Transformations', in R. Wallis (ed.), *Sectarianism: Analyses of Religious and Non-religious Sects* (London: Peter Owen, 1975), 35–49. This formulation I find more convincing than the distinctions drawn by J. T. Richardson, 'An Oppositional and General Conceptualization of Cult', *Annual Review of the Social Sciences of Religion*, 2 (1978), 29–52. Since this essay was written in 1979, the attempt has been made to draw a sharp distinguishing line between religious bodies that might be called 'sects' and those that might be called 'cults'. The argument takes these as classificatory and not as ideal types. Rodney Stark and William Sims Bainbridge have suggested that what they choose to call sects, that is splinters from the indigenous religious tradition, proliferate in social contexts where religion is strong. In contrast, cults are said to be 'something new vis-à-vis the other religious bodies of the society in question': 'Of Churches, Sects, and Cults: Preliminary Concepts for a Theory of Religious Movements', *Journal for the Scientific Study of Religion*, 18/1 (1979), 125. Cults are said to succeed in

religious traditions, plural loyalties, which in the West are characteristic only of cults, constitute a more general phenomenon. It is not surprising, then, that for want of a better concept, sociologists have continued to use the term 'new movements'. But what, apart from a denotative list of actual movements, are we talking about: what do these social phenomena have in common that allows us to lump them together? We are led to three broad, related questions. What is new about new movements? Do new movements fulfil similar functions even in diverse cultural and historical contexts? To what extent is any given new movement capable of maintaining its own intrinsic character as it spreads in space and persists in time? It is to some preliminary considerations that might eventually lead to partial answers to these questions that I now turn. What follows is, then, essentially exploratory, and I refer to specific movements illustratively rather than analytically.

The Newness of the New

Salvation

The very idea that movements are new indicates the importance of considering them in the context of an already existing religious tradition. All new movements of necessity offer something unavailable in older religions. Basically, they offer a surer, shorter, swifter, or clearer way to salvation. Whatever its specific cultural content

cultural contexts where indigenous religion is weak. It may be observed, however, that the basis for distinguishing so-called sects from so-called cults is far from being entirely satisfactory. By no means are all small groups within the broad indigenous traditions created by schism from within existing bodies, and none of the largest American sects—Mormons, Seventh-day Adventists, Jehovah's Witnesses, or Christian Science, began as schismatic bodies. (It may be noted in parentheses that A. A. Hoekema, *The Four Major Cults* (Grand Rapids, Mich.: Wm. B. Eerdmans, 1963), perhaps the leading theological writer on minority movements, refers to all four as 'cults', in direct contradiction of the Stark–Bainbridge criteria.) The term cult is used in other ways, which the Stark–Bainbridge thesis ignores, but which can be well accommodated by the definition supplied by Wallis, namely, that, unlike the sect, the cult is not exclusivistic, accepting pluralistic legitimation. This formulation makes possible the retention of the common-sense usage, whereby we can refer (within Roman Catholicism) to the cult of Our Lady of Fatima; or the cult of the Sacred Heart; or to Opus Dei; or (within Protestantism) to Moral Re-Armament or Charismatic Renewal. Those who subscribe to these persuasions do not do so to the exclusion of wider or additional religious commitments. The distinction proposed by Wallis is analytical and not, as is the instance of exotic provenance, a mere incidental item.

may be, sociologically salvation is, in essence, present reassurance of the possibility of overcoming evil, in whatever way evil is theologically or culturally defined. Salvation is the commodity in which all religions deal, whether it is release from witches, illness, disgrace, bad luck, early death, punishment after death, or damnation to recurrent lives of misery. Using salvation in this sociological sense, we have a general phenomenon, a category that encompasses many different cultural contents. The appeal of new movements is the offer of a more convincing reassurance about salvation than was hitherto available. New movements are thus likely to encourage optimism, at least among those who subscribe to them, about prospects of overcoming the evil and the untoward. Even of movements that have sought to rationalize experience, in which the deity becomes a more transcendent, less immediate entity, this generalization appears to hold. If Calvinism made God transcendent, removing him from the stage of life, none the less, for believers, the effect of Calvinism was to make God's will, if inscrutable, in some sense ultimately rational. Salvation became more certain—if not in the sense that a man could assert his assurance of election (although even in pristine Calvinism the record is not unequivocal), then at least in the sense of knowing his obligations in both faith and morals. Calvinism swept away the arcane, mysterious, and quasi-magical apparatus and activities, with respect to which the lay individual had neither knowledge nor control.

The fact is that, in established religions, the salvation prescribed is often remote and difficult, is associated with the process of institutionalization of religious sytems, which not only affects church activities and their relationship with other social institutions,[5] but which occurs also in ritual and doctrine. In the older religions, routines and rituals acquired increasing formality: activities that once had intrinsic purpose persisted even after purpose was lost and action retained only symbolic significance. The virtue of the deeds of the saints became transferred—by the latent and recrudescent disposition towards the magical—to their bones. But when nirvana is a thousand lives away, or when schoolmen calculate the specific value of relics and elaborate the penalties of

---

[5] The *locus classicus* for the discussion of institutionalization is in T. O'Dea, 'Five Dilemmas in the Institutionalization of Religion', *Journal for the Scientific Study of Religion*', 1 (1961), 30–9.

post-mortem purgatory with ever-increasing scholastic refinement, laymen are likely to look for a more ever-present help in their daily troubles. New movements cut through both ancient forms and routines and the recondite schemes of sacerdotal systems. They offer more proximate salvation. The successive development in Japanese Buddhism from the Nara period to the doctrine of salvation by faith in innate enlightenment in Tendai, and its further extension to reliance on the mercy of the Amida Buddha in Jōdō Buddhism, and then, with Shinran in the Jōdō Shin Shū to the concept that the Amida Buddha had already accomplished the salvation of all men,[6] illustrates a process in which salvation, initially more difficult to attain, is progressively made into a present reality. The supersession of Calvinism by Arminianism, the shift from determinism to free-will salvation by faith, and the subsequent doctrine of assurance in Methodism, illustrate a not dissimilar trend, and one that might be described as an evidence of the increasingly demotic character of successive new movements in religion.

Elitism and scepticism

It is not only remoteness and obscurity in traditional soteriologies that prompt lay demands for short, surer paths to salvation, and so to present reassurance, it is often also the effect of spiritual élitism and its not infrequent concomitant, clerical scepticism. Old religions tend to encourage the evolution of spiritual hierarchies, and the élites that emerge protect their own interests as the possessors of what is usually claimed to be at least a superior, if not an exclusive, wisdom concerning the divine, acquired by specialized techniques (study, prayer, meditation, chant, visions, trance, possession among them). Such superior knowledge and sanctity legitimize the performance of these élites for the lay public, performances offered as indispensable for laymen in the search for salvation. With their own indispensability established, priests have shown two divergent tendencies, each of which engenders lay discontent. One is the élitist preoccupation with minutiae in ritual and with metaphysical speculation in teaching—concerns that are narrowly specialist and which distance priests from laymen in

---

[6] On Shinran, see A. Bloom, *Shinran's Gospel of Pure Grace* (Tucson, Ariz.: University of Arizona Press, 1981).

rendering the terms of salvation both obscure and dependent on priestly interpretation.

A second, perhaps alternative, tendency is that priests have often shown themselves to have a considerable capacity for scepticism about the doctrines that they are supposed to profess and the rituals that they perform. Occasionally, a cleric has spoken out against the claims of the religious system that he serves, and has sometimes taken this so far as to lead out a new religious movement. Periodically, priests have shocked the laity by publicizing in unprecedented ways the limitations of priestly belief in widely held popular assumptions which laymen have supposed that priests believed.[7] Perhaps more often, priests have developed a personal cynicism concerning the claims made for the priesthood of heightened spirituality and sanctity. The phrase 'trahison des clercs' did not become a commonplace without the phenomenon that it denotes having been widely observed. Priestly disenchantment, apathy, indifference, weariness in well-doing, spiritual laxity, and moral turpitude have occurred recurrently in all the ancient religions. These things, combined with spiritual élitism and the claims to a monopoly of indispensable functions, have given impetus to new religious movements.

Mobility and therapy

New movements arise to offer more proximate salvation and also to offer wider access to it. They have frequently attacked the distinction between priest and laymen, whether in asserting a 'priesthood of all believers', as in Protestantism, or in the contemporary radical claim in Catholicism to a shared ministry of laymen and clerics, with Christ the only priest; or in the diminution of clerical distinctiveness, as when priestly celibacy is set aside, as occurred in Anglicanism, Lutheranism, and, *inter alia*, in the Jōdō Shin Shū school of Buddhism. Thus, spiritual élitism is assaulted, a new voluntarily recruited public is given wider access to spiritual opportunities, and there is prospect of more rapid spiritual

[7] For priests who have engendered new movements, one need think only of Luther and Wesley. A priest who revealed the extent of clerical scepticism towards literal belief still dear to many of the church-going laity was Bishop J. A. T. Robinson, in his book, *Honest to God* (London: SCM Press, 1963). The public response to that book is discussed in R. Towler, *The Need for Certainty* (London: Routledge and Kegan Paul, 1984).

mobility. Salvation is now to be obtained by simpler techniques, and paradoxically they become, by an iron law of institutionalization, the basis for new distinctions between specialists and laymen. The simpler techniques become an avenue for rapid spiritual—and often social—mobility for a new style of religious specialist.

When ordinary people seek reassurance—that is to say, when they consider salvation—they tend to do so at the prompting of urgent need. They are impatient of doctrinal refinements and uncomprehending of abstruse soteriological considerations that stand between them and the assistance and reassurance that they seek. When doctrines become too metaphysical, they have typically had recourse to the palliatives, remedies, prophecies, and panaceas of ancient magic, and such magic has, even despite the type of hostility that it encountered in Christendom, lingered on.[8] New religions cater to the same need, sometimes by a virtual return to something like the same nostrums, but at other times by new rationalizations of men's problems and the means to their solution. It should not, then, surprise us when new religions offer therapies for mental or physical distress. In doing so, they pick up an ancient function of man's concern with the supernatural, but they realize it by contrasting their claims with those of conventional religion. Thus, what is 'new' may be something restored, reformed, or revived (as in revivalism, fundamentalism, or Charismatic Renewal); or it may be wisdom newly garnered from other half-known cultures (as in the Krishna Consciousness movement, the Divine Light Mission, or 3HO);[9] or it may be presented as

---

[8] The evidence is particularly impressively presented for Sri Lanka: see R. F. Gombrich, *Precept and Practice: Traditional Buddhism in the Rural Highlands of Ceylon* (Oxford: Clarendon Press, 1971); and M. M. Ames, 'Magical Animism and Buddhism: A Structural Analysis of the Sinhalese Religious System', *Journal of Asian Studies*, 23 (1964), 21–52.

[9] On Krishna Consciousness, see G. Johnson, 'The Hare Krishna in San Francisco', in C. Y. Glock and R. N. Bellah (eds.), *The New Religious Consciousness* (Berkeley and Los Angeles: University of California Press, 1976), 31–51; S. J. Gelberg, *Hare Krishna, Hare Krishna* (New York: Grove Press, 1983); E. Burke Rochford, jun., *Hare Krishna in America* (New Brunswick, NJ: Rutgers University Press, 1985); K. Knott, *My Sweet Lord: The Hare Krishna Movement* (Wellingborough: Acquarian Press, 1986); and F. J. Daner, 'Conversion to Krishna Consciousness', in Wallis (ed.), *Sectarianism*, pp. 53–69. On the Divine Light Mission: J. Messer, 'Guru Maharaj Ji and the Divine Light Mission' in Glock and Bellah (eds.), *New Religious Consciousness*, pp. 52–72; and J. V. Downton, jun., *Sacred Journeys: The Conversion of Young Americans to Divine Light Mission* (New York: Columbia University Press, 1979); on 3HO, A. Tobey, 'The Summer

something modern and scientific (as in Christian Science and Scientology).[10]

From scarcity to abundance

The characteristics of new movements—their offer of a proximate salvation; the implicit assault on spiritual élitism; their availability to a wider public; the accessibility of their techniques; the spiritual mobility that they facilitate; and their use of therapeutic claims— may all be described as life-enhancing for the ordinary man. In some respects, one might even postulate a broad, loose, evolutionary trend towards the demotic. Religions develop intellectual and metaphysical orientations, but old religions began in ways similar to the contemporary new movements—as is evident both in the appeal of physical healing and in the promise of a new kingdom in early Christianity. The new religions in America have been described as offering man a new partnership with God, in which man acquires an increased capacity 'formerly reserved for the gods, of not only discovering reality and truth, but of creating them symbolically and experientially'.[11] But the process is not unique to the new Eastern mysticisms now popular in the United States. Mormonism, which began in 1830, declared that men had the opportunity to evolve into gods, and it reiterated the sentiments of another new movement of the time, Universalism, in claiming that practically everyone would attain the heavenly afterlife. (Nor may one forget the biblical promise to early Christians that they, as children of God, were also joint-heirs with Christ[12]—Christ whom Christians also came to regard as God.) Similarly, in the 'old new' religions of Japan, Tenrikyō and Konkōkyō, the highest deity became more available and more concerned with the affairs of ordinary people, providing healing, solace, and the regimen of an ordered life in rapport with spiritual forces.[13] The new religions

Solstice of the Healthy-Happy-Holy Organization', in Glock and Bellah (eds.), *New Religious Consciousness*, pp. 5–30.

[10] On Christian Science, see B. R. Wilson, *Sects and Society* (London: Heinemann, 1961), 119–215; on Scientology, R. Wallis, *The Road to Total Freedom: A Sociological Analysis of Scientology* (London: Heinemann, 1976).

[11] R. Wuthnow, *Experimentation in American Religion* (Berkeley and Los Angeles: University of California Press, 1978), 191.

[12] Romans 8: 17.

[13] On Tenrikyō, see C. B. Offner and H. van Straelen, *Modern Japanese Religions* (Leiden: Brill, 1963), 41–60; R. S. Ellwood, jun., *Tenrikyō: A Pilgrimage Faith*

offer more, and offer it more immediately to more people: they overthrow the old scarcity mentality which older religions often manifest in making salvation difficult of attainment, remote, and expensive of effort, time, and money. In the new religions there is a brighter prospect of spiritual abundance.

We may speculate whether such an offer is related to the general improvement in the lot of mankind. As higher living standards and greater life security, at least in more advanced countries, make the religious repertoire of sacrifice and self-denial less compelling and less relevant, at least in the material sense, so it may be that the spiritual appetites undergo change, demanding different titillation and different sustenance. The 'transcendental *Ausgleich*' of traditional Christian theodicy is apparently less necessary in a world in which the ills that men suffer are, in considerable measure, of a different kind from those experienced in the formative period of the great religions. Men seek compensations at different points of experience and in different material and symbolic terms. The new religions are, in this sense, adaptations to changing human circumstances and the changed expression of spiritual needs.

Fervour, discipline, rational organization

The anti-élitism and the open, accessibility of new religious movements is often accompanied, when movements are in their pristine state, by at least an element of the ecstatic, whether or not that is a feature of the religious tradition within which, and against which, they arise. New religions tend to set spontaneity, immediacy, and sincerity over against the cultivated and measured responses of conventional religion. They call for total allegiance rather than for mere regular and regulated religious ˙ observance. Thus they mobilize enthusiasm at a level which is not usually attained in traditional religion and which, when it does abnormally occur there, is a source of embarrassment to other believers, with their moderated expectations concerning religious performance. Just as new religions are life-enhancing, so they explicitly enhance emotional

(Tenri: Oyasato Research Institute, 1982). On Konkōkyō, see D. B Schneider, *Konkokyo: A Japanese Religion* (Tokyo: ISR Press, 1962); H. N. McFarland, *The Rush Hour of the Gods: A Study of New Religious Movements in Japan* (New York: Macmillan, 1967), 97–122. Valuable insight into both movements is provided in Susumu Shimazono, 'The Living Kami Idea in the New Religions of Japan', *Japanese Journal of Religious Studies*, 6/3 (1979), 389–412.

responses. In the longer run, they all face the dual problem of how to maintain, but also how to contain, the initial enthusiasm. That exercises intended to sustain enthusiasm may themselves become routinized is evident in the history of religions—whether in the sponsored revivalism of Finney and his successors; or in the recurrent invocation of the Holy Spirit in both Pentecostalist sects and in the Charismatic Renewal movement; or in the stimulated excitement with which the pilgrims of Sōka Gakkai go to Taisekiji.

Thus, sustaining, rather than containing, expressions of enthusiasm often becomes the main concern of new movements, and this within a relatively short time. The phenomenon of routinization is well understood. It begins as an initial following is converted into a stable membership, engaging in regular devotions, making regular subscriptions, accepting specific obligations, giving public acknowledgment to specific teachings, and obeying certain social, moral, and administrative stipulations. Movements must balance the ecstatic (in however dilute a form it is permitted to persist), since it marks the mobilization of emotional commitment, with the imperative of orderly, systematic, organized, and sustained patterns of behaviour by which alone a new movement is assured of stability, unity, continuity, and growth. Whether the process of routinization is effected by social control within the movement— that is by explicit rituals, the supervision of officials, and sometimes even by magical sanctions—or whether it is achieved through the encouragement of self-control, personal discipline, and accountability of individual believers each to himself, are variables that may be culturally determined. Movements that fail to achieve routinization, and which fail to develop a sense of boundary maintenance, tend to fail as new religions. In such cases, where we perceive a loose, ill-defined set of practices and ideas spreading within a population that is never weaned of its traditional commitments, we have a fashion rather than a movement. Charismatic Renewal is an example of just such a congeries of beliefs, practices, and partial organization. It is not yet clear whether its ultimate destiny is to become an independent movement, or whether it is to remain a party that will change the church, or will pass away as a style of worship fashionable for a limited period.

(In passing, we may note that boundary maintenance is itself subject to cultural variation. In cultures with a pluralist tradition, in which there is no emphasis on exclusive adherence to any one pattern of religious belief and practice, or in which such exclusivity is heavily compromised, the ideal-typical construct of a new movement as a separate, self-contained entity, demanding the total and sole allegiance of its members, is not substantiated, nor even approximated by actual empirical cases. Indeed, even in Western societies, where exclusivity is the norm, new movements may compromise: organizational principles, rather than the claim to a monopoly of truth and the exclusiveness of correct practice, may suffice to distinguish movements, as in the Methodist schisms of the nineteenth century, or in the Pentecostal sects of the early twentieth.[14] The newest movements in Western societies have arisen at a time in which boundaries have increasingly been challenged, and in which discrimination has given place to a vogue of indiscriminateness in a wide variety of social phenomena, and especially so among the young, to whom in large measure the new movements make their strongest appeal. We must wait to see whether movements that reject boundary maintenance, such as Transcendental Meditation and Charismatic Renewal, persist, wither, or are absorbed.)

Routinization is a normal feature of the development of new movements. It occurs because stability of commitment, consistency, and calculability of member dispositions are ultimately even more vital than enthusiasm for the persistence of any movement. Fervour and discipline must thus go together, the one justifying the other. In persisting movements, a new balance of emotional control is struck at a far higher level of dedication—at least as far as the generality of the membership is concerned—than is encountered in all but exceptional cases in conventional religions.

Discipline is itself an earnest of the new order which the new religious movement proclaims, intrinsically as a movement, in its own activities and operations, but also as a precursor of the world-wide order which, in one realm of experience or another, here or

---

[14] Methodist schism is treated in R. Currie, *Methodism Divided* (London: Faber, 1968), 17–82. Division and diversity in Pentecostalism have been too extensive to admit of single treatment in one work: various issues emerge, albeit sometimes only incidentally, in W. J. Hollenweger, *Handbuch der Pfingstbewegung*, 10 vols. (Geneva: n.p., 1965–7); and id., *The Pentecostals* (London, SCM Press, 1972). For a more detailed account of some important divisions and issues, see R. Mapes Anderson, *Vision of the Disinherited: The Making of American Pentecostalism* (New York: Oxford University Press, 1979), 153–94.

hereafter, is to come into being. It is by no means always the case that new religious movements represent more rational procedures than do the traditional religions. In the nature of things, there must always be a strong non-rational element in any religious system, given the superempirical character of the goals that are canvassed, and thus the necessarily arbitrary nature of the procedures that are specified for their attainment. This said, however, we have noted that new religions tend to simplify the techniques and procedures stipulated for the achievement of superempirical goals, and this simplification may, in certain circumstances, be something of a rationalization. Contemporary new movements in particular arise in social conditions in which the external secular world is itself undergoing a long-sustained process of rationalization, and these new movements are thus all the more likely to be influenced by this wider availability of rational techniques which may be used to attain certain organizational ends, and to be infected by the general spirit of rational planning which so generally obtains. New movements, being less inflexibly bound to traditional arrangements and precedents, easily adopt more modern and more rational systems. Particularly where their concerns transcend those of a local culture, or where essentially secular procedures of propaganda, recruitment, evangelization, fund-raising, member-deployment, and assembly are available, new movements are likely to embrace the most modern secular techniques. If teachings are arbitrary, organization may, none the less, be created in accordance with entirely pragmatic criteria, and, in many respects, may manifest a surprisingly secular character.

We have noted this tendency in various Western sects,[15] and although it can be no accident that it is among movements of American origin that this disposition is most pronounced, it may be observed to have become an increasingly universal tendency. The cell and cadre structure of Sōka Gakkai is not dissimilar in style and purpose from the strictly rational arrangement of house-canvassing and study groups of the Jehovah's Witnesses. In each of these two movements, so different in origin, beliefs, and background, there is, none the less, a vigorous demand for recruitment which requires members to make a rational use of their time and energy in the service of the cause, in the clear conviction that this is the highest

----

[15] See Ch. 7 above.

service one can perform for others. Older religions would find such well-coordinated and pragmatic patterns of action less than congruous with their general style, ethos, and their conceptions of spirituality.

Obviously, rational procedures may be variously mixed with entirely arbitrary elements that stem from the received supernaturalist content of a movement's doctrines or ideology. Thus, in Christian Science, to take a conspicuous example of a faith with a metaphysical belief system that claims totally to transcend the rational empirical evidences, this admixture occurs. Officials are appointed, employed, and paid according to the same rational criteria that obtain in business and bureaucratic systems. Even the movement's healing practitioners, whose therapeutic techniques consist essentially in denying normal empirical evidence and the rational procedures relative to them, contract their services and receive remuneration in accordance with the normal practices of the commercial world. A movement ignores such rational desiderata at its peril: the schism in Christian Science led by Mrs Augusta Stetson in New York in the 1910s and 1920s, which sought to divest itself utterly of all non-spiritual elements that 'material organization' entailed, did not survive for so very long.[16] Whilst new and more charismatic movements may experience some difficulty in embracing entirely rational procedures, as these movements have grown, the need for system, order, and routine have become more apparent, tending to circumscribe arbitrary and *ad hoc* decisions and the excitement of charismatic caprice.[17]

In the foregoing, we have not attempted to construct an ideal-type of the new religious movement: the concept is too unspecific and too relative for any such exercise. New religions are too diverse for such a formulation, even when their main characteristics are denoted in terms of considerable abstractness. Different new religions adopt diverse organizational arrangements and espouse widely divergent values. A movement like Sōka Gakkai is manifestly a mass movement with a vigorous public presence, taking its place in

---

[16] The Stetson schism in Christian Science and the founding of the Church Triumphant is discussed in A. K. Swihart, *Since Mrs Eddy* (New York: Holt, 1931).

[17] For a case in which a charismatic leader has by apparently capricious changes of policy managed to ensure that the process of routinization was effectively impeded, see R. Wallis, 'Charisma, Commitment and Control in a New Religious Movement', in R. Wallis (ed.), *Millennialism and Charisma* (Belfast: The Queen's University, 1982), 73–110.

the national life of Japan.[18] In complete contrast, the Krishna Consciousness movement is deliberately a minority movement, appealing explicitly to one section of the community, and more or less self-consciously casting itself, in the Western societies where it was first launched, in the role of the exotic import unconcerned about the general social order of those societies. Sects such as the Seventh-day Adventists and Jehovah's Witnesses reassert many traditional social values in idealized form, in contrast to the explicit rejection of traditional ideals by a movement such as Scientology. The Children of God (Family of Love) draws its members out of the wider society into segregated communities in preparation for the end of the present dispensation, whereas, in various ways, Transcendental Meditation, Scientology, and Perfect Liberty Kyōdan offer principles and therapies to help their votaries to get more out of life within the existing social order.[19]

New movements, then, have in common only their newness at a given point of time. For any specific purposes of analysis and prediction, we should need refined typologies, even though there is some value in looking at new movements as a generic class. That so many and such diverse religious manifestations emerge more or less contemporaneously in itself points to inadequacies in traditional religion in the context of social systems and national cultures that are undergoing disruption, and points, too, to the latent discontents prevailing within advanced societies. New religions indicate an area of need among the population: some of these needs may be spontaneously felt; others, some people may be easily induced to recognize within themselves once they are sensitized to them. The

---

[18] On Sōka Gakkai, see McFarland, *Rush Hour of the Gods*, pp. 194–220; J. W. White, *The Sōkagakkai and Mass Society* (Stanford: Stanford University Press, 1970); H. Dumoulin (ed.), *Buddhism in the Modern World* (New York: Macmillan, 1976), 251–70. For the political influence of Sōka Gakkai, see A. Palmer, *Buddhist Politics: Japan's Clean Government Party* (The Hague: Nijhoff, 1971). For the movement's development in America, see R. S. Ellwood, jun., *The Eagle and the Rising Sun: Americans and the New Religions of Japan* (Philadelphia: Wesminster Press, 1974), 69–110.

[19] Transcendental Meditation is discussed by Wuthnow, *Experimentation*, pp. 15–43; see also, W. S. Bainbridge and D. H. Jackson, 'The Rise and Decline of Transcendental Meditation', in B. Wilson (ed.), *The Social Impact of the New Religious Movements* (New York: Rose of Sharon Press, 1981), 135–58. Brief accounts of Perfect Liberty Kyōdan are to be found in Offner and van Staelen, *Modern Japanese Religions*, pp. 82–8; H. Thomsen, *The New Religions of Japan* (Tokyo: Tuttle, 1963), 183–98. A popular treatment is provided by M. Bach, *The Power of Perfect Liberty* (Englewood Cliffs, NJ: Prentice Hall, 1971).

new religions speak to a variety of conditions of men: their success indicates the spiritual, social, and cultural defects of the times. When traditional religionists say that new religions arise from a spiritual malaise, we need not gainsay them: but we should be clear that the new religions are not themselves that malaise—rather it is located in the current social situation. The new religions, however they might be evaluated—and such evaluation is not our concern— are responses to the malaise, not its symptoms or its source.

The Question of Contextual Diversity and Functional Similarity

Japan and the West

The new religions do not, except in the most general sense, fulfil the same functions in the various cultural and historical contexts in which they arise. Thus, for example, the new religions in Japan appear to act as important *loci* of allegiance occupying a space between the total society (including the state) and the individual. They undertake a variety of intermediary functions, providing welfare, education, medical care, a sense of involvement, a focus of loyalty, meaning, and orientation, and a point of identity for people living in a newly urbanized world in which the older intermediate agencies of social structure, and particularly the traditional household, have largely disappeared. Thus, perhaps especially for those—housewives for example—uninvolved in the life of a company to which loyalty is to be given, a movement such as Risshō Kōsei-kai provides an encompassing focus.[20] Would it be too much to see in the new religions of Japan the type of institution which Durkheim prescribed for modern society when he (mistakenly) ascribed to professional guilds the function of mediating between modern man and the state?[21]

These functions of Japanese new religions differ from those of new movements in the West, which cater to an individuated public, often recruiting isolated people searching for much less structured and much more metaphysical support, for personal therapy, encounter, and a lighter, often more contractual commitment of a

[20] For Risshō Kosai-kai, see Dumoulin (ed.), *Buddhism*, pp. 245–51; Thomsen, *New Religions of Japan*, pp. 117–26; McFarland, *Rush Hour of the Gods*, pp. 173–93.

[21] E. Durkheim, *Professional Ethics and Civic Morals*, trans. C. Brookfield (London: Routledge and Kegan Paul, 1957), 1–41.

more adventuring kind. To say more, we must have more detailed profiles of those who are recruited, and closer accounts of the processes of induction and socialization.[22] How are the predispositions of individuals who are recruited to a given movement matched to its particular facilities and orientation? What is the fit between the previously felt needs of those who become members and the facilities to meet such needs provided by specific movements? On these questions, all our plausible theories, including the relative deprivation thesis, are weak.[23] Only with detailed individual studies can such theories be put to the test. We cannot rule out the possibility that, in some measure, movements may 'awaken' needs in particular individuals, giving them increased specificity in the terms of the movement's own ideology, and so defining the situation for prospective adherents, supplying both the sense of needs and the means of their fulfilment. One can see such a relationship in traditional religions, most conspicuously perhaps in the inducement of a sense of personal sin by evangelical Christianity, and the offer of techniques for the elimination of the sense of guilt and the control of conduct, with the goal that what religion defines as sin might be eradicated. Clearly, what is called sin must have some objective reality, and it might be argued, at another level, that this reality was indeed constituted by socially deleterious conduct; but part of the object of religious agencies— even those with libertarian ideologies—has always been to establish a measure of control over votaries, and in traditional situations that religious control coincided in large part with the social control functional for the wider society. What new religions do is to raise the consciousness of their adherents to a reformulated and redefined understanding of their needs and deficiencies. Stating the problem in these terms does not solve it: we still need to know why people should accept the proposed definition of their situation and the proffered solutions.

Relating general and particular

Functionalist explanations of new religious movements tend to relate the phenomena that are general in given cultures, but they

---

[22] See, for examples, Chs., 8 and 9 above.
[23] The concept of relative deprivation is set out in greatest detail in C. Y. Glock and R. Stark, *Religion and Society in Tension* (Chicago: Rand McNally, 1965), 242–59.

frequently fail to discriminate between the different postures of the new movements themselves. Thus, if urbanization, the new technology, the development of role-articulated social systems, the corresponding process of institutional differentiation, and the creation of impersonal social contexts—if these are all general circumstances of the situations in which new movements emerge, how are the discontents that these conditions precipitate related to the specific teachings, practices, life-style, and orientations of the very diversified new religions? Of course, broad patterns of social change are mediated by multiform processes to particular regions, classes, groups, and individuals, and this allows for considerable variation of effect. Yet we cannot be sure that these effects are themselves related in any systematic or determinate way to the specific intrinsic orientations of the movements. Even employing a value-added logic of the kind advanced by Smelser[24] takes us little further than the level at which action occurs: religious movements are all value-oriented movements, concerned with more basic things than the mere provision of facilities. Our problem is to account for the differences in their value-orientations. Can we even eliminate the element of randomness in the distribution of adherents to movements, which may obtain even though those who join do so voluntarily? Individuals suffer situational constraints, and those constraints may propel them towards one movement rather than another, and may have nothing to do with their basic personality dispositions.

Facilitating circumstances

Obviously, certain broad facilitating circumstances condition the emergence of new movements. The diminution of religious persecution is a *sine qua non*. Toleration, initially for dissenters objecting marginally to the main tradition, gradually extended to permit choice that is limited only by considerations of conventional morality, and to protect individuals from constraint and from unacceptable therapies. Of course, official prohibition, as in the Soviet Union and other eastern European countries, does not eradicate religious movements: proscribed organizations persist, and sometimes flourish.

[24] Value-added logic is a concept developed in sociological analysis by N. J. Smelser, *Theory of Collective Behaviour* (London: Routledge and Kegan Paul, 1962), 80–123.

The breaking of links between traditional religious systems and national, regional, local, and familial communities provides the gap in which new religions can grow. The impersonal context of modern society facilitates the attraction of socially anonymous individuals to new communities, whether these are religions that seek to revive personal relationships and affectivity, as do Pentecostals; to celebrate impersonality and capitalize on it, as do Christian Science or Scientology; or to heal its effects in the fashion of the Human Potential movements.[25] The impersonality of the social context affects the process of communication in religion. Literacy is perhaps the single most important facility. Even though movements have from time to time used radio and even television, in various parts of the world, neither of these media appear to have been significant ways of recruitment. Jehovah's Witnesses, who once used radio, gave it up for better methods. In Africa, the Seventh-day Adventists broadcast their Voice of Prophecy, but my evidence is that very few were influenced by radio to join that church. These mass media are, after all, even more transitory than the feeblest piece of printed ephemera, much of which has recurrent use in being passed from hand to hand. Personal communication, however, appears to have special significance for movements with a strong supernatural content. Transmission face to face by word of mouth in door-to-door canvassing, as undertaken by Witnesses and by Sōka Gakkai; work through informal group networks, supplemented by circulation of literature, appear to be the most effective methods of recruitment. In impersonal contexts, the little touches of personal warmth and friendly association are effective— sometimes leading to the creation of sect-based surrogate communities within the wider society.

Therapy has had a varying role both as a conditioning factor and as a function of the new movements. Physical healing has frequently been part of a movement's promise, but in societies in which there has been steady improvement of medical care, and in which social provision is made for it, the demand for healing through recourse to supernatural agencies has probably diminished

---

[25] For a general discussion of this genre of movement, see Donald Stone, 'The Human Potential Movement', in Glock and Bellah (eds.), *New Religious Consciousness*, pp. 93–115. For a more detailed discussion of one particular movement, S. M. Tipton, *Getting Saved from the Sixties* (Berkeley and Los Angeles: University of California Press, 1982), 176–231.

significantly. Faith-healing of physical ills is less canvassed in advanced societies, except for ailments regarded as incurable by medical means, or as too vague or too trivial for such treatment. In Japan, the new movements are less exclusivistic than those of the West, with regard not only to doctrines but also to alternative curative practice, and some, such as Tenrikyō and Perfect Liberty Kyōdan, have increasingly combined the facilities of materia medica with their own resources for diagnostic and curative practice. In the West, the emphasis has shifted from physical to psychic well-being, and this not only in explicitly mind-healing movements and movements concerned to enhance 'human potential'. Even among Jehovah's Witnesses, a movement without explicit therapeutic provision or expectation, 'peace of mind' is perhaps the most common response elicited when Witnesses are asked what are the principal blessings that they have experienced since becoming believers.[26]

Religious discipline and social control

Especially in the West, there are marked variations in the functions of new religions with respect to social control and socialization. Both were important functions of traditional religion: in societies where secular morality was underpinned so centrally by religious sanctions, religion supplied the vital agencies of attitudinal control. In Christian cultures, religion increasingly defined the mores and in certain respects did so even more powerfully after the Reformation: the moral man was, for a time, the religious man. Subsequently, religion declined as an agency of social control, partly as it concentrated more on the internalization of values and as it emphasized the individual's responsibility for his own conduct in an evangelical scheme of personal salvation. With the processes of secularization and the rationalization of social life, social control became less a function of morals and more a matter of techniques. Men were controlled less by inbuilt inhibition and external moral censure, and more by mechanical instruments which measured or regulated in 'objective' ways the individual's obligations, and extracted performance from him. Works' clocks, conveyor belts, traffic lights, electronic eyes, and data retrieval systems belong, at different points, to the process by which society is technically de-

[26] These findings derive from my own unpublished research.

moralized.[27] The need for supernatural sanctions wanes, and even reliance on internalized pressures of conscience apparently diminishes —certainly in the economic sphere. As old religion in the West surrendered its control and socialization functions, only the new fundamentalist groups sought to take them up: for the newer mystical faiths, such things became irrelevant. If the new religions emphasize discipline, it is not discipline for the well-being of the wider society, but only a spiritual exercise for the benefit of the individual believer himself, and sometimes for the communal life of the group.

Diffusion and Integration

Questions of identity and function

New religious movements were once no more than deviations from older traditions of the culture to which they were indigenous: whatever was new about them, their continuities with parent religions were far more evident. Today, national, regional, and cultural barriers have been eroded, and new movements spread from their native culture to others. By vigorous proselytizing, Pentecostals, Mormons, Witnesses, Seventh-day Adventists, and others have become world-wide movements, newer in some contexts than in others. Sometimes they have been very effective in other societies: the Witnesses in Zambia; the Adventists in western Kenya; the Pentecostals in Chile.[28] Clearly, there are questions to be raised about their functions in different societies, and even about the cultural identity of the movements themselves, and that which they confer on their following.

Other movements appear to flourish especially by transfer. Thus the Krishna Consciousness movement and the Healthy-Happy-Holy Organization (3HO) are regarded as less authentic in the

---

[27] For a fuller discussion of this argument, see B. R. Wilson, 'Morality in the Evolution of the Modern Social System', *British Journal of Sociology*, 36/3 (1985), 315–32.

[28] On Jehovah's Witnesses in Zambia, see N. Long, *Social Change and the Individual* (Manchester: Manchester University Press, 1968); on Pentecostals in Chile, see C. Lalive d'Epinay, *Haven of the Masses* (London: Lutterworth Press, 1969): W. J. Hollenweger, *Die Pfingstkirchen* (Stuttgart: Evangelisches Verlagswerk, 1971), 285, estimated that the proportion of the Chilean population involved in the Pentecostal churches to be 36 per cent.

societies from which they sprang (Indian, Hindu, and Sikh societies respectively), than they are in the societies in which they have sought to recruit (American and European societies). However, in the West, they have now revealed some capacity to appeal to immigrants from those Indian homelands in which they are still not regarded as fully orthodox. Even so, they subsist almost entirely as alien growths, less transplanted than deliberately cultivated as exotica in alien host societies.

Some movements have less capacity for transfer except among emigrants from the society in which the movement itself emerged: those migrants become ethnic minorities in other places. Ethnic sects are always likely to be viewed with suspicion as potentially subversive of a host culture which expects to absorb and assimilate immigrants rather than to house distinctive minorities that use an alien religion to reinforce ethnic identity. But not only ethnic religious movements find themselves suspect: any sect is likely to be seen as the purveyor of alien ideology or as the agent of another country, as evidenced by the Soviet reaction to the Jehovah's Witnesses, and the hostility to the Children of God and the Unification Church in several countries. Politicians recognize the implicit threat of enclaves in which alien values are nurtured, even if, in practice, they need rarely fear that such movements will effectively challenge the operation of the state and the economy.

Modern social values and the declining role of religion

It has been a commonplace of modern sociological theory to argue that social systems depend for their integration on value concensus, and that such consensus attains its ultimate expression and legitimation in religion. The latest form of this thesis, perhaps in acknowledgment of the decline of supernaturalist orientations in both social structure and popular consciousness, locates these values in civil religion—the more or less explicit symbolic celebration by its members of their society, and often, indeed, of the state.[29]

---

[29] The concept of civil religion was initially expounded by R. N. Bellah, 'Civil Religion in America', *Daedalus*, 96/1 (1967) 1–21 (following Rousseau). He saw it as the subordination of the American nation to transcendent ethical principles which provided a religious dimension to national and especially to political life. Behind this religion stood biblical archetypes. A diverse literature has since been devoted to this thesis, and the concept has been applied to various cases and exhaustively explored,

Yet, today, states have tarnished reputations in the eyes of many of their citizens; and society becomes too amorphous in many ways, too similar in its basic dependencies to other societies, and too bound up with them economically for 'our society' to be much of a focus of identity, even less of pride. It is difficult to say just what are the supposed values that distinguish a given society, or in what ways they are rooted in religion. The prevalent values of modern society appear to be procedural rather than substantive, and to be sanctioned and legitimized by pragmatic considerations rather than by the absolute standards derived from the supernatural. When intrinsic societal values are surrendered to the purely technical imperatives of economic efficiency, and when states and their rulers fail the test even of honesty and common decency, then the social system itself ceases to be a focus of loyalties. The old religions— whatever the virtues that they canvass—lose all influence on social and political structures. Like Protestantism, they fall into palsied desuetude, or like Catholicism, they manifest overt internal value-conflict and accelerating decline. The emergent new religions provide new focal points of commitment, and even if they are marginal, as they certainly are in the West, their existence is itself of the utmost sociological significance. They evidence extensive discontent with the values and facilities of the wider society, the discontents of secularization which have superseded, perhaps, the earlier discontent with traditional religion.

Will such new movements become a source of new values for society as a whole? Not, certainly, if they appeal only to sectional minorities, nor if they remain so widely diverse in orientation and structure; nor yet again if they fail to acquire purchase on any facet of the institutional order. They persist in offering their solutions in what may be called the evangelical mode, as if private virtue and personal discipline could transform modern society. That vision might have been plausible in Victorian England; it is scarcely so

almost as if to retrieve a remnant of religion in the operation of what is acknowledged to be increasingly secularized society. See Bellah's later revised thoughts in R. N. Bellah, *The Broken Convenant* (New York: Seabury, 1975); and R. N. Bellah and P. E. Hammond (eds.), *Varieties of Civil Religion* (New York: Harper and Row, 1980); G. Gehrig, *American Civil Religion: An Assessment* (Storrs, Conn.: Society for the Scientific Study of Religion, 1981); and for a perceptive discussion, pertinent to new religious movements, D. Anthony and T. Robbins, 'Spiritual Innovation and the Crisis of American Civil Religion', *Daedalus*, 111/1 (1982), 215–34.

now. Making men new appears to have little impact on the inexorable cost-efficiency criteria of modern economics and technology; private virtue appears to be irrelevant to public performance and to modern organization. The new religions may achieve much for individuals in their personal lives, they may even create new subcultures into which some men can permanently, and others temporarily or occasionally, retreat from the abrasiveness of the impersonal society of the modern world. But as yet we have little reason to suppose that they have, or that any one of them has, any likelihood of transforming the structure of society and the alien experience that it produces into the encompassing community of love, of which—inside the new religions and out—men still so vividly dream.

11

Factors in the Failure of New Religious Movements

THE application of the concepts of failure and success to religion is a problematic exercise. Since religion is a matter of faith, its goals might be expressed in transcendental or metaphysical terms. Such goals are regularly represented as supramundane. What, it might be asked, does it profit a religious movement if it 'shall gain the whole world and lose [its] own soul'? The attainment of Nirvana by all the world's Theravada Buddhists, and hence the extinction of Buddhism, could be seen as success. Just as the Christian Church exists for men *in this world*, so does Buddhism, its doctrines and organization. In Buddhism, as in Christianity, ultimate success comes when the world passes away. Christian religion is for man under the relative natural law, in the period between the fall and the resurrection: it is a social phenomenon with transcendent goals. When those goals are attained, that phenomenon—the church, its material structures, social organization, creeds, and catechisms will all pass away. The sociologist, however, has no brief to deal with metaphysical ultimates: his concern is with the limited goals of social organizations, even though he may not totally ignore the speculative end and final expectations of religious believers.

Those expectations are sometimes expressed in terms that do admit empirical appraisal, however. Does a religious movement fail when the prophecies it endorses fail? Have the Shakers—to take one example—who are now reduced to a mere handful of believers, failed, since Christ has not come, sickness has not been eliminated, and the sin of sexuality is perhaps even more rampant than when Mother Ann Lee first pronounced against it? Or has the world, in some way, become a better place for their having been?—which is the way that they themselves are disposed to explain away apparent failure. To take religious groups seriously, we must take their prophecies, their own criteria of self-appraisal, and even their rationalizations into account. Nor can we simply assume that growth means success and that decline means failure. Not all movements seek unconditional and unlimited growth, and those that do may pay for it at the cost of abandoning pristine teachings and organization to accommodate the influx of joiners. Even virtually extinct sects are sometimes accounted a success: a historian of the Muggletonians, a sect which arose in England in 1652 and which has but one member still remaining, has written, 'Theirs is a success story, not in terms of a mass movement, but in terms of longevity. In those terms it is incontestably a success story; the more so when one realizes the astonishingly low level of interest shown by Muggleton himself, and by those who came after him, in the business of recruiting new members.'[1]

To take a sociological—and one might say, commonsensical—approach, one might begin to assess failure by the extent to which religious movements achieve their purposes (or wrongly forecast God's). Yet, such is the subjectivity of the product of religion that even objectively stated goals—'to save the world'; 'to redeem the race'; 'to clear the planet'; 'to gain eternal life'; 'to eradicate sin'—are often unavailable to empirical investigation. Religious leaders rationalize their experience. While some movements do not seek to recruit, such growth is—except for highly ossified sects—rarely total eschewed. When growth does not occur, the movement's mission may be interpreted in qualitative rather than quantitative terms: the mere possibility of one sheep recovered may be worth leaving the ninety-and-nine at risk. For the sociologist, however, numbers, endurance, maintenance of commitment, persistence, or attainment of goals, become necessary indicators of relative success or failure, even allowing that performance may also be appraised in terms of the criteria which a movement has itself constructed with respect to its social goals.

Among these sociological criteria, an analytical distinction may be posited between exogenous and endogenous factors, even though this division may not always be easily recognized empirically. The endogenous factors deserve greater attention, and in what follows I review five areas in which, on historical evidence, failure has occurred: ideology; leadership; organization; constituency; and institutionalization. These categories bear considerable convergence with the criteria suggested by Rodney Stark in his discussion of how success is to be appraised, although I omit explicit discussion of

[1] W. Lamont in C. Hill, B. Reay, and W. Lamont, *The World of the Muggletonians* (London: Temple Smith, 1983), 114.

what he calls 'medium tension'.[2] Tension with the world (or with the church, as the world's ostensible religious representation) is implicit in any new (hence deviant) religious movement. New movements are likely to find need to be firm about their members' commitment—to be strong they need to be strict.[3] Their severity will in itself promote tension. But just what constitutes 'medium tension' may be discernible only retrospectively, and to employ a category of this kind might bring one close to tautology.

Ideology

The failure of ideological pronouncements to find confirmation is an obvious Achilles' heel of any religious movement. For many such propositions there are defence-mechanisms: prophecies are postponed, or they are applied to another sphere of existence, or they are taken as having an essentially, if less obvious, symbolic significance. What does it mean to tell people, 'Blessed are the poor in Spirit, for they shall inherit the earth'? After 2,000 years that prediction is manifestely still unfulfilled, and the actual words have come to be regarded as poetic utterance rather than literal promise. The promise that 'the peacemakers shall see God' is presumably for a life hereafter, and, as such, is an untestable proposition. These elements of ideology are largely rhetorical, as little heeded, even by the devout, as the injunction to 'Take no thought for the morrow, what ye shall eat and what ye shall drink'. A movement may, then, survive even though its ideological and rhetorical promises should fail. Even where prophetic utterance has been amplified by specific time-bound calculations, there is abundant, and abundantly celebrated, evidence that ideological falsity does not occasion organizational failure. People continue to believe, and continue to support the movement which mobilizes that belief.

The study by Festinger and his associates might not in itself be adequate to establish this point, so local was the sect that he studied, and so few its votaries.[4] One might equally not be

---

[2] R. Stark, 'How Religions Succeed', in D. G. Bromley and P. E. Hammond (eds.), *The Future of New Religious Movements* (Macon, Ga.: Mercer University Press, 1987), 11–30.

[3] D. Kelley, *Why Conservative Churches are Growing* (New York: Harper and Row, 1972), 95.

[4] L. Festinger, H. W. Riecken, and S. Schachter, *When Prophecy Fails: A Social and Psychological Study of a Modern Group that Predicted the Destruction of the World* (New York: Harper and Row, 1956).

altogether persuaded by the application of that thesis to early Christianity itself. John Gager, who has made that application, argues that cognitive dissonance was perhaps in itself a fillip to the success of the early Christians—in having themselves been proved wrong concerning the imminence of the second coming, they were all the more eager to get others to espouse that belief, so vindicating themselves.[5] The causes for the expansion of early Christianity remain in contention, however, and whilst Gager's thesis is ingenious and plausible, it remains a speculative hypothesis, and one offering a radically divergent appraisal from that of Stark.[6]

There is considerably better evidence for Gager's point in more recent movements, and perhaps most dramatically in the case of Seventh-day Adventism. The Adventists, already disappointed by the failed predictions that the second coming was to occur in 1843 and 1844, created their own separate denomination committed to adventism only after prophecy failed, and only after the secondary elaboration of the causes of that failure, with respect both to the portent of prophecy and what was now believed had happened (in another sphere) on the revised date in question, and what it was now incumbent on them to do. In a sense, they pleaded justification (something *had* happened on the specified date, albeit in heaven and not on earth): but they also blamed themselves for failing to be prepared for what they had expected to happen: (had they somehow held it back?). What it was perceived now had to be done, perhaps to facilitate the coming to pass of what had been prophesied, was to obey the hitherto unheeded injunctions of Scripture, namely to honour the Sabbath on the seventh day, and to keep the dietetic prohibitions of the Old Testament.[7]

[5] J. G. Gager, *Kingdom and Community* (Englewood Cliffs, NJ: Prentice Hall, 1975).

[6] See Stark, 'How Religions Succeed'.

[7] On the early history of the progenitor of the Adventist movement from which the Seventh-day Adventists emerged, see, for the general social and intellectual context, W. R. Cross, *The Burned-Over District: Enthusiastic Religion in Western New York, 1800–1850* (Ithaca, NY: Cornell University Press, 1950); and D. L. Rowe, *Thunder and Trumpets: Millerites and Dissenting Religion in Upstate New York 1800–50* (Chicago, Calif.: Scholars Press, 1985). On Miller's prophetic career, see W. R. Judd, 'William Miller: Disappointed Prophet', in R. L. Numbers and J. M. Butler, (eds.), *The Disappointed: Millerism and Millenarianism in the Nineteenth Century* (Bloomington, Ind.: Indiana University Press, 1987), 17–35; and, in the same volume, J. M. Butler, 'The Making of a New Order: Millerism and the Origins of Seventh-day Adventism', 189–208; and id., 'Adventism and the American Experience', in E. S. Gaustad (ed.), *The Rise of Adventism* (New York:

Jehovah's Witnesses, less dramatically perhaps, are also a testimony to the capacity of true believers to set at nought evidences of failure: after setting 1914 as the occasion of the advent, Witnesses came to believe, despite lack of physical evidence, that the second coming did indeed occur then. Later, despite strong expectations that 1975 was the last possible date for the manifestation of Christ on earth, they found justification for the continued delay by revising the basic datelines from which their calculations proceed: instead of dating from the hypothesized date of the creation of Adam, as they had done hitherto, they now came to believe that the appropriate date would be from the time of the completion of the conjugal family with the creation of Eve.

Similarly, the Southcottians in Britain might also have been expected to abandon hope once the prodigious swelling in the body of their prophetess turned out to be not the man-child that she had predicted, but only an acute case of dropsy which killed her.[8] Yet, successors arose to continue this prophetic tradition, and Joanna Southcott, far from being discredited, was recognized as the first of a succession of God-anointed prophets by those who persisted in, or were newly recruited to Christian Israelite beliefs.[9]

The failure of ideological promise, then, may not in itself cause a movement to decline: indeed, the opposite has been argued. Even the falsification of categorical and specific prophecy may be irrelevant to a movement's continuance, growth, and wider diffusion. On the historical evidence—and other cases could certainly be cited—we must look for structural rather than ideological deficiencies to account for the occasions when a movement fails. This point holds even though ideology often prescribes (or powerfully influences) organizational structures. The interrelationships may be close. Thus, on theological (that is, ideological) grounds, and in deference to the transcendental

---

Harper Row, 1974) 173–206. A fuller account, including an exposition of Millerite exegesis, is provided in the curious and essentially apologeticist work of L. E. Froom, *The Prophetic Faith of Our Fathers: The Historical Development of Prophetic Interpretation* iv (Washington, DC: Review and Herald Pub. Assoc., 1954).

[8] For an account of Joanna Southcott, see J. F. C. Harrison, *The Second Coming: Popular Millenarianism, 1780–1850* (London: Routledge and Kegan Paul, 1979), 86 ff.

[9] Ibid. 135–60; and for an American off-shoot of the Southcottian tradition, see R. S. Fogarty, *The Righteous Remnant: The House of David* (Kent, Ohio: Kent State University Press, 1981).

charisma claimed for Jesus, there is an implicit limit on the charismatic claims made by or for the leaders of any Christian movement: the charisma of such leaders must, of necessity, be weak if the claims of Christ are not thereby to be diminished.[10]

The stronger the charismatic claims made for leaders of movements that also claim to be Christian, the more the claim to the title 'Christian' will be disputed, as can be seen with respect to Joseph Smith, jun., and Mormonism; Mary Baker Eddy and Christian Science; and Sun Myung Moon and the Unification Church. In each case, the claim of these movements to be Christian has proved contentious. Or to provide a second example, the theology of Christian movements often incorporates biblical specifications for church organization and ecclesiology (usually on models found in the New Testament) and these are taken to be mandatory for the sect, and may even constitute its specific *raison d'être*. This point holds in general for the Christadelphians; the Brethren (Open and Exclusive); and, most explicitly for the Churches of God.[11] Such ideological constraints on organization may severely limit a movement's adaptability, of course, but ideological commitment does appear to be remarkably durable, even when it might consign a movement, as a matter of principle, to an inflexible pattern of organization. It is, however, at the level of organizational structure and not at the level of ideology *per se* that we must look for direct causes of failure.

Leadership

Economists regard as a principal factor in the limitation of growth of the firm the incapacity of management and the consequent failure of control and communication. We might relate the failure of religious movements to limitations of management or leadership. Not all religious movements neatly approximate the Weberian ideal-types of leadership: those which do may enjoy greater stability

[10] For some discussion on the concept of derived charisma, see B. Wilson, *The Noble Savages: The Primitive Origins of Charisma and Its Contemporary Survival* (Berkeley and Los Angeles: University of California Press, 1975).

[11] On the links between ideology and organization in sects, see B. R. Wilson (ed.), *Patterns of Sectarianism: Organization and Ideology in Social and Religious Movements* (London: Heinemann, 1967), and for the Churches of God as an exemplary case, see, in that volume, G. Willis and B. Wilson, 'The Churches of God: Pattern and Practice', pp. 244–86.

than those which do not.[12] Various Christian sects in the past have been exemplars and expositors of a democratic tradition and have rejected any of the strong forms of leadership, favouring unanimity as the basis for decision-making, consensus as the guarantor of an ethic, and brotherhood as the model for internal relationships: such has been the basis of their polity. Yet, movements with these ideals have often fallen prey to competition and rivalry for informal status among the stronger personalities of the fellowship. Not infrequently, factually powerful if theoretically non-existent informal leaders have emerged, their position depending on the subtle operation of consent which might suffer disruption on a wide variety of counts, from differences in ideology to purely organizational arrangements. In these movements, nothing more profound than personality differences and jealousies appear to be the most frequent causes of such struggles, however wrapped about these issues may be in a tissue of ramifying ideological controversy.[13] Such movements tend to be schismatic, and schism is, in itself, widely acknowledged to constitute failure in Christian communities since unity in the followers of Christ is a purported ideological imperative. And objectively speaking, schism amounts to failure for all religious leaders.

Outside radical Protestantism, democracy is a rarely encountered polity in new religious movements. Charismatic leadership, in a strong or somewhat diluted form, is widely prevalent. In the strong instances we find the messiah-figure, the uniquely endowed guru, or the special vehicle transmitting to mankind a message from beyond. Such figures are much more at risk in the modern world than has usually been the case in time past. The speed and ubiquity of communications, the degree of public exposure, the exaggerated style of debunking and symbolic deflowering in which media men compete, are all very much at enmity with charismatic claims. Whereas a leader like Mrs Eddy could remove and insulate herself from the outside world, admitting only selected visitors now and then as suited her, and choose to teach only an occasional and very

---

[12] The ideal-types of authority are its legitimation by reference to one of the following principles: (1) tradition; (2) charisma; (3) rational legality—of the bureaucratic type.

[13] This point could be repeatedly exemplified from the history of the various fellowships of Brethren, but for an explicit discussion of the problem, see the case of the Christadelphians described in B. R. Wilson, *Sects and Society* (London: Heinemann, 1961), 236–80, 338–42.

special class of pupils the principles of Christian Science, the modern charismatic leader finds it more difficult to escape overexposure.[14] Like L. Ron Hubbard, he might take to the high seas or to a remote and secret location, remaining so far out of sight that, like Hubbard, he might be presumed dead.[15] Like Bhagwan Rajneesh, he might take a vow of silence, which would at least partly protect him from journalistic enquirers.[16] Like Moses Berg of the Family of Love (formerly the Children of God), he might prefer to communicate in writing to his following. Yet, charisma depends on some measure of exposure: it needs signs, and cannot persist purely and merely as myth.[17] Here and there, now and then, at least, the leader must be seen or heard—all the more so in movements that emphasize his personal qualities on which the very prospect of salvation rests, albeit less so where, as in Scientology, the leader produces a set of principles for others to follow. Yet, in all cases, whatever the claims to supernature of the charismatic leader, his charisma must maintain its anthropomorphic quality, even if the leader is literally supposed to be God. Christianity, eager to proclaim its founder to be God, has always had to remember that he was also man, and his humanity has had to be constantly acknowledged even by those most committed to his deity: the problems of Christology are merely the paradigm case—much refined by protracted polemics and sophisticated rhetoric—of the

[14] Accounts seeking to justify Mrs Eddy's self-chosen seclusion in her later years abound in the numerous official biographies and memoirs: see e.g. L. P. Powell, *Mary Baker Eddy: A Lifesize Portrait* (Boston: Christian Science Publishing Society, 1930), 177–248; and A. L. Robertson, *et al.*, *We Knew Mary Baker Eddy* (Boston: Christian Science Publishing Society, 1943); and the unofficial but hagiographic book by N. Beasley, *Mary Baker Eddy* (London: Allen and Unwin, 1963), 231–4. Less restrained accounts are given in E. Bates and J. V. Dittemore, *Mary Baker Eddy: The Truth and the Tradition* (New York: Knopf, 1932); and H. A. Studdert-Kennedy, *Mrs Eddy: Her Life, Her Work, Her Place in History* (San Francisco: Farrallon Press, 1947).

[15] An account of Hubbard's retreat to sea, his recluse-like existence in California, and his death is given in S. Lamont, *Religion Inc.: The Church of Scientology* (London: Harrap, 1986).

[16] On Bhagwan Rajneesh, see J. Thompson and P. Heelas, *The Way of the Heart: The Rajneesh Movement* (Wellingborough: Acquarian Press, 1986), 23; for an analysis, see R. Wallis and S. Bruce (eds.), *Sociological Theory, Religion and Collective Action* (Belfast: The Queen's University, 1986), esp. 206–7.

[17] The charismatic strategy of Moses Berg is the specific focus of R. Wallis, 'Charisma, Commitment and Control in a New Religious Movement', in R. Wallis (ed.), *Millennialism and Charisma* (Belfast: The Queen's University, 1982), 73–140; see also Wallis and Bruce (eds.), *Sociological Theory*, pp. 129–54.

problems inherent in all charisma. Without such reiterations and exemplifications of the humanity of the deity, the nature of authority must change, as it does when the leader is removed from the scene. The occasions for the public appearance of the charismatic leader are in themselves necessarily stage-managed. The leader presents himself, not on the terms of the public, nor even those of his followers, but on his own terms and at his own times. Exposure is a risk. A charismatic leader may capitalize on the claims made for him: he need never explain himself, indeed there is some advantage in his inexplicability and unpredictability. His followers will rationalize his idiosyncracies and aberrations. None the less, outsiders may seize on just these vulnerabilities to discredit charismatic claims. The role of the charismatic leader is unstructured: there is no job description; no set patterns; few, if any, appropriate models; and uncertain expectations. Yet, this very uncertainty renders such a man vulnerable as it simultaneously confers upon him the widest area of autonomy and discretion.

The public's readiness to see charisma deflated is the simple counterpoise of unbelief to the commitment of a movement's votaries. This readiness has undoubtedly grown in modern society, in which the charismatic manifestations are increasingly confined to the fringes, in which there is dependence on systems and not on persons, in which objectively tested routine procedures and forward planning are relied upon rather than the exceptional competences of individuals. The charismatic becomes the bizarre: few men believe that social problems can be solved even by the collective will, let alone by the supposed extraordinary will-power of one gifted and divinely inspired individual. The charismatic leader easily becomes the object of public ridicule.

The image of the charismatic leader depends on a mythology of origins; on the incidence of portents and signs; exceptional experiences; on his or her having had the opportunity to assimilate past wisdom; on hearsay stories of stamina, energy, untutored insight, and untrained exceptional abilities. Above all, he must be above normal human failings and beyond the need of such therapeutic or miraculous powers as he is supposed to possess and which he applies to others. With such an image, the charismatic leader is always at risk. He may not suffer ill-health, nor yet, in any common way, indulge in the pleasures of the senses. Yet, one after another of the leaders of new movements, in being exposed to public view, has been found wanting by the media. Contrary to expectations, Maharaj Ji married; Mr Moon was imprisoned for tax evasion; Mrs Eddy wore spectacles; Father Divine died; L. Ron Hubbard did not get a university degree—all in defiance of the things claimed for them or by them. Such items, seized on by journalists, discredit charismatic claimants in the eyes of the general public, and ultimately may tarnish the image even for some followers. Charisma is difficult to prove, and claims to it are easy to refute. Since so many new religious movements depend on such claims, their easy deflation is a factor in their failure.

Organization

A characteristic difficulty of new movements, encountered long before the problems of institutionalization begin, is the accommodation of necessary organizational procedures and arrangements to the transcendental, mystical, and spiritual elements of the movement's message. The problem is not merely one of the routinization of charisma, although that may become a part of it. Rather, it lies in the conjoining of modern, rational methods with the inspirational and charismatic. This difficulty is particularly acute for new movements, and it is a factor which may occasion their failure. For older and established bodies, in which spiritual claims have become tempered and moderated, in which the operation of spiritual power is only symbolically expected, and in which ritual has regulated emotion into orderly rhythms and anodyne responses, these problems are very much less evident (although they have their analogue in the accommodation of tradition to modern rational planning). New movements, which reject the traditional religious forms that have evolved in old churches, are free to adopt up-to-date, modern techniques for the dissemination of their message and their other purposes. Such techniques, however, are impersonal, uninfused with spirituality, and unsacralized by long usage or traditional encrustations of sanctity. They carry the full imprint of secular purposes and pursuits, and sit uneasily with claims of charismatic power and religious concern.[18]

The media quickly detect and exploit the divergence between the spiritual message and the practical organization of new religious

[18] For a fuller discussion of this point, see Ch. 7 above.

movements, finding scandal in what, on reflection, must of necessity be brought into some relationship if a movement is to operate at all. Traditional religious bodies are also quick to criticize these apparent discrepancies between high spiritual proclamations and mundane and material arrangements, even though the difference between their own situation and that of new movements lies only in the long-established legitimation of their own way of proceeding, and in the antique respectability of their forms, nomenclature, property, and role-designations. The new movements are quickly accused of being 'rackets', and financial arrangements and unconventional attitudes to sexual relations (whether more lax than those of the normative standards of the wider society, as in the case of the Family of Love and the Rajneesh movement, or more austere, as in the case of the Unification Church) are publicized as evidences of duplicity, ulterior purpose, and corruption. The media forget that the established churches themselves are necessarily administrators of extensive corporate wealth, including endowments, shareholding in industries of many kinds, land-ownership, and government stocks; that they have often had a dubious reputation as landlords, and that their financial management is conducted according to strictly economic criteria rather than, shall we say, in accordance with the prescriptions of the Scriptures to 'consider the lilies of the field . . .' When the Ginseng factories and shops, the titanium industries, and the fishing industry of the Unification Church were singled out as evidence of undisclosed economic interests and the exploitation of workers, the Press forgets that the Roman Catholic and Eastern Orthodox churches—long before there was a Press to complain—had thousands of voluntary workers, controlled in the minutiae of their everyday lives and committed to a condition of celibacy and dissociation of the sexes which was of far longer duration than that required in the Unification Church or the International Society for Krishna Consciousness.[19]

[19] In a miscellany of ill-assorted charges, *The Times*, 13 Dec. 1977, attacked as exploitation the use by the Unification Church of its votaries as salespeople. Condemnation of the movement's development of factories has been frequent and widespread in the Press: e.g. *The Times*, 4 Apr. 1978 and 6 Apr. 1978; *South China Morning Post*, 10 Jan. 1982; and J. F. Boyer, *L'Empire Moon* (Paris: L'Decouverte, 1986). A more objective commentary is found in D. G. Bromley, 'Financing the Millennium: The Economic Structure of the Unificationist Movement', *Journal for the Scientific Study of Religion* 24/3 (1985), 253–74. The tendency for some sects to develop their own economic institutions is, of course, characteristic not only of

New movements, however, lack the legitimation of tradition, lack the reputation for assumed moral excellence credited to the older churches, which also raise funds by regular collections—the most ubiquitous of religious practices—by public appeals, and the sale of various products, and even by begging for worthless items which others might then be persuaded to buy. Fund-raising from the general public is not an invention of the new movements: the Salvationists and Seventh-day Adventists have an established tradition in this respect, and long before they made their bids for free-will giving, the older churches exacted compulsory tithes from the god-fearing and godless alike. Yet, for such activities, condoned as legitimate and even desirable in the long-established churches, the new movements are regularly condemned and this promotes a hostile public image which may reduce a movement's acceptability, and so its prospects of success.

The balance between practical planning and devotional or worshipful activities often differs between old and new religions. In movements with a strong intellectual commitment—for example, Jehovah's Witnesses and the Unification Church—much more attention is given to practical activities than to devotions. The Witnesses spend their time, even when corporatively engaged, largely in learning techniques for evangelization, and in the purely intellectual exposition of their beliefs. Not much time is spent in praise or worship.[20] The Moonies assemble less often and with less regularity for specifically worshipful activity than do congregations of conventional churches, and their occasions together combine the social and the devotional. They spend much more time in fund-raising, witnessing, and 'Home Church' activities (undertaking practical tasks in their designated neighbourhoods) or in the movement's economic subsidiaries.[21] Such a different allocation

---

contemporary new religious movements. It occurred among sects originating in the last century: see, for example, J. Heinerman and A. Shupe, *The Mormon Corporate Empire* (Boston: Beacon Press, 1985).

[20] A vivid account of the congregational life of Jehovah's Witnesses, even though now outdated in a few details of organization, is to be found in A. Rogerson, *Millions Now Living Will Never Die: A Study of Jehovah's Witnesses* (London: Constable, 1969), 124–42.

[21] For a detailed study of the time spent in various activities by a community of Moonies, see K. Dobbelaere and B. R. Wilson, 'Het sektarisch antwoord op het begrip vrije tijd: het tijdsbudget van Belgische Moonies: een Gevallen Studie', *Vrijtijd en Samenleving*, 4/2 (Aug. 1986), 133–65.

of corporately spent time also elicits the criticism of those used to more conventional and compartmentalized religiosity. The 'fanaticism' of these sectarians is condemned, and the poverty of their liturgical forms is advanced almost as a proof that they are 'not really religions at all'. Conversely, groups in which strictly devotional activity is emphasized—the Krishna Consciousness movement is a convenient example—and which spend long hours in chanting, are regarded as engaging in a worthless and meaningless activity, of being impractical and almost self-hypnotized.

If Krishna devotees are regarded as manifesting almost atavistic superstition, even more suspicion is engendered by the practical efficiency and the development of computerized techniques in the promotion of the goals of the new religious movements. The explicit association, in Scientology, of spiritual perceptions, on the one hand, and technological apparatus and jargon appears to amount almost to an affront to those for whom religion and tradition are inextricably intermingled, and for whom the patina of age is readily mistaken for the halo of sanctity.[22] This conjunction of religious goals and technological means, which helps the *Watchtower* (the fortnightly produced by Jehovah's Witnesses) to be the magazine of perhaps the widest circulation in the Third World, is mistrusted just because, for the public at large, efficiency and religiosity are not easily associated with each other, and appear as an incongruous combination. Obviously, efficiency and modern techniques do not constitute a factor that promotes failure for a new religion, but for those who wish to promote such failure undue efficiency can serve as a basis on which to impugn authentic spirituality.

Although new movements adopt the techniques and procedures current in contemporary secular society—from careful accounting to the use of computers—they are not as efficient as modern business corporations. Although they meet condemnation because they utilize the impersonal, rational, electronic devices of the modern world, which are readily identified as being in some sense secular in themselves, they often suffer from lack of trained

[22] The Church of Scientology stakes its claim to superiority over older religious systems (Christianity and Buddhism) on the grounds that it has evolved entirely rational methods for therapy on the basis of research discoveries of its founder, L. Ron Hubbard. The Church has a 'Religious Technology Center', and has registered as trade marks the words 'Scientology' and 'Dianetics'.

personnel to make the fullest use of such equipment. New movements recruit devotees to man their administrative roles, and such people cannot make up with religious zeal what they lack in technical competence. The Divine Light Mission appears, from published accounts, to have disrupted its own efficiency by this mixture of rational systems and the irrational dispositions of its personnel.[23] Moonies are frequently urged or ordered to change their jobs within the movement, transferring sometimes from one centre to another, and this procedure defies the consistency needed in the rational deployment of manpower. New movements tend to regard too rigorous a commitment to efficiency, particularly where personnel (as distinct from equipment) are concerned, as in some way inimical to spirituality. Amateur enthusiasm is matched with professional technology, and whilst a new movement may meet condemnation for its commercialism and its concern for profitability, it may simultaneously suffer from an inadequacy of specialist trained staff. Older movements do, in practice, go further in training their personnel, even if, for traditional reasons, they have not legitimized their functions nor felt able to acquire all the accoutrements of modern business enterprise.[24]

Constituency

In pluralistic societies, new religious movements have shown a strong tendency to recruit their following from one particular constituency, and the appeal of a movement to one such constituency

[23] See for an account, J. Messer, 'Guru Maharaj Ji and the Divine Light Mission', in C. Y. Glock and R. N. Bellah (eds.), *The New Religious Consciousness* (Berkeley and Los Angeles: University of California Press, 1975), 52–72, especially 68. Another illustration of an admixture of rational elements with emotional commitment occurs in the Church of Scientology. As Wallis notes, 'The Org[anization] is a highly bureaucratized structure although it retains distinctive patrimonial characteristics . . . The employees of Hubbard's Org are not merely officials but also disciples': R. Wallis, *The Road to Total Freedom: A Sociological Analysis of Scientology* (London: Heinemann, 1976), 136–7. The officials, as devotees, are not merely reprimanded for incompetence if they fail to keep up their 'stats' (the number of enrolments for courses) but are charged with *ethics* offences, and subjected to demeaning punishments by stigmatization and even ostracism within the organization. Thus, the system, although vaunted as totally committed to rational procedures, relies on a mixture of modes of compliance—normative, remunerative, *and* coercive.
[24] For a discussion of these problems in a very different context, see P. M. Harrison, *Authority and Power in the Free Church Tradition* (Princeton, NJ: Princeton University Press, 1959).

may undermine its appeal to other sections of society. At times, the focus of that appeal might be clearly predicated in a movement's teachings. It is not surprising, emerging when they did and couching their doctrines and discourses in intellectual literary form, that Christian Science, Theosophy, and the Vedanta movement should have attracted something of a leisure class—middle-aged, increasingly functionless, relatively well-to-do women. Once a movement becomes type-cast in this way, the likelihood of recruiting effectively and widely outside the class which already predominates may well be limited. That impediment arises, on the one hand, from the perception of those already in the movement of the kind of outsiders who might be likely to be suitable recruits, and from the relationships and lines of communication that their own social circumstances make available to them. On the other hand, the perception of outsiders of 'just what sort of people' belong to a given movement affects their predispositions towards it. Thus recruitment of more of the same kind is facilitated and the interest of those who differ is prejudiced. The new religious movements of recent times have appealed very largely to middle-class youth. While any distinctive self-perception and very specific social image produce their effect on recruitment, in this case that effect is further reinforced by the particular character of the young as a constituency.

A movement with a highly disproportionate membership of one sex, one age-group, one social class, one ethnic category, or one ecologically based constituency, but particularly if it is composed from one age-group or one sex, has maintenance problems. The age-based sect becomes a feature of a stage in the life-cycle of adherents, having as its primary source of further recruitment only the pre-conversion friends of its votaries or those of their generation. Adherents, when they get older, drop out as sect experience becomes less congruous to their total life situation: or, in sects that recruit the middle-aged and the elderly, they die. The mood and tone of the movement, being especially congenial to one age-group, or, in a rapidly changing society, to those of a particular generation, become somewhat less than congenial to others. The movement, resting on a narrow social base, has limited viability socially, no matter what measure of internal coherence its homogeneous constituency confers upon it. In the longer run, such a movement, depending on the recurrent socialization of a similar age-group, has a much more limited sense of continuity than a movement which encompasses whole families of people of all generations. It is, of course, true that a movement with a constituency that requires constant renewal by conversions, and which embraces people who are likely, on average, to remain for a relatively short time (i.e. young people dropping in and dropping out, or, in other movements, older people joining but then dying) can trade on the short-term enthusiasm of neophytes. But when turnover is high, certain features of stability may be difficult to attain.

Not all movements seek to be encompassing of all sections of society, of course, and many are ideologically committed in ways that cannot possibly accommodate the ordinary family with all its extra-religious, day-to-day mundane preoccupations—educating the young; acquiring property; contracting mortgages, pensions, hire-purchase agreements, and the like. There are movements that do not seek to proselytize, or do so in very discreet and restricted ways—the Exclusive Brethren, the Quakers, and the Unitarians among them—none of which can, therefore, be said to have failed because they have not gained mass adherence. But these are all movements that embrace whole families and successive generations. Many new movements do not embrace whole families, and many are unlikely to enjoy the natural recruitment of the next and subsequent generations. In failing to do so, they put at risk their own appearance as 'normal'. To gather one age-group or one sex into a body that proclaims itself as a way of salvation is to impair credibility. In societies that encourage equal opportunity and non-discrimination, the public at large expects even salvation to be equally available.

The intrinsic problems that arise when the constituency of a religious movement is grossly biased towards any particular age-group are most evident when that constituency is predominantly the very young—adolescents and young adults. In recent times, new religions have deliberately sought to recruit precisely this class. The threat is widely perceived outside, particularly because parents and others continue to perceive young people who are not yet married and 'settled down' as in one way or another still under tutelage, still not wholly 'mature': indeed, their acceptance of a new religious persuasion is taken as virtually a proof of lack of judgement. When a movement both recruits the very young and demands total allegiance, the threat is regarded as particularly acute, and there is some degree of convergence of these two characteristics in many contemporary movements. New religions have generally been most successful in recruiting those who lacked secure social roles, and those least securely bound in to enduring patterns of relationships, and particularly to work relationships. In different historical contexts, such groups might be the poor; new immigrants; ethnic minorities; or even dislocated élites or leisure classes.[25] In the early twentieth century, middle-aged women generally conformed to this condition. In more recent times, those susceptible on these grounds have been the very young. Those in these insecurely located groups are the people who can most easily abandon existing commitments and who are best able to adopt new life-styles, even finding it possible to transform their entire way of life and outlook on the world.

Not all of today's so-called new religious movements demand such total allegiance, but those most readily identified by the media and by the general public do so—often prescribing that devotees should live within the sect's communitarian system and should relinquish previous roles and obligations. Even movements such as Transcendental Meditation and Scientology which, at least initially, and for most of their clientele generally, require only segmentary involvement, also have special cadres who commit themselves totally to the movement, and who man the organizational and teaching echelons. The demand for total allegiance is part of the radical message of salvation which, in one form or another is what all of these various movements claim to offer. Inevitably, what must be abandoned is the normal preparation for later-life roles, except as envisaged within the movement. Since training the young is indispensable for the manning of work roles in the wider social system, it is this aspect of new religious commitment which stimulates the most vigorous opposition from those with settled obligations in society. Education is a peculiarly esteemed facility of

[25] An instance of a movement (albeit not a sect) which appears to have disproportionately attracted a dislocated élite is the (variously organized) British Israelites, whose dominant thesis is that the British (or the English-speaking peoples generally) are the desendants of the lost tribes of Israel to whom God's promises as recorded in the Old Testament will one day be fulfilled. For their ideology and their social constituency see J. Wilson, 'British Israelism', *Sociological Review*, 16/1 (Mar. 1968), 41–57; and id., 'British Israelism: A Revitalization Movement in Contemporary Culture', *Archives de sociologie des religions*, 26 (1968), 73–80.

modern society, and its disruption by religious conversion is perhaps the single most telling complaint against the new religions with their youthful constituencies. If the Moonies and the Krishna Consciousness movement had sought to recruit mainly post-menopausal women, public reaction would have been quite different. Clearly, persecution and public pressure alone are not in themselves directly the case of failure in new movements, but a tarnished image is itself a handicap to success, and that image of today's new movements is directly attributable to the particular type of constituency that they have attracted.

Institutionalization

Finally, among these endogenous factors we must take account of the general question of institutionalization of procedures. H. Richard Niebuhr made the socialization of the second generation his primary argument in enunciating the dictum that the sect became a denomination in the transmission from the first to the second generation.[26] Whilst, as a generalization, this thesis is easily falsified, none the less, the process that Niebuhr indicated is a crucial one for all movements that expect to establish a stable commitment from continuing families. New religious movements in our own time, however, are not usually marked by the recruitment of whole families. Movement appeal is more highly individuated and almost generation specific. If families come into being, they do so, in the majority of cases in these movements, only after individuals have been converted. These movements then face decisions about how the young are to be socialized, and about the appropriate institutional provisions for that to occur, and, as sociologists long ago noted of older sects, these considerations may have their influence on the preoccupations of a movement, shifting the emphasis from proselytizing and conversion towards the evolution of a system of a relevant education for their young.[27] In the case of the contemporary new religious movements, teachings must be adapted to the needs of a different age-group from that to which the movements made their initial selective, indeed almost

[26] H. R. Niebuhr, *The Social Sources of Denominationalism* (New York: Holt, 1929).
[27] L. Pope, *Millhands and Preachers* (New Haven: Yale University Press, 1942), emphasized this aspect of the process by which a sect evolved into a denomination.

exclusive, appeal. The family itself, as the major socializing agency, is likely to acquire enhanced importance, factually if not ideologically, and movements that once addressed their message to single individuals must now speak to married couples preoccupied with and needing guidance about the rearing of children.

The dominant modes of the new movements are, on the one hand, the communal organization, and, on the other, the 'self-enhancing' therapeutic system. The principal difficulty for religious communitarianism is that of establishing stable patterns of life within their self-consciously created communes. These, after all, have called themselves out from the wider society on the basis of a shared ideology and strength of fellow-feeling part of the basis of which was the conviction of the inadequacy, or even the corruption, of the institutions of modern society. The evidence of history concerning such communities, most of which comes from the America of the eighteenth and nineteenth centuries, is that they were more likely to persist if they were religious than if they were secular. But even religious communitarian bodies did not have a good record of long survival, a few exceptions such as the Shakers notwithstanding—and at that time, when cheap land was available, there was also the possibility of vicinal segregation as a protective device for self-preservation. Unlike the monasteries of old, communitarian sects are supported neither by the religious ideology of the secular society nor the goodwill of the population at large. They exist as somewhat embattled enclaves, lacking the stability of life-time commitment and permanent vows as well-legitimized and sanctified devices for eliciting and sustaining commitment. Given that long-term celibacy is rarely demanded, the eventual exigent claims of partnership and family are always likely to conflict with the primacy claimed by and for the religious community, so jeopardizing its viability.

The difficulties of the self-enhancing therapeutic movements are understandably different. They are vulnerable because their hold on their clientele is itself so narrow. The basic client–practitioner relationship of all such movements makes difficult the creation of a solid core of support that will withstand outside onslaught and internal attrition of interest. If the therapy is purchased, then the customer has a right to become 'cured and discharged', discontented, apathetic, or too busy to bother further. The therapeutic movements depend on marketability of product, and that product faces increasing difficulty as therapeutic styles and the diagnoses of ailments change over time. The difficulty is manifest in the history of Christian Science and other New Thought movements. Mrs Eddy reinforced the arrangements for the healing practice that she etablished by imposing a traditional church-style organization on her movement. Thus, Christian Science became much more than a loose association of practitioners and their clients, which appeared a likely prospect in its early years. Hierarchy was established, property was acquired, unofficial publications were circumscribed, and all the features of institutional organization were brought into being, together with the distinctly churchly characteristics of congregational involvement. Although somewhat susceptible to the hazards typical for therapeutic movements, Christian Science fared better than most, displaying more durability and stability, despite early threats, than perhaps all of its New Thought imitators, most of which failed effectively to reinforce client-practitioner arrangements with a stable church structure.[28]

Some External Considerations

Some of the foregoing issues necessarily allude to exogenous factors—the reaction to new movements of the media and the general public, for example—which have their own impact on the purely internal elements of a movement's ideology, organization, life-style, and interpretation of its role in the world. The important exogenous factors in the relative success or failure of a movement include: the extent of the hostility of the media, the public, and the authorities; confusion of movements in the public mind; the transitoriness and changeability of the contemporary *Zeitgeist*; and the decline of stable relationships in modern society. Before turning briefly to these items, the incidence of purely adventitious factors must be recognized, since these may, at times, have a significant impact on particular movements. Although the illustrative cases relate to more conventional Christian sects, there are analogous factors which might at some time arise for particular new religious

[28] For various aspects of this issue, compare the evidence offered in C. S. Braden, *Spirits in Rebellion: The Rise and Development of New Thought* (Dallas: Southern Methodist University Press, 1963); Wilson, *Sects and Society*, pp. 157–74; and R. Wallis, *Salvation and Protest: Studies of Social and Religious Movements* (London: Frances Pinter, 1979), 25–43.

organizations. The occurrence of the two World Wars was undoubtedly of importance for religious bodies that had espoused conscientious objection to military service as one of their principles. Such groups suddenly found themselves forced either to reinforce or to abandon positions that hitherto (at least in Britain, where conscription was unknown until 1916) had been purely theoretical. Conscription imposed on all young men in these sects a crisis of conscience, and so reinforced sect solidarity by leading the weak to disfellowship themselves (by accepting conscription) and the strong to intensify their sect identity and to reinforce their long-term commitment (by going before a tribunal).

Issues which bring a sect into confrontation with the authorities always have consequences, positive or negative, for the sect itself. Up to a point, confrontation heightens sect self-awareness, and even though, in such a case as this, some members may be lost, there ensues a general reinvigoration of the movement, which is the common experience for a sect of a process of moral conflict. Paradoxically, there appears to be no such benefit when developments in the wider society lead to some incidental confirmation from external, secular sources of the wisdom of some facet of sect teachings. Such confirmation goes unnoticed in the wider society, while confrontation leads to public rebuke and enhanced tension. Thus, contemporary dietetic wisdom largely confirms the views advocated since the last century by the Seventh-day Adventists— namely, the preferability of cereals and fruit to the overmuch use of sugar, meat, and synthetic substances; and abstinence from tobacco and alcohol. But the movement has not benefited particularly from this shift in medical and, subsequently, public opinion. Conversely, the impact of conscription on the Christadelphians was to establish more firmly the boundaries of the sect, to create internal cohesion, and to give the movement a very practical goal to pursue and a persistent and recurrent cause to fight as each individual member had to establish his religious bona fides in the courts. Of course, the obverse of this increase in internal consolidation was that the sect was brought into a measure of public dispute and opprobrium. Up to a point, all this reinforced the sectarian ethic and the commitment of members who sought or gave support one to another in this situation. In this case, there was a further consequence, however. The courts wished to treat with those who could claim authority in the movement. But the Christadelphians eschew all formal (human) leadership, even to the point of rejecting normal organizational offices and designations. None the less, to fight the cause of their young conscientious objectors, a self-appointed committee came/ into being. Throughout the war, its activities were welcome and its irregularity overlooked, but when, after the war, it sought to perpetuate itself and to exert some authority in the movement, bitter divisions occurred and schism ensued. Thus, external pressures led to a movement's successful consolidation, but the internal consequences of responding to external circumstances subsequently led to considerable disruption.[29]

Whilst adventitious issues of the kind already referred to may provoke public hostility, they relate to one particular aspect of the sect's ethos and activities. These specific instances of tension may be differentiated from the more general climate of hostility which sometimes develops against a movement. Occasions of escalating moral panic have periodically occurred, sometimes focusing on one movement but not infrequently expanding to embrace whole categories of movements—categories which exist in the public mind, but which do not relate to any intrinsic ideological or organizational similarities among the sects concerned. The success or failure of movements is affected by the climate of rumour, innuendo, the confessions of disaffected members, and the often misinformed reporting of the newspapers. Against such an encompassing climate of opinion, a sect can do very little in the short run. Counter publicity and litigation are dubious and expensive weapons for a movement to employ, as both the Scientologists and the Unification Church have discovered:[30] being a source of controversy in the courts is in itself a potential source of negative public reaction, and a new movement may, by initiating litigation, further damage its own image, even if it wins in court.

The proliferation of contemporaneous new religious movements has led to confusion of one with another, arising both from public ignorance and from the fear that induces an unwillingness to acquire too close a knowledge of such things. The events in Guyana

---

[29] This issue is discussed in detail in B. R. Wilson, 'Apparition et persistance des sectes', *Archives de sociologie des religions*, 5 (1958), 140–50.

[30] As instances: the cost, running to hundreds of thousands of pounds of the unsuccessful libel action brought by the Unification Church against the *Daily Mail* in 1980; and the pronouncement of Mr Justice Latey who, gratuitously, gave an open court judgment, following a private hearing, in which he declared Scientology to be 'corrupt, sinister and dangerous': *The Times*, 24 July 1984.

which led to the induced mass suicide by the members of the People's Temple, and the murders committed by the Manson so-called 'sect' in California, had their consequences for other new movements whose tenets and life-styles were totally different. Guilt by association produces a general negative public reaction towards all new religions, even though these movements are associated with one another only in the minds of outsiders who—ignorantly like the newspapers, or with greater sophistication as among academics —seek to propound some general theories concerning whole ranges of similar phenomena.

The very number of contemporary new movements indicates, in at least a general way, some commonality of circumstances in the general background against which they have arisen. It cannot be said without qualification that the number of movements leads to a type of competition within an available area of recruitment, since divergent elements among movements may be significant in their specific appeal, and yet, for movements arising to market therapeutic techniques, or movements dealing with the occult, there may be a certain competitiveness that may lead to differential success or failure, as there certainly is among the various 'human potential' movements. There may be a tendency for movements working in one catchment area to outbid one another, to adopt styles that exaggerate certain features of the existing social ethos in either a positive sense (i.e. by legitimizing hedonism) or a negative sense (asceticism and alienation). Broadly, the new religions of Japan endorse hedonistic values—very evident in Sekai Kyūsei Kyō (The World of World Messianity); Perfect Liberty Kyōdan; and, to some extent, Sōka Gakkai: and so do the Rajneesh Movement, Scientology, and Transcendental Meditation. In contrast, distrust of contemporary hedonism is evident in the Krishna Consciousness movement and the Unification Church. In the hedonistic culture of contemporary society, one perceives that some new movements may be tempted to vie with others in promises of gratification. It is difficult empirically to establish that the sheer profusion of movements has been a factor in the failure of any one of them, but such a development is theoretically possible, and to some extent the emphasis in the appeal of particular movements may have been influenced by the activities—and the apparent success—of others, and this especially so for those movements which draw their members from those sections of society in which there exists an eclectic enthusiasm for new spiritual or occultist ideas, in what has been termed the 'culture milieu'. Direct evidence of borrowing ideas or practices is not easily established, but there can be no doubt that many of the human potential movements were influenced by Scientology. In its initial phases this was clear, and admitted, in the creation of the movement then known as The Process.[31]

The new movements have individually divergent relationships with contemporary culture, in their acceptance or rejection of its various facets. Yet all movements operate within this cultural context, and bear in some degree its imprint, even if their main thrust is in opposition to it. Even if a movement condemns contemporary society for its materialism, hedonism, for the demands for instinctual gratification, the spontaneity of expression, and the rejection of inhibition, none the less, in order to communicate with its audience it tends to go some way to conceding to some of these values. Certainly in its own organization, it may embrace the latest techniques of modern technology and communication. Sometimes, the clientele is recruited at least in part from sections of the public which have been intensively exposed to extreme forms of contemporary subcultures. Such was the case with the recruitment of ex-hippies by various charismatic 'Jesus' groups in the early 1970s, with the Family of Love (also known as the Children of God), and Krishna Consciousness.[32] But the imprint of a particular cultural climate also entails the possibility that a movement may become outmoded and irrelevant as the cultural context undergoes change. If movements become frozen in certain postures this may eventually cause them to fail. On the other hand, in so far as they embrace change, they also risk being held up to ridicule for volatility, expediency, and opportunism.

To avoid failure, a movement must at least retain members (even if it abandons active proselytizing). Yet, movements recruiting young people, at a stage in their lives when they have forged no

---

[31] This point was directly conceded in conversation with me by the founder of the movement called The Process. A general account of that movement at a later stage of its development (in America) is provided in W. Sims Bainbridge, *Satan's Power: A Deviant Psychotherapy Cult* (Berkeley and Los Angeles: University of California Press, 1978).

[32] The relationship of the Krishna Consciousness movement to the counter-culture, and in particular to Hippies, is explored in J. Stillson Judah, *Hare Krishna and the Counterculture* (New York: Wiley, 1974).

permanent identity, no stable roles, no permanent relationships other than those inherited by birth, are particularly vulnerable not only to the lack of experience of permanent regular commitments among their clientele, but also to the fact that in contemporary society, abiding relationships are much less the norm than once they were. We may see this in the increase of casual cohabitation, the presumed greater transitoriness of marriage, and the rising incidence of divorce; in the growing disposition for people to move house; in the increased frequency with which priests and religious, supposedly bound for life, abandon their orders; and in the Christian mission field, which is no longer peopled by individuals who have undertaken a lifetime's obligation but by people on limited, perhaps only three-year contracts. In part, modern culture —with its emphasis on individual autonomy, cultural pluralism, changes of personal style, the right to one's own choices and one's changes of mind—militates against the espousal of permanent, stable, enduring values and relationships of the kind that have characterized successful religious bodies in the past. These contemporary features obviously affect all religions in Western society, old and new, but for new movements, which depend so much more on young recruits, unsocialized in the more persisting values of the past—the values of persistence—the prospect of failure by virtue of unstable commitment may well be even more powerful than for movements that have acquired an established form and *modus vivendi*, no matter how archaicized they may appear to have become.

12

Unificationism:
The Moonies in Belgium

(WITH K. DOBBELAERE)

THE Unification Church has been accorded an importance in western countries quite out of proportion to its size, principally because of the attention of the mass media. Orchestrated press campaigns have typically alleged that Moonies induce converts to break off contact with their families; deceive donors and potential converts about their identity; and 'brainwash' their recruits. The media have both fed and in part created public and political concern: yet, outside the Far East, there have never been more than about 12,000 Moonies. This general situation is reflected in Belgium, where press comment has been extensive even though the Church recruited only about sixty Belgians in its first decade of operation (up to 1982), with only half that number active in the country at any one time.[1] To assess whether press and public disquiet were justified, we examined the organization, development, and activities of Moonies in Belgium to determine who had joined, how they were attracted and recruited, and the consequences for family relationships.[2]

As elsewhere, the Unification Church in Belgium enjoys considerable autonomy, having first depended for assistance in evangelism (but not for financial support) on Austrian missionaries, who began work in 1968–9. The Belgian Church began properly in 1973, when a Belgian couple were converted in Denmark; returning, they recruited others and, by 1976, there were twenty members. By 1982, about sixty members (not all Belgian nationals) had joined,

---

[1] The attitudes of the Belgian Press are recorded in K. Dobbelaere, G. Voet, and H. Verbeke, 'Neue religiöse Bewegungen im spiegel der Belgischen Presse' in M. W. Fischer and J. Neumann (eds.), *Toleranz und Repression: Zur Lage religiöser Minderhieten in modernen Gesellschaft* (Frankfurt am Main: Campus Verlag, 1987), 230–44.
[2] For the theology and history of the Unification Church, see E. Barker, *The Making of a Moonie: Choice or Brainwashing?* (Oxford: Blackwell, 1984), and works cited there.

but about twelve of these had subsequently left. Fourteen others left Belgium to do Church work abroad. At various times, the Church had had small cells in Louvain, Ghent, and Liège: in 1982, only Liège survived in addition to the Brussels centre where twelve members were normally resident. We interviewed all eighteen Belgian nationals remaining in Belgium and three resident foreigners.

Activities

The main activities of Belgian Moonies were witnessing; fund-raising; and business. Street witnessing was consolidated by inviting contacts to the centre and, later, to a weekend 'workshop' of lectures in Unification theology. Periodically, the leader sent a member on a 'forty-day condition' to witness in a strange town, while fending for himself, begging for food and lodging, and so deepening his spiritual experience. Fund-raising comprised soliciting donations for literature or small decorative items. Business amounted to a shop selling ginseng products, and an incipient (but eventually abortive) effort to sell machine-tool equipment. Witnessing was the prime task, since it offered people the chance to opt for salvation. Fund-raising was vital for community maintenance but was also seen as spiritual work for members which afforded outsiders the opportunity to contribute towards God's Kingdom.

All members undertook street witnessing. There was considerable division of labour, but long-term specialization was limited. Exchange of roles, with frequent recourse to *ad hoc* decisions about who should do what, reduced potential boredom and threats to group unity. Even so, usually for months at a time, major activities were assigned to designated teams.

The Belgian Moonies agreed to record for us in detail, over a two-week period, the way in which they spent their time.[3] To each of the three main activities we have added the time spent in planning, evaluation, and incidental travel which each entailed. On average, each of the twenty-one members spent 9 per cent of a twenty-four hour day in witnessing; 7.6 per cent in fund-raising; and 7.8 per cent on Church business. Of all the time spent witnessing, nearly one third was spent on following up contacts at the centre, and a further 5 per cent of it was spent at workshops.

[3] For further detail see K. Dobbelaere and B. Wilson, 'Het sektarisch antwoord op het begrip vrije tijd: het tijdsbudget van Belgische Moonies: een Gevallen Studie; *Vrijtijd en Samenleving*, 4/2 (Aug. 1986).

Street fund-raising was an important source of income, but the ginseng shop accounted for 40 per cent of the Church's financial needs, and one member, exceptionally, although living in the centre, retained secular employment and contributed her salary to its maintenance.

Whilst seeking to deepen spiritual life, the Moonies emphasized practical tasks. The missionary herself observed, 'People can get too spiritual—they have to be reminded sometimes of the need for gardening and cleaning'. These two sides of Moonie life were combined in Home Church work, the goal of which was unification with the wider society. Each worker selected a neighbourhood of 360 houses, lived in the community and offered help to local residents. The purpose was not to recruit but, as a spiritual exercise, to give practical service to others.

We spent a day with one Home Church worker, visiting old, sick, or handicapped people for whom she undertook cleaning, shopping, errands, and whom she helped to keep their hospital appointments. For a Vietnamese family of six living on the wages of one working daughter, the worker arranged to use the Moonie van to help them move house. She regularly begged stale food from shops, both for the centre and to distribute to the poor. House repairs and painting were examples of jobs done by another worker. Home Church work was the part-time effort of three members: it occupied just over 2 per cent of the total time of the whole membership.

Commensality and Devotions

Moonies differ in their activities from other church congregations. Comparison with other communally-organized conventual orders might be more relevant, but it would show that Moonies spent less time on devotional and scholastic activities. Although communally organized, Moonies are not primarily inward-looking: proselytizing and seeking outside support are central concerns. The explicitly spiritual side to Moonie life is very evident at communal, especially evening, meals (which accounted for over a third of all the time spent on meals). Then, the group reassembled, evaluated the day's activities, and reaffirmed spiritual commitment. Group unity was reasserted over and above the departmental concerns of the different working teams. The Moonies rarely ate alone or away from the centre: only 8 per cent of all the time spent on meals was spent on meals taken alone outside the centre. Commensality, although not a sacramental activity, reinforced the spiritual ethos: prayers and holy songs were usual before and after the meal.

Neither study (which occupied less than 1 per cent of members' time) nor prayer (less than 6 per cent) was a commanding concern. The collective emphasis on meals contrasts with the practice of prayer, much of which occurred privately in nearby churches at intervals during witnessing or fund-raising. Private prayer accounted for nearly three-quarters of all the time spent on prayer. Thus, Moonies were not narrowly 'religious' in pursuing a devotional life. Their commitment was to foster a close relation with God in the context of activity in the world. As the administrative leader said, 'We want to bring God into daily lives, not just to live like monks.' Prayer was not a sole or specifically conducive means for saving the world, and the Moonies did not favour narrowly liturgical religion.

Who Were the Moonies?

Of the twenty-one Moonies interviewed, eighteen had been converted in Belgium and two abroad (the remaining interviewee, a Japanese, is not included in our discussion). All but three of these twenty people were in their twenties or early thirties: fourteen were women and six men. Two were already married to each other when they joined, at the age of about 40. A third, of the same age, had joined with her husband who, however, had left the Church. A fourth had joined with his wife, but she had left: they had decided to divorce. The remaining sixteen members were all single, and all of them had joined before the age of 25, including two at 19, two at 20, and three at 21.

Only two members had terminated education before the age of 18; eight had continued until 18; five until 21; and three beyond that. Two were still pursuing education as adults. Belgian Moonies were thus educationally a higher than average group. Occupationally, they had been less successful. Seven women had had jobs as secretaries or clerks, some having acquired some supervisory responsibility, although this was not general. Two women were housewives; three were students, one a schoolgirl, and one had been a chemistry laboratory assistant. The men included a student; a physical education teacher; a photographer; a waiter; a gendarme-trainee; and one who had been engaged in editorial work.

The pattern of employment suggests considerable change of jobs and restlessness, insecurity, and uncertainty about whether what they were doing was worthwhile. The physical education teacher had originally wanted to teach academically; the waiter was an Italian immigrant who had returned to Belgium to avoid military service; three of the secretaries, young as they were, had had more than two jobs; and the man in editorial work had had spells of unemployment; another girl (born in Australia) had hoped to be a ballet-dancer, and had turned to part-time acting whilst employed by her father's company as a secretary. The Home Church worker who was likened to a nun by one of her contacts had indeed trained for that role when young. The medical student had had a very troubled scholastic career, with illness, depression, and parental lack of confidence in him as part of his pre-Moonie history. The photographer, although enjoying some inherited wealth, had not had a regular job and had for some time been supported by his now estranged wife. Uncertain career prospects, however, may be a not uncommon phenomenon, and these Moonies may not be exceptional in that respect.

Five individuals came from working-class families, with parents who included two miners, a truck-driver, a poor farmer, and a cook. Ten described themselves as middle-class with farmers, a pharmacist, shop-keepers, and small businessmen among their fathers. Five considered their families upper middle-class or upwardly mobile people, and had fathers who were high-ranking civil servants, prosperous farmers, and a journalist—altogether, a higher proportion of the better-to-do than a random sample of the population.

Ten certainly, and one probably, had spent their early lives in villages, and a further five in small towns. Only four had been brought up in big cities, two of them outside Belgium. Thus, the Belgian 'big city' was a different environment for most of them. Belgium is a small country with a high population density, and large cities are not far from any village. None the less, respondents frequently emphasized the difference between village life and life in Brussels, and village origins appear as a predisposing factor for some who became Moonies. The majority first encountered the Moonies in Brussels or some other big city where they were living alone. Seventy-five per cent of the unmarried had left the parental home, wholly or partly, before they met the Moonies: only three left home to become Moonies. Some had left home for educational purposes, others to seek or take up a job. Fifteen of the twenty had first met the Moonies on the street, ten of them in Brussels (and almost always not in their home town).

Self-Appraisal

These data are augmented by the Moonies' accounts of their own lives and attitudes. Despite rationalization and secondary elaboration in accounts in which, months or years later, respondents recall their early lives and their first encounters with the Moonies, such accounts matter. The 'testimony' is almost institutionalized behaviour for Moonies, as for many other sectarians who undergo radical conversion and who learn a language in which to 'make sense' of their past.[4]

Two thirds regarded their childhood as happier or at least as happy as that of others: none said it had been unhappy. Forty per cent had had 'lots of friends' and had engaged in numerous social and sporting activities: most of the rest claimed few 'real' friends, and often only one at any given time. Several expressed disillusionment with the quality of friendships, a feeling frequently reinforced by contact with work colleagues or fellow students.

Although 40 per cent declared that they were not experiencing personal problems in the period before joining, unspecified 'trouble' and uncertainty had affected four of them. General family problems—among them, choosing to live away from home in Brussels (prior to contact with the Moonies)—had troubled three others. Some were lonely.

Disillusionment, Personal and Religious

At college, Irene, daughter of a farmer who studied mass communications, found 'These students, the boys had every day a different girl. I was shocked by that. I couldn't do the same . . . I asked one boy how he could be like that, and he said I was too idealistic.' A hotel trainee, Guido, declared

---

[4] The implications of this proposition are set out (for Jehovah's Witnesses) in Ch. 9 above.

The environment in which I had to live in Belgium was atheistic and corrupt—centred on pleasure—among others, sexual pleasures . . . I did not have real friends. I felt that through my work I would be involved in amusements with women. My colleagues were very much centred on women, but that did not correspond with what I was looking for.

I was always very lonely.

At 15, Carla had started work

in a parfumerie . . . I had up to then looked for real friends but I had always been disappointed and exploited. In the parfumerie, there was a different atmosphere—people joking about bad things; no respect for each other, or for religion.

I tried to make friends, but there were no real friends.

One of the older already married converts, Rachel, said

We had left our old habits and friends [by going on a two-year educational course to Copenhagen] . . . now we were free—we realized this long afterwards. It was a difficult way of life—very simple, no radio, no TV, no friends, and my husband was very busy . . .

About taking her first secretarial job, Roos said

I started this job with ideals, energy, enthusiasm, but after some time, I became aware of the very different relationships between people—between the bosses and the secretaries there was a false relationship: some married people were having extra-marital relations with the secretaries, and people made relationships with others solely for their own advancement. There were hypocritical relationships. There was thus a confrontation between the values for which I was searching and the values among these people around me.

Family bereavement in two cases and personal accident and illness in two others had produced not ony shock but a need for some general explanation of the purpose of life. Such events stimulated the search for meaning which appears to have been in the background history of many Moonies. At least half had been consciously searching, and, although not all had been conventionally religious, anxieties about ecology, third-world hunger, drug addiction, and war had been important to the majority. In the interviews, diverse expressions of concern and of searching were provided and disillusionment about existing religion. Roos said

I read many books about people who were looking for an ideal world . . . it was normal for us to have long discussions. I felt a malaise because of the gap between our ideals and what actually was. In the village, I had seen problems only on the village level . . . I had heard about drugs and alcoholism, family problems and pornography, but now I was discovering these problems in actuality. So I began to wonder if anywhere there were people or a society who were looking for an ideal world.

Irene said

When I was 17 a group of Jesus people came from Holland. They said you had to give yourself up to Jesus and decide. I realized that I had never decided to do that . . . I always felt that we lived in a mediocre way in the Church . . . I wanted to live like Jesus lived . . . Later I went to Taizé, to 'Fire and Flame'. Such meetings . . . gave me strength, but I was disillusioned about it when I got back and felt that I could not realize it. I felt a contradiction between aspiration and what I was really like.

Peter, a photographer, said 'My wife and I had become vegetarians . . . A lot of people tried to show us ways towards God and a healthy life . . . and how to learn to know oneself. And that was just what we were looking for.' Fernanda, a clerk since quitting school, from a family of non-believers who conventionally attended Catholic rites of passage, observed, 'I didn't understand the suffering [in the world]. If God exists why is there all that suffering. I also thought of going to the Third World—hunger, etc.' Michel, a university student, stated, 'Before meeting the Moonies, I was depressed because of the situation in the world [1978]: deforestation, atomic energy, water pollution. I was afraid of disasters and the menace of war, the number of deaths. . .' Valerie, the daughter of a farmer who engaged his family in the social, political, and religious life of the community, said, 'I was looking for the meaning of life and I revolted against suffering: why did it exist? Why were some people dominating others, e.g. the Third World dominated by the rich.'

All (including the foreign nationals) had come from Roman Catholic homes, nine with strong religious influences, but nine only conventionally religious. Before joining, three had wanted to take up missionary work. One girl and one man expressed their earlier concern to help people: another girl had been converted to Protestantism in Australia by an older woman and had helped her with her social work. Another had also been inspired by an elderly social worker, and had joined her in voluntary work among lonely and rejected people, including prostitutes. The older woman, who had trained as a nun, said, 'When I saw the way the nuns live, it didn't appeal to me any more.' Such disillusionment with conventional Christianity was a recurrent theme.

Louise, who studied computer analysis, said 'There was an evolution with respect to religion in my life. Even the priest had asked me if I didn't want to become a nun. I was very angry.' After being very involved in church life and especially with the church youth group, she dropped away and 'in the end I did not practise [religion]'. Rachel, abroad with her husband while he followed an educational course, said, 'we ceased attending church. There was much missing . . . I had always believed in God, and I was disappointed to have nothing to show the children . . . We asked why, after 2,000 years of Christianity, there were so many problems . . . so many sins.'

Priests and teachers of religion who failed to answer searching questions were specifically commented on by three members. Another, Peter, complained of the religious practice of his family, expressing disgust at their comfortable home life.

At home we had all imaginable comfort, and I thought that this was impossible. I was disgusted to attend mass: about 11 o'clock mother often said, 'Zut, we shall have to go to mass'—Tradition! This theatre didn't interest me. From my sixteenth or seventeenth year, I didn't got to mass— without my parents knowing it. After six months, I told them, and they didn't like it. At the beginning of my photography studies, I watched nature and I felt something internally which I was not able to communicate to anyone else, then I went to church by myself—at a time when there was no mass going on—where I found myself close with God, that is, nature.

Some, clinging to religious ideals, continued to pray, but were discontented with religion. Jenny, a chemist, said, 'Every day I prayed a little bit. I tried to live according to the Gospel—but I realized that I didn't succeed completely. Something was lacking. I was not perfect. I felt that I wasn't a real Christian . . .' Roos, despite disillusionment with social life and her work colleagues, said, 'Almost every morning before going to work, I stopped in a church to pray, mostly because I didn't want to give up my ideals and thoughts and the values in which I believed.' The hotel worker had been similarly disposed, often fasting out of religious conviction.

Idealism and Action

For others, conventional religion seemed feeble compared to the lives of contemporary virtuosi—Schweitzer, Mother Theresa, Gandhi, and Martin Luther King were specifically mentioned—or compared to active effort to overcome injustice and suffering. They were idealists, eager to do something to make the world a better place. Nine of the twenty had participated with a high degree of commitment, some of them as leaders, in various voluntary organizations and caring activities: helping the aged; organizing youth activities; and mission-support societies.

Of her peripheral involvement for a time with the Children of God, Helen, the Australian girl, said, 'The singing and relationships were fine, but I saw that this did nothing to change the world, and it wasn't enough to attract me.' Irene, who had taken up voluntary community work with a 60-year-old woman, said, 'I was interested in that sort of work and although I thought it was good to read the Bible, eventually you had to go out and do something.'

The motivations that prompt people to become Moonies are not a simple reflection of their backgrounds. What the Moonies offer is also a part of the explanation. What attracted them to Unificationism was the chance to be active in the world, seen as being close to God and as helping God—help of which he was said to be very much in need. 'When I met the Unification Church, I realized that God is not almighty but is a suffering God, and I wanted to help him. I was not interested in religion, only in people with a higher purpose,' said Ingrid, who lived in Austria and who was puzzled by the suffering and misery of people. Regina, the daughter of an Italian immigrant, said, 'I was touched by the community life, and by what they wanted to realize—the work in the neighbourhoods. I was touched by the fact that people devoted themselves as they did . . .'. These ideals and disillusionment with formal religion had their complement in the search for active religious commitment in which idealism could find expression.

Encounter and Engagement

Expectably, members typically acknowledged that they had been attracted to the Unification Church from their first encounter, even if their interest had not always developed rapidly. Some said they felt they belonged from their very first introduction to *Divine Principle*. Others had been ambivalent about some teachings and, in some cases, had joined, left, and rejoined. The intervals between contact and membership is summarized in Table 20.

TABLE 20. *Interval between first encounter and membership*

	Men	Women
Less than 6 weeks	—	2
6–10 weeks	4	4
10–20 weeks	2	4
20 weeks–9 months	—	1
9 months–1 year	—	3

Interested individuals were invited to a 'two-day workshop' of lectures, discussion, spiritual songs, and social involvement with members, usually held within weeks of the first encounter. Only a small proportion of those who participate in such weekends join the Church. In the period 1980–2, the Belgian Church organized ninety-two workshops, at which 223 persons attended. Only 4.5 per cent of those attending actually joined the movement. Clearly, workshops were not very successful agencies of recruitment, and the very small proportion of attenders who became Moonies effectively discredits any implication that workshops were occasions for 'brainwashing'. We sought to discover the impact of attending a workshop, and to this end we asked about the period of time that had elapsed between the time of the workshop and the date at which the respondent had been received into membership. Table 21 summarizes these findings.

TABLE 21. *Interval between two-day workshop and membership*

	Men	Women
At once	1	1
Within 1 week	—	2
1–4 weeks	2	2
4–10 weeks	—	4
10–20 weeks	1	2
8 months	—	1
Not applicable[a]	1	2
Not stated	1	—

[a] These members joined before 2-day workshops were held in Belgium.

Ingrid had not been attracted after the first encounter: 'I continued contact [with a schoolfriend who became a Moonie] but it was not easy for her to bring me to the centre—I was not really interested in religious groups, whom I thought were not dealing with reality.' Irene found the experience deeply disturbing: 'After meeting the Moonie and hearing ideas about atoms and energy, I went back to talk to her for three successive days.' On the third day she was introduced to the first chapter of *Divine Principle* concerning Adam and Eve.

I didn't believe that. But they talked further and as they left, I became physically sick that day thinking about it. [At the workshop] I was very impressed the first time, but I began arguing a bit. I believed in evolution and not in Adam and Eve. I was moved by the mission of Jesus. I had believed that Jesus had come to earth to die, and now I learned something else. That evening, after the first day [at the Paris workshop] I was crying— all my old beliefs were destroyed.

Isadora, a secretary who had never finished her studies and who had had a difficult childhood after her mother died, resisted invitations to revisit the centre. After two visits she was asked again:

I said that I would come if I liked. I felt that they insisted but I wanted to be free. I didn't want to become a member without really wanting to . . . [Later, after joining] I took a room for six months [that is, left the centre] . . . and studied *Divine Principle*. After six months, I came back—I knew that I would come back . . . I always came on Sundays, on my own initiative. I gave myself some time to think it all over . . . to live six months out of the centre was no problem . . . it also proves that one can leave.

For at least one other, Valerie, the very name of the Moonies was enough to deter her. After introductory discussions at the centre, she commented

I had always heard such bad things, negative things, about the Moonies. [Earlier] the second time I came, I had said, 'But is it not a sect here?' She said it was a Christian group. Then, I asked about Moon. But she did not answer my question—luckily, otherwise, I would not have come back. Today, I say 'luckily' for God worked a lot at that moment. He was surely very much scared at that moment. It was only at the Conclusion [the final chapter of *Divine Principle*] that they spoke to me about Moon . . . I did not trust it, even though I liked to come. When I knew, I didn't come back any more. I knew a lot of bad things about the movement. In March, I came [to the centre] twice—and then they didn't see me again for some time because I had to think it over . . . I think it was in April that Roos asked me if I sometimes prayed. I was astonished, and she gave me a Bible to read . . . After that unconsciously—now can I say it—I started, on an unconscious level, a relationship with God . . .

The general stereotyped idea that those invited to Moonie centres are brainwashed is not substantiated by these accounts. Certainly, like all committed believers, Unificationists are anxious to introduce their ideas to potential new members, but the challenge of a new belief-system to which an individual is converting may—as recounted in one of the cases—be deeply disturbing. Such a consequence is not in itself an evidence of undue coercion, much less of any technique which, in any accurate usage, can be called brainwashing. Workshop participants and long-established members do retain a freedom of choice concerning their commitment. The implausibility of brainwashing—if that term, derived from Chinese treatment of American prisoners in the Korean War, is used with any degree of integrity—was confirmed by our participation in a workshop. The workshop, which was a village cottage close to other houses, did not have facilities for coercion or incarceration: anyone could have left at will. Meals were jovial community occasions for four or five Moonies and participants. The circumstances lent themselves neither to manipulation nor to the exercise of constraint. And there remains the fact that religious conviction entails normative compliance as a voluntary response: such compliance cannot be elicited by coercive means.

Family Relations

Mass media and politicians have sometimes charged the Unification Church with breaking up families. The charge is a vague one, but strong religious convictions are likely to induce people to abandon conventional social arrangements. That occurred in early Christianity, in monasticism, and in a wide variety of sectarian movements. The Unification Church has a special attraction for young people, many of whom have recently left home. Moonie converts have often left their jobs or abandoned higher education. Among Belgian Moonies, this tendency was not evident: in one case, a member was urged to complete his medical training, and another who had abandoned higher education was persuaded to resume her studies. How commonly does becoming a Moonie lead to the severance of family relationships? Respondents described their relationships with parents before and after their conversions. (See Tables 22 and 23.)

TABLE 22. *Relations with parents before joining*

	Men	Women
Closer or better than average	2	4
Good (traditional) but not deep	1	6
Some trouble	1	4
Bad	—	2

TABLE 23. *Relations with parents at time of interview*[a]

	Men	Women
Improved	—	2
Same	4	5
Deteriorated	—	3
Varied	—	2
No statement	1	—

[a] 3 older members omitted.

Almost invariably, there is parental opposition to Moonies. Only one respondent discussed with both parents his decision to join: five discussed it with one parent. The extent to which these potential converts were already growing away from their parents is perhaps reflected in the fact that five of them discussed the decision with friends; eight with other kinsfolk; two with priests; two with colleagues or other acquaintances. Six did not discuss it with anyone.

Most members, however, had retained contact with their parents. Almost all made visits, a few of them monthly. Others telephoned or wrote. Over all, the unmarried Moonies spent, on average, more than 4.5 hours during the two weeks of our time-budget registration on family relations, visiting, telephoning, and letter-writing. In three cases there was continuing hostility: in other instances, relationships, bad at the time of conversion, had improved. Irene's father had said when she joined,'What are you doing to us?', and had hit her: later, happy and confident about her involvement, he said, 'How can Moon be so bad if you have become a better girl?' Helen declared

Relations with my parents are now very good—excellent in fact. In the beginning my father was calm and perhaps shocked. At the beginning my mother was upset, but it was also due to the distance. It hurt her that I wanted to stay here [Brussels] permanently. This was for one and a half years, but then she changed. I made the effort to write more and more, and we began a relationship through letters. The day I left Australia, we weren't even speaking. I said, 'Goodbye', but it was very strained. I realized, when I read *Divine Principle*, how much I misunderstood her—and I cried and cried when I realized. I apologized and asked questions. I realized that I didn't even know her, and now I feel that I know her better than ever. We have very good relations.

This is, of course, exceptional, but other parents moderated their early opinions. Some visited the centre, and although some were critical, others were impressed by the Moonies' activities despite reservations about the movement.

Conclusions

From our evidence, the general depiction of Moonies by the mass media was not confirmed in Belgium. Moonies were, indeed, mainly young people. They were of better than average education. Involvement did frequently result in the convert giving up his job, but in only one (possible) case did it lead to the abandonment of a course of study, while in two other cases, the Moonies persuaded converts to continue or resume higher education. There was some evidence of previous instability (although we have no means of knowing whether this was of an exceptional incidence) and considerable uncertainty of purpose. Converts had a high level of social concern and commitment, and earlier uncertainty of purpose may have been attributable to excessive idealism. Membership provided them with opportunities to express these dispositions. Among those who became Moonies there was considerable disillusionment with the quality of young adult relationships and widespread disenchantment with the Church among both the seriously and the nominally religious. The Catholic Church had failed to satisfy young people who, on the face of it, might have become its committed supporters.

Almost always, parents were expectedly apprehensive about a son or a daughter joining the Moonies. In some instances, their opposition diminished as time passed, but this appears almost invariably to have been because personal parent-child relationships improved, or, more marginally, because parents found the calibre of other adherents impressive, and their activities laudable, and not because they were attracted to Unification doctrines or to the Revd Moon.

13

Scientology:
A Secularized Religion

WHETHER a particular ideological or therapeutic system can properly be designated a religion is an issue that is not solely academic. In order to acquire charitable status or to have premises registered as a place of religious worship, official recognition that an organization is a religious body is, in England and other English-speaking countries, a matter of real importance at law. New movements—among them Scientology—have sought to have their religious status acknowledged, and in so doing have brought into prominence fundamental questions about the definition of religion, as the judgment delivered by the Australian High Court demonstrates.[1] What becomes apparent from such a case is that religion itself is a phenomenon which changes, and the conception of what constitutes religion must, therefore, also change. In practice, there is a distinct cultural lag before legal conceptions catch up with changes in social reality.

Historically, the understanding within a given society of what constituted religion was confined, within fairly narrow parameters, to that system of supernatural reference which had slowly grown up and which modern societies inherited from their past. Part of the Christian tradition was to regard any alternative to this system, or any deviation from its prescripts, as unacceptable and untrue and, for a long time, as therefore not really religion at all, at least not 'true religion'. But as conceptions of the supernatural were increasingly challenged and diversified, and as these old-time religious certainties were shaken, a new and widening relativism came to prevail: what was recognized as religion came steadily to encompass a wider variety of diverse representations of the supramundane. The line between religion and non-religion (which might include forms of paganism, magic, and heresy) was still drawn, but just where it was to be drawn became a matter of

[1] For a fuller discussion, see Ch. 4 above.

heightened uncertainty. Gradually, that uncertainty might be resolved, in particular instances, by specific legal judgments, but such judgments left unresolved the genuine intellectual issues. The range of what were sometimes arbitrary legal decisions, and the self-confessed incompetence of judges to discriminate among religions, or, indeed, to determine what constituted religion, has produced a situation which demands—but as yet has scarcely received—a total reappraisal of social categories. Categories that are specific to one culture, impregnated as they are with the particularities of one received religious inheritance, cease to be adequate bases for the appraisal of claims to religious status of new ideologies, movements, or organizations in a world in which the old orthodoxies which endorsed those categories no longer command much allegiance. If—to leave other considerations aside—the law is to be applied impartially, then old concepts have to be replaced by a repertoire of more encompassing, essentially more abstract, terms which can embrace the contemporary and increasing diversity of idea-systems that are advanced by their exponents as 'religious'.

The processes of cultural change that have produced the hiatus between traditional conceptions of religion and many of its diverse contemporary forms are numerous. Many of them are facets of the process of secularization that has occurred in Christendom and, indeed, within Christianity itself. Various currents may be identified, which cumulatively led towards more secularized forms of religion. The rise of the natural sciences, the development of a new sense of history, and the effects of higher criticism induced a decline in biblical literalism and put Christianity into a new perspective. The conception of God gradually became less anthropomorphic. New 'rational' variants of Christianity, deistic and unitarian, challenged traditional faith. The stern doctrines of God as vengeful judge sentencing the majority of mankind to damnation gave place to increased emphasis on a God of love and the free-will Arminianism of the Methodist and revivalist traditions. As living standards improved, so life was less convincingly depicted as merely a vale of tears, and the focus of salvation shifted from exclusive concern with the next world to increasing demand for religious benefit in this one, whether expressed in terms of a Social Gospel or evidenced in the decline of the old ascetic ethic. The idea of religion as an agency of progress and self-improvement became associated with the pragmatism of the industrializing nineteenth century, with claims that Christianity also 'worked'. These claims became emphatic in the attempt to build out of Christianity a new therapeutic agency, as variously evidenced in Christian Science and the diverse New Thought movements, in the faith-healing claims of fundamentalists, in spiritualist healing, and in the resurgence of a healing ministry in the established denominations.[2] Finally, the expanding knowledge of other world religions, and the growing, if not always very well-informed, admiration for Buddhism, led to a relativizing of the claims of Christianity to be *the* religious truth.[3]

Whilst all of these developments placed in question the old legal formulas that concerned religion, it is the emergence of a conception of Christianity as a tool for self-improvement that is most at issue here. The late nineteenth and early twentieth century saw the burgeoning of a more utilitarian approach to religion. If religion was generally conceded to be good, then it followed that it was 'good for you'.[4] It could be approached instrumentally, demonstrated, and, eventually, marketed and virtually bought and sold in a way far more explicit than was revealed by the traditional mode of the inevitable payment for services which necessarily underlies the relationship of religious functionaries and their clientele public. In America in particular, the emphasis on religion as a very present help in trouble, as a form of immediate salvation from besetting ills, was widely canvassed. American inspirational literature shifted from the joys of contemplative reverence to the possibility of harnessing religious power for everyday concerns, emphasized within the mainstream denominations by such writers as Norman Vincent Peale, Mgr. Fulton Sheen,

[2] This modern concern with healing was essentially a reassertion of an aspect of Christianity that had been largely eclipsed. Healing is clearly a core concern of the synoptic gospels, and closely associated with the idea of salvation. For a theological discussion, see J. N. Lapsley, *Salvation and Health* (Philadelphia: Westminster Press, 1972).

[3] See P. C. Almond, *The British Discovery of Buddhism* (Cambridge: Cambridge University Press, 1988), for an account of the developing appreciation of Buddhism in late nineteenth-century England.

[4] This attitude found institutional expression in Christian Science, of which a sociologist noted, 'Christian Science taught the promised land was here and now; not only did it teach that there was no death or disease, but also that mortal man (in his immortal essence) had the power to achieve his goal on this earth': H. W. Pfautz, 'A Case Study of an Urban Religious Movement: Christian Science', in E. W. Burgess and D. Bogue (eds.), *Contributions to Urban Sociology* (Chicago: University of Chicago Press, 1964), 288.

and Rabbi J. Liebmann.[5] Within the course of four decades, the early 'power of positive thinking' had burgeoned into a whole array of 'human potential' movements cast in language which might be either quasi-religious or avowedly secular, but offering a range of benisons of an essentially practical kind.[6] These movements manifested the profundity of the shift from a God-centred belief system to an emphasis on man's own resources, even if those resources could be released only through the application of some more or less religious apprehension of the way things really worked.

The secular context, as represented in the buoyancy of the American economy and the general cultural optimism prevailing there, affected the orientation of these new styles of religion. So, too, did the development of psychology and, more specifically in the twentieth century, of psychoanalysis. What in particular psychoanalysis added was the assumption that human behaviour was not to be seen as sin or saintliness, but as the more or less involuntary, or at least largely predetermined, consequence of psychic forces. Thus, blame and, more widely, moral responsibility were eliminated from the assessment of human action. What had been immoral was now to be regarded at worst as illness. As this amoral reinterpretation of behaviour entered into general intellectual thinking, so new religious movements were absolved from justifying suffering as part of God's moral economy. Suffering and any manifestation of the untoward was to be relieved, perhaps eliminated as alien to the way things should be, or the way God intended them to be.

Scientology emerged in a context in which the old moral rigour of Christianity in America was already widely relaxed, and in

[5] For a discussion of this current within religion, see L. Schneider and S. M. Dornbusch, *Popular Religion: Inspirational Books in America* (Chicago: University of Chicago Press, 1958).

[6] Of the growing and diverse literature on Human Potential Movements, see in particular, D. Stone, 'The Human Potential Movement', and R. Ofshe, 'Synanon: The People Business', in C. Y. Glock and R. N. Bellah (eds.), *The New Religious Consciousness* (Berkeley and Los Angeles: University of California Press, 1976); S. M. Tipton, *Getting Saved from the Sixties* (Berkeley and Los Angeles: University of California Press, 1982), esp. 176–281; P. Heelas, 'Californian Self-Religions and Socializing the Subjective', in E. Barker (ed.), *New Religious Movements: A Perspective for Understanding Society* (New York: Edwin Mellen Press, 1982), 69–85; R. Wallis and S. Bruce, *Sociological Theory, Religion and Collective Action* (Belfast: The Queen's University, 1986), 157–90; and P. Heelas, 'Exegesis: Methods and Aims', in P. Clarke (ed.), *The New Evangelists: Recruitment, Methods and Aims of New Religious Movements* (London: Ethnographica, 1987), 17–42.

which at many points religious ministry had embraced the new therapeutic orientations. The founder of this new movement, L. Ron Hubbard, a wartime naval officer, film producer, and science fiction writer, had originally published a prospectus in a science fiction periodical for a new type of therapy, dianetics. It was apparently based on psychoanalysis, communications technology, and some general ideas derived from engineering. Dianetics was not initially offered as a religion, but as a form of mental therapy. It attracted widespread interest. Subsequently, this system was incorporated into a more encompassing metaphysical body of doctrine, Scientology.[7]

Scientology picked up ideas already current in other systems of metaphysical thought. Like Christian Science, it rejected the idea that man is his body. The body, for Scientology, was merely a temporary vehicle occupied by a 'thetan', which is an individual expression of an ultimate reality, 'theta'—a primary substance of thought, the life-source, the ground of all Being. Very loosely defined, the thetan is the soul, but Scientologists emphasize that the thetan is the real being, the continuing identity which transcends the body which it inhabits. It is held to be immaterial and immortal, and so as having infinite creative potential. It is not part of the physical universe, but has a latent capacity to control that universe, which is comprised of Matter, Energy, Space, and Time (MEST). According to the theory, thetans in the distant past created the material world as a plaything, much in the spirit of the play of the Greek gods, or of the adolescent Krishna. Incautiously, however, they became victims of their own involvement with the physical, so allowing their creation to limit their own abilities. Since the thetan became encumbered with MEST it came to acquire a 'reactive mind', a mind which responds irrationally and emotionally to anything which recalls painful and traumatic past experiences. Thus, a painful experience is held to produce an 'engram', a persisting impediment to rational thought on any issue that evokes the original experience.

This, then, is the basic thesis which explains human inadequacies.

---

[7] For two contrasting but equally objective and admirable treatments of Scientology, see R. Wallis, *The Road to Total Freedom: A Sociological Analysis of Scientology* (London: Heinemann, 1976), and H. Whitehead, *Renunciation and Reformulation: A Study of Conversion in an American Sect* (Ithaca: Cornell University Press, 1987).

Scientology is devised to discharge these engrams, and to this end there is a trained auditor who interrogates his patient, registering emotional reactions to questions with the use of an E-meter, a simple device with a dial on which a needle registers emotional response as communicated through two metal canisters which the patient grasps in his hands. The engrams are discharged once the subject can be talked about without an emotional response. Once all these 'blocks' to clear thinking have been eliminated the patient is declared to be 'clear', that is, believed to possess a thoroughly rational mind and total recall. However, an early extension of the theory claimed that engrams were implanted not only by experiences in this life or in antenatal circumstances, but persisted also from past lives, from times when the thetan occupied other bodies. Thus, Scientology embraces a theory of reincarnation: in that present consequences (effects) accrue from past actions (causes) there is a close analogy to a doctrine of *karma*. By the recall of past 'overt acts' (that is, harmful acts) through the process of auditing, the thetan can be released from their influence, and so be 'at cause' over phenomena, that is can realize its potential to control its own environment and determine its own well-being.

In further explanation of the wider metaphysical system, Scientology divides existence hierarchically into eight 'dynamics'. The first dynamic is the self-dynamic, represented in the urge of the self to exist. Second, is the sex act and the family unit. Third, is a group dynamic, which recognizes the existence of groups and nations. The fourth dynamic is the maintenance dynamic, for mankind as a whole to maintain its existence. Fifth is a dynamic embracing the entire animal kingdom and all living entities. Sixth is the urge towards existence of the entire physical universe (MEST). The seventh dynamic is 'the urge towards existence as or of spirits', and this includes all spiritual phenomena. Finally, the eighth dynamic is 'the urge towards existence as infinity . . . the Supreme Being . . . the God Dynamic'. The goal of Scientology is for all of these dynamics to survive. Once this elaborated theory had been expounded, it became possible for the Scientologist to perceive that his own therapeutic concerns were but a fragment of the total, and to recognize that the present individual life of the thetan was merely an episode of its total life, and this again but a part of the totality of the eight dynamics.

It has to be said that those who take up Scientology are not attracted specifically by this elaborate metaphysical system: the appeal is rather the promise of personal therapy. That therapy claims to bring individuals into harmony with reality, so assisting them to communicate and to attain affinity with others. One aspect of this enhanced capacity for communication lies in the thetan's acquired ability to communicate with its own past, to recognize the nature of past experience, and so to perceive how false and traumatic impressions have been created. With such self-knowledge, the thetan is expected to experience improvement in ability and in its 'emotional tone', that is to say graduating from grief or apathy up the 'tone scale' to enthusiasm and exhilaration. Auditing is the technique by which the individual gains release from his engrams, rises in the tone scale, and enhances his intelligence. Eventually, he should overcome his entanglement with the MEST universe and be 'self-determined'. This condition of 'exteriority' is the ultimate ideal: in itself, it is not unlike the concept of nirvana.

It will be evident from this brief exposition that Scientology deals in concepts that are quite remote from those of Christian orthodoxy. Yet it is also evidence that it, too, seeks to purvey a commodity that might readily be called 'salvation'. Can it be said, then, that Scientology is a religion?

What Scientology claims to have done is to have rationalized the path to salvation. Hubbard has indicated that there is a continuing track from the wisdom of the Vedas and of Gautama Buddha to Christianity.[8] All of these have been ways in which men have sought salvation. In contrast, however, to a religion such as Buddhism, where only the occasional individual might attain 'release' in one lifetime; and where there was no precise specification of the appropriate procedures to attain that result; and where there was no clear possibility of replication of the process in which random factors intervened—it is maintained that in Scientology there was a standardized, routinized procedure and increasing predictability of

---

[8] He declared that Scientology 'has accomplished the goal of religion expressed in Man's written history, the freeing of the soul by wisdom', and that it was 'a far more intellectual religion than that known to the west as late as 1950': L. R. Hubbard, *The Creation of Human Ability* (London: Scientology Publications, 1954), 180. He regarded Christianity as in some respects less advanced than Buddhism, referring to the Christian conception of a day of judgement as 'a barbaric interpretation of what Gautama Buddha was talking about, the emancipation of the soul from the cycle of births and deaths': id., *The Phoenix Lectures* (East Grinstead: Publications World Wide, 1968), 29–30.

soteriological results. In this claim, we may see the full influence of secularization: there is an attempt to discipline, regulate, and routinize access to the supernatural sphere. Scientology provides technical devices by which to increase the production of salvation: to reduce mystery to formulae.[9] As such, of course, this endeavour is not new. Wesley prescribed regular spiritual exercises for his followers, much as had the founders of religious orders, and Methodism, as the name suggests, urged a routine commitment to religious practice. But whereas the techniques canvassed by Methodism were described in religio-emotive language, Scientology has sought clinically to divest its terminology of all non-neutral connotations.

Exactly the same tendency can be discerned in the firmly specified routines of auditing, the idea of which is the employment of standardized procedures ('standard tech' in scientological jargon) which progressively probe deeper levels of consciousness. The auditor may appear like a confessor but, unlike a confessor, he does not rely on his own spiritual apprehensions or on his own personal appraisal of the needs of the 'pre-clear' (patient). Instead, he follows in close detail the prescribed procedures, never commenting or elaborating except to acknowledge responses. Thus, Scientology seeks to eliminate the purely incidental, adventitious, idiosyncratic elements in spiritual ministrations by instituting a systematic and controlled approach to the promotion of spiritual enlightenment and self-knowledge. There is a conjunction of technical means and spiritual goals. Just as Christian Science adopted some of the ideals of science in application to religion, so Scientology bears the imprint of the technological age in which it came into existence. It is explicitly committed to the ideal of rational thought and self-examination, and to the elimination of untoward and incidental emotion. In this sense, Scientology takes its place in the evolution of religious ideologies as a rationalized and thus secularized system of belief which rejects emotion and emphasizes reason.

Yet, Scientology is not science.[10] It deals in certainties, that is in

---

[9] Hubbard declared that Scientology has 'brought the first religious technology to overcome the overwhelming backlog of spiritual neglect': L. R. Hubbard, *The Character of Scientology* (East Grinstead: Publications World Wide, 1968), 10.

[10] In 1965, Hubbard wrote '. . . I must face the fact that we have reached the merger point where science and religion meet, and we must now cease to pretend to deal with material goals alone': L. R. Hubbard, *Scientology: A New Slant on Life* (East Grinstead: Publications World Wide, 1965).

dogma, not in doubts. It is concerned with absolutes. Its definitive goals transcend empirical proof. Its ultimate belief-system is essentially metaphysical. It constitutes a religious system set forth in the terms of scientific discourse.

The initial goal of therapy is to release the thetan from the confines of the reactive mind, but the ultimate goal is to so rehabilitate the thetan that it achieves a stable state where it no longer has a reactive mind. Thus, the individual is to move from the preoccupation with the proximate and immediate goal of his own survival (the first dynamic) to an increasingly expanded recognition of the possibilities of salvation, as he progressively identifies with the family, associations, mankind, the living world, the universe, spiritual states, and the infinity of God. The final goal of the thetan is the attainment of something of a god-like condition. It is a type of goal that is characteristic of human potential movements, but it is not unlike some conceptions of ultimate salvation found in other contexts (most explicitly perhaps in Mormonism).[11]

Secularization affects religious bodies, not only marginalizing them within the social system, and by causing changes in religious commitment within a population, but also by making it likely that new religious expression will necessarily emerge in new forms and employ new language. New religious impulses will evolve new patterns of organization, and will posit new patterns of relationships with other secular institutions. In an increasingly rationalized society where pragmatic dispositions prevail, new religious agencies are likely to claim their own practicality and to make explicit their functions for the wider social system—particularly by therapeutic and remedial, capability-enhancement techniques. Given such likely change of orientation, what must be expected is that doctrine (theology), worship, ethic, leadership patterns, and organizational structures will all acquire characteristics quite alien to those of earlier religious manifestations.

[11] Parley Pratt, one of the early leaders of Mormonism, wrote that man possessed God-like attributes which 'need only cultivating, improving, developing, and advancing . . . in order to arrive at the fountain "Head", the standard, the climax of Divine Humanity': P. Pratt, *Key to the Science of Theology* (Liverpool and London, 1855), 32, cited by T. O'Dea, *The Mormons* (Chicago: University of Chicago Press, 1958), 128. The thesis is often summed up in the Mormon dictum, 'As man is now, God once was; as God is now, man may become.' A not dissimilar emphasis on man's potential divinity is found in another nineteenth-century American religion, Christian Science, which emphasizes that man is made in the image and likeness of God, and need not suffer sin, sickness, or death.

In doctrine, a movement like Scientology takes further trends evident in main-line theology. Modern theologians have increasingly rejected the idea of a 'God up there' or even 'out there'.[12] They have abandoned anthropomorphic conceptions in favour of such concepts as the ground of Being 'the ultimate concern', and they have gone so far as to urge Christians to forget all traditional ideas about God—even the word itself.[13] Some of the objections of atheists are accepted by these theologians—'if such a being [as the Old Man in the Sky] did exist, he would be the very devil'.[14] Bishop Robinson, in his celebrated book published in the early 1960s, declared that 'to say that "God is personal" is to say that personality is of *ultimate* significance in the constitution of the Universe'.[15] Theological opinion has sometimes been represented as being in advance of that of the lay public, but that is true only of the (steadily declining) body of the church-going public: public opinion polls tend rather to support advanced theological views. Successive polls have shown that increasing numbers of people have abandoned anthropomorphic conceptions of God in favour of the idea of God as a force or a spirit. When these trends are surveyed it is not surprising that any metaphysical system embraced by a new therapeutic movement for its underpinning should be stated in secularized, contemporary terms. Although modern theologians did not directly influence L. Ron Hubbard, his conceptions of God are very like theirs.

It follows that when the conception of what God is undergoes such radical change, then man's attitude towards him and relationship to him must also experience change. In particular, it follows that there must be some reappraisal of what is understood by worship. If there is no longer a definite Being conceived as more or less in the human image, then such traditional dispositions as reverence, humility, submission, veneration, and gratitude may have become inappropriate responses. Where no distinct and definable object of worship can be found, intimations of regard suitable towards 'superior' human beings (monarchs, in particular) become incongruous. Thus, although a new movement may expound metaphysical premises and represent the supernatural in

---

[12] Bishop J. A. T. Robinson, *Honest to God* (London: SCM Press, 1963), 41, 43.

[13] These ideas are expressed by P. Tillich, *The Shaking of the Foundations* (Harmondsworth: Pelican, 1962), 63–4.

[14] J. Wren-Lewis, cited by Robinson, *Honest to God*, pp. 42–3.

[15] Robinson, *Honest to God*, pp. 48–9.

these terms, it may not elicit traditional worshipful dispositions with respect to that system. In particular, congregational activity may be inappropriate, and shared gestures of obeisance may make no real sense, once symbols have become more explicitly abstract and disembodied.

Fundamental changes in doctrine and conceptions of worship are accompanied by transformation of the religious ethic. The ethic of Scientology derives from its therapeutic emphasis on accepting responsibility for one's own destiny and on the need for individual guidance. Although ultimately, in its goal of 'clearing the planet' (that is, of eliminating the reactive, irrational dispositions of all mankind), Scientology embraces a very general soteriological purpose, in practice, as Hubbard emphasized, the primary concern is to improve the condition of individuals. Therapy comes before world-saving. In common with other 'human potential' movements, Scientology is a this-worldly philosophy, concerned with life-enhancement and positive thinking. Whereas traditional religions, coping with a world of hardship, legitimized suffering and advocated asceticism, the new religions that have emerged in recent decades in a world of relative affluence and hedonism, accepted the enhancement of personal benefit and of personal ambition as worthy religious goals. The ethic of Scientology conforms to these essentially modern ethical prescriptions of contemporary secularized society.

A further significant aspect of the secularization process lies in the demise of a distinctive form of religious leadership, sacralized to its tasks. The necessity of a sacerdotal class has been recurrently challenged by new movements, and some of the movements emerging within the Protestant tradition have gone further and rejected any form of specialized religious ministry. Obviously, informally if not formally, a leadership structure prevails in every social and religious movement, but the tendency in secularized movements has been to disavow the need for explicitly religious or spiritual competences in their leaders, but to make leadership roles available to those whose abilities are attested by essentially secular qualifications.

Scientology designates itself as a church, and that description embraces the entire organization which, over all, bears little resemblance to a traditional church structure. The most explicitly church-like facets of the movement lie in its chapel services and, to some extent, in the activities of its chaplains, but these, it must be said, are not central to the movement's operation. The core activity is auditing. Sociation is generally loose, impersonal, and informal. Chapel congregations are not the salient pivot on which the organizational structure rests. Church services are only occasional, not particularly solemn, not well attended, and far from being the main nexus of attachment of individuals to the movement. Thus, Scientology conforms to the concept of a privatized religion which relies hardly at all on communal expression or community activity. New forms of association complement a new metaphysic, a new ethic, the use of new techniques, described in new language, and constitute, if the word can be used at all, a new conception of worship.

The judges of the Australian High Court, in the case in which a scientological organization claimed to be a religious body and therefore exempt from certain species of taxation, accepted that Scientology was a religion, and in our discussion above we have noted certain similarities between some scientological doctrines and those of other movements—bodies that are generally recognized as being religions. We have made random comparisons and analogies where salient and conspicuous features of Scientology have made them appropriate. To ground the issue more securely, however, we need a more systematic and extended analysis of the characteristics of this movement than concerned the Court, or than has concerned us so far in the foregoing. We need an appraisal of the extent to which Scientology is in conformity with a comprehensive inventory of the characteristics that constitute typical religion.

The purpose in pursuing this question is not merely to decide on the appropriate label to attach to Scientology, nor even to attempt to settle its eligibility to qualify, as a religion, for tax-exempt status. Rather, the point is to examine the measure to which an ideology and the organization that sustains it can embrace the rational and secular orientations that characterize contemporary society, whilst yet effectively claiming to be a religion.

Were there a readily accepted general definition of religion, our task would be simple, and this essay otiose. Since religion is found in all societies and is widely diverse in character, a definition that covers all cases must be stated in encompassing terms, terms, as we have noted, of considerable abstraction. As social science has superseded theology in providing definitions for social (and religious) phenomena, so concrete and culturally specific references have been replaced by just such abstract and generalized formulations. Of necessity, it is a definition or a characterization of this type that we must now seek, since to carry over terms used within or about one specific religion in the description of others is clearly inappropriate. Concepts evolved within one religious tradition misrepresent the functionally equivalent but formally and substantively distinctive elements in another tradition—grossly and ignorantly exemplified in such usages as 'the Buddhist church'; 'the Muslim priesthood'; or, in reference to the Trinity, 'the Christian gods'. Abstract formulations are needed in order to avoid such contamination by the particularities of any one religious tradition.

For normal purposes a brief working definition of religion might suffice, be it acknowledged that such a definition necessarily elides issues and features that religionists of a specific tradition might see as central. Such a working definition might declare religion to be 'a set of beliefs, attitudes, and dispositions concerning, and activities directed towards, superempirical entities, states, objects, or places'. There are many such general definitions in the literature. But such an all-purpose, summary statement is inadequate for the present enquiry. What appears to be more useful is to set out a probabilistic inventory of elements: probabilistic in the sense that these items are frequently observable of known religions and thus might be expected to be found in any hitherto unexamined phenomenon that we might wish to call 'religion'. Thus, what follows does not purport to be a universally applicable definition which exhaustively embraces all (and excludes none) of the salient and essential features of all religions: such an encompassing definition is unattainable. It is rather an enumeration of features and functions that are frequently found in phenomena that in normal usage we recognize as 'religions'. We need not declare any of these items to be *sine qua non*, and we may concede that some are more probable than others, but without a considerable representation of them, we might seriously doubt whether what we had in hand was indeed a religion.

A Probabilistic Inventory

(1) Belief in an agency (or agencies) that transcends normal sense perception, and which may also include an entire postulated order of being.

(2) Belief that such an agency not only affects the natural world and the social order, but operates directly upon it, and may have created it.

(3) The belief that at some time (past, present, or future) explicit supernatural intervention in human affairs has occurred, or does or may occur.

(4) Belief that supernatural agencies superintend human history and destiny: when anthropomorphically depicted, these agencies are credited with definite purposes.

(5) Belief that man's fortune in this life and in afterlife (or lives) depends on relationships established with, or in accordance with, these transcendental agencies.

(6) Belief that whilst transcendent agencies may arbitrarily dictate an individual's destiny, the individual may have the possibility, by behaving in prescribed ways, to influence his experience either in this life or in future life (lives) or both.

(7) There are prescribed actions for individual, collective, or representative performances—namely, rituals.

(8) There are placatory or supplicatory procedures by which individuals or groups may seek special assistance from supernatural sources.

(9) Expressions symbolic of obedience, gratitude, obeisance, or devotion are required in particular circumstances, often in the presence of symbolic representations of the supernatural agency (-ies): such manifestations of attitude constitute worship.

(10) Language, objects, places, edifices, and seasons are designated as particularly identified with the supernatural, and may themselves become objects of reverence.

(11) There are specified occasions of celebration and mortification (fasting, penance) and pilgrimage, and re-enactments or commemorations of episodes in the earthly life of deities, prophets, or great teachers.

(12) Occasions of worship and exposition of teachings are claimed to encourage a sense of community, goodwill, fellowship, and common identity and reconciliation among devotees.

(13) Moral rules are enjoined upon believers. The area of their concern varies: they may be couched in legalistic and

ritualistic terms, or canvassed as being in conformity with the spirit of a less specific, higher ethic.

(14) Solemnity, seriousness of purpose, sustained commitment, and lifelong devotion are normative requirements.

(15) Adherents accumulate merit or demerit, and a moral economy of reward and punishment operates. (The precise nexus between action and consequence varies: it may posit automatic effects of given causes; judgement and punishment by supernatural agencies; the possibility of demerit being cancelled by self-surrender; ritual acts; vicarious atonement; confession and repentance; or special supernatural intercession.)

(16) A class of specialist religious functionaries are licensed as custodians of sacred objects, places, and scriptures; and/or as instructors in doctrine, ritual, and/or as moral exemplars or mentors.

(17) Specialist functionaries are paid for their services, whether by tribute, specific rewards, or instituted stipends.

(18) Required beliefs and actions, systematized and legitimized by authorized functionaries, are claimed to provide all necessary knowledge to explain the origin, operation, meaning, and purpose of life and the world; and as means to evoke and assuage emotions.

(19) Beliefs, rituals, and institutions are legitimized by reference to tradition and/or revelation, and innovation is justified as restoration.

(20) The truth-claims of teaching and the efficacy of ritual are accepted as matters of dogma, without empirical test. Goals are ultimately transcendent and faith is demanded both for goals and for the arbitrary means for their attainment.

The foregoing inventory is set forth in terms of considerable abstraction: as indicated, each item might cover a variety of substantive cases describable in the first-order language of a given culture. But, as will be evident, the inventory is rendered cumbersome by the necessity of encompassing what may be regarded as evolutionary divergences in religion. Thus, although placatory action is evident in only vestigial forms in contemporary religions, it is accommodated (in item 8) with supplication, because placatory acts are common in tribal religions. Evolutionary divergences must be accommodated, however, since different religions have developed at different rates of change, and some retain, residually, elements that elsewhere have been superseded or even explicitly disavowed. In considering the case of a religion which first developed in the nineteenth or twentieth century (say, Christian Science and Scientology, respectively) we may perceive that the more overtly magical, placatory, and even ritualistic elements inherited from older, major religious traditions, have virtually disappeared (although, as a matter of empirical fact, this is not invariably the case with new religious movements, some of which claim to 'recover' or even 'discover' facets of religious practice and belief that are of an arcane, occult, or magical character).

Initially, Scientology was not presented to the world as a religion.[16] Dianetics, its precursor, was designated a mental therapy, and Scientology a science rather than a religion, but even as early as 1953 there was a new approach and the movement was reorganized as a church.[17] It has been contended that that change may have been dictated by expediency. As a church, Scientology would be protected in the United States from prosecution should anyone seek to declare its use of the mails to be fraudulent. But even

---

[16] Hubbard made various pronouncements on the status of Scientology, some of which suggest that whilst it is itself a religion it none the less remains tolerant of religious diversity among its following. In *Scientology 8–80* (Silver Springs, Md.: Distribution Centre, 1952), 8, he wrote, 'Scientology is not a therapy for the sick, although from Scientology such a therapy may be derived.' It was rather a science, 'knowing about knowing'. In *The Creation of Human Ability*, p. xi, he declared that a Scientologist was expected to have 'no specialized political or religious convictions beyond those dictated by wisdom and his own early training'. In *Scientology: A New Slant on Life*, p. 17, he called Scientology 'a philosophy', but in *Phoenix Lectures*, p. 35, he wrote, 'Scientology is a religion in the very oldest and fullest sense'; and in *The Character of Scientology*, p. 12, after describing Scientology as the technology of religious practice, he continued, 'A technology of religion should service the basic fundamental urge and requirement common to all and any religions without regard to denominational divisions.'

[17] This point, which is made contentiously by those who have doubted the religious status of Scientology, is alluded to by Whitehead, *Renunciation*, p. 70, where she writes, 'It is not difficult to see the move to churchly status as simply one more defensive maneuver, especially when Hubbard is quoted as slyly remarking, "Of course anything is a religion that treats of the spirit. And also, parliaments don't attack religions".' G. Malko, *Scientology: The Now Religion* (New York: Delta, 1970), 64–5, quotes this exchange, '. . . asked . . . why he had turned Scientology into a religion', Hubbard answered, ' "To some this seems mere opportunism . . . Why should Scientology ally itself to religion? There are many, many reasons. Amongst them is that a society accords to men of the church an access not given to others. Prisons, hospitals and institutions . . . cannot do otherwise than welcome men of the church."'

if it could be conclusively shown that Scientology took the title of 'church' specifically to secure protection at law as a religion, that would say nothing about the status of the belief-system, and it is with the belief-system that we are here specifically concerned.

Scientology (as Dianetics) began as a form of therapeutic practice and subsequently developed a legitimizing philosophy which might be religious. All religions evolve. Early Christianity began with therapeutic practice and acquired its doctrinal rationale only subsequently. Christian Science began with healing and only gradually acquired its final doctrinal statement. Prophetic exegeses were widely canvassed by those who became Seventh-day Adventists years before that movement crystallized into a separate denomination, and the gifts of the Spirit were cultivated and manifested long before any separate Pentecostalist sect emerged. Like these and other religions, Scientology evolved. We have outlined the metaphysical system which Hubbard steadily unfolded following what he called his 'researches'. Man was a spiritual being, a thetan, fundamentally good and both desirous and capable of survival, but, by his past forfeiture of his abilities for rational thought, his entanglement with MEST, and his accumulation of an engramatic reactive mind, had become a seriously endangered species. Through Scientology, he might now recall and confront the traumatic events of earlier life and past lives, and eliminate their emotional residues which are the source of his present problems: thus, he has the opportunity to alter the 'karmatic' effects of past actions.

As in other religions, the initial preoccupation of many of those who are drawn to Scientology is proximate salvation from immediate experience of evil: the prospect of therapy appeals before the appreciation of the more mystical, metaphysical, spiritual teachings which explain that therapy. That appreciation develops as growth in the faith, but may be likened to the 'strong meat' of Hebrews 5: 12–14, not suited to the needs of neophytes. Those who acquire knowledge of this metaphysical system learn that the ultimate goal is to become an 'Operating Thetan', a being which exists outside the body in a condition described as 'exterior to all physicality'. Such a condition resembles that which at least some Christians would acknowledge as that of the saved soul. That status of ultimate salvation is achieved by the 'standard tech' of scientological procedures, which Hubbard has also likened to the *upaya* (right method) of the seventh stage of the Bodhisattva way of salvation in Mahayana Buddhism, the point at which the believer becomes a transcendental Bodhisattva who dedicates himself completely to the liberation of others by freeing them of their suffering, and who, like the Operating Thetan, is no longer tied to a physical body. Thus, the Scientologist should move from the initial goal of therapeutic relief from the confines of the reactive mind to an ultimate position where he no longer has a reactive mind, and from a position where his preoccupation is with his own survival (salvation) to an identification with progressively wider groups as expressed in the eight dynamics. The ultimate goal is the attainment of something like a god-like condition.

The agent, who facilitates this process, who practises the *upaya*, is the auditor, who is held to be trained in skills to help others, and to help them to help themselves. His task is to deal with the 'pre-clear' neutrally and clinically. Scientological auditing is not the purveyance of random advice given at the personal discretion of confessors of variable competence, but a systematic and controlled endeavour to elicit self-enlightenment and spiritual knowledge. In its prescribed auditing techniques, and in its underlying philosophy, Scientology conjoins technical means to spiritual goals. The emphasis on technique, the use of technical apparatus and scientific language, and the insistence on systematic procedures are directed to spiritual and soteriological ends. However, the scientific style of scientological discourse need not be taken as evidence against its claims to be a religion.

The ideal of standardization and similar concepts in Scientology illustrate the penetration of the religio-therapeutic sphere of assumptions, styles, and methodologies drawn directly from the world of science. Religion in this period becomes instrumental in a way which characterizes magic, although with an apparently more scientific mode of explanation. The way to salvation is rationalized, depicted not in emotion-evoking liturgies but in emotionally-anaesthetizing 'standard tech'. Scientology, in effect, claims to have brought a new technology to the production line of salvation, and it is in the reduction of the sacred to the scientific that Scientology might appear to come close to blasphemy, since it desacralizes language, actions, relationships, and institutions that are normally assumed to be intrinsically sacred, and as such, 'essentially' religious. Scientology exemplifies that religious tendency which seeks to introduce order, discipline, and method into spirituality, as occurred with Methodism and, using a different model, with the Salvation Army. At a philosophical level a reconciliation of religion and reason was attempted by the Unitarians, and between religion and science, by Christian Science. The saved individual in Scientology is the individual who is completely rational and totally in charge of himself, as Hubbard says, 'at cause'.

The elimination of the expressiveness of conventional religion is perhaps the greatest weakness of Scientology. Whereas normally religious agencies control emotion by summoning responses and channelling them into acceptable paths, so establishing and sustaining motivation and commitment to the faith and to its organization, Scientology, in its impersonal, rational, and technical style, seeks to dispel emotion, thereby weakening collective commitment. It has eliminated worshipful association. A God who is not a person, nor even represented in language appropriate to persons, who is rather 'a ground of Being', requires no worship. It is even difficult to know what worship of such a God might comprise. However, worship and conceptions of deity are not the determining criteria of religion. Other systems of thought and action that are undeniably religions have functioned without them. If Scientology is to be counted a religion, it is clearly not on the basis of its theism or its commitment to worshipful activities that the case will be judged.

Scientology is concerned with salvation, initially as a therapy for the individual, but ultimately with the survival of the thetan in a world cleared of irrational impulses. The key term used by Scientologists is 'survival', and although that word has about it the ring of people conscious of atomic warfare and ecological issues, it is a concept that is entirely cognate with salvation. The thetan is seen as anterior to the human body and as having a potential to survive it. In its final analysis, survival is related to the survival of the eighth dimension, the Supreme Being. A Scientology chapel service seeks to enhance consciousness of that ultimate reality. It may not be an occasion of conventional worship, but it is an occasion for the reinforcement of recognition of what can be termed, non-scientologically, the supernatural.

Given this general understanding of Scientology, we may now assess its characteristics in the light of the probabilistic inventory set out above, which will serve as a measuring rod to assess its claims. No religion will conform to all the items in the inventory, but a high degree of convergence must amount to prima-facie grounds for regarding that candidate as a religion. We note those points in which Scientology conforms to the model as *Accord* or *Qualified Accord*; those on which there is no correspondence as *non-Accord*.

(1) Thetans are agencies that transcend normal sense perception, and Scientology alludes to, even if exiguously, a supreme being. *Accord.*

(2) Thetans are held to have created the natural order. *Accord.*

(3) Thetans occupy human bodies, hence intervene in the material world. *Accord.*

(4) Thetans operated before the course of human history, but are not represented as having been in control, nor is the supreme Being represented as having definite purposes. *Non-Accord.*

(5) The future of the thetan will be profoundly affected when release is gained from the reactive mind, and the present life of the individual will be affected by the same process. *Accord.*

(6) The individual's destiny can be altered by auditing, certainly in this life and, if not completely cleared, in the lives of the bodies which the thetan may later occupy. *Accord.*

(7) Rituals in the sense of worship are minimal and rudimentary in Scientology (as among Quakers), but they do exist. In the wider, anthropological sense of the term 'ritual', the process of auditing is a highly routinized procedure with rigorous rules. *Qualified Accord.*

(8) There are no placatory acts in Scientology: the individual seeks aid by techniques that purport to be discovered principally by scientific research. *Non-Accord.*

(9) Expressions of obedience, gratitude, obeisance, and devotion to supernatural agencies are absent, except in the truncated rites of passage used in Scientology. *Non-Accord.*

(10) There is a distinctive language which reinforces values internal to the group, but, in common with other late Protestant movements, sacralization is not a function of Scientology. *Non-Accord.*

(11) There are no mandatory celebrations or expressions of collective penance, nor as yet any acts specifically commemorative of the founder. *Non-Accord.*

(12) There are few collective rites, but exposition of the movement's teachings and recordings of the founder's lectures provide a common *Weltanschauung* and promote the sense of a common cause and identity. *Qualified Accord.*

(13) Scientology initially lacked a moral dimension, but concern for moral propriety has grown as the implications of its metaphysical premisses have been realized. Since 1981, a moral code which resembles the Decalogue has been articulated, and makes explicit the long-maintained concern to avoid 'overt acts' (harmful acts). The doctrines of the reactive mind and reincarnation embrace ethical orientations similar to those of Buddhism. *Accord.*

(14) Scientology strongly emphasizes seriousness of purpose, sustained commitment and loyalty to the organization and its members. *Accord.*

(15) The teaching of reincarnation meets this criterion fully. The accumulative reactive mind corresponds to demerit for the thetan, and such demerit can be reduced by the application of scientological techniques and by the element of 'confession' embraced within auditing. *Accord.*

(16) Auditors act as 'confessors', and they and all staff members are charged to preserve Scientology theory and practice from contamination, and in this sense are custodians. *Accord.*

(17) Auditors are remunerated. *Accord.*

(18) The body of metaphysical teaching purports to explain the meaning and purpose of life, provides an elaborate psychology; and accounts for the origin and operation of the physical universe. *Accord.*

(19) Scientological teaching is claimed as the result of research combined with the wisdom of ancient religion, and implicitly also a revelation by (if not to) L. Ron Hubbard. *Qualified Accord.*

(20) The truth claims of Scientology are beyond empirical test, but the efficacy of auditing is claimed to be pragmatically provable. The goals of Scientology are ultimately transcendent and rest on faith. *Qualified Accord.*

It must be apparent that not all items in this inventory need be accorded the same weight. For example, the placatory element (item 8) is typically part of earlier—quasi-magical—aspects of religion which have largely disappeared from religion in more advanced societies. In general, Scientology may be seen as being close to various highly evolved religious forms: it has few of the preserved and vestigial elements characteristic of ancient religions that have survived from more primitive conditions of society. Religion clearly takes on the colour of the culture in which it evolves, and it undergoes change over time and distance in broad congruity with its social context. Typically, modern religions reflect concern with subjective, psychic well-being rather than with positive otherworldly objectivity. Scientology embraces both these elements, but its main appeal is undoubtedly initially the prospect of therapeutic benefit. As with other religions emerging in the context of modern, secularized society, worship is less significant than is the acquisition of assurance and competence.

In its main thrust, Scientology is this-worldly, concerned with life-enhancement. Whereas more traditional religious sytems which sought to help men cope with a world of hardship and suffering legitimized personal sacrifice, modern religions are more likely to endorse the hedonistic values of contemporary society as legitimate goals. In Scientology, both initial goals and the means employed to attain them reflect the degree of rationalization that obtains in the wider society. Our probabilistic inventory suggests that Scientology must indeed be regarded as a religion, and this in respect of the metaphysical teachings it canvasses (and not because it describes its organization as a church), but it is a religion which mirrors many of the preoccupations of contemporary society. Religion, however, invariably offers men salvation in terms that they can understand and which are relevant to their circumstances. In this sense, Scientology appears as a congruous religious orientation for modern society. If one were to set forth the norms, values, and technical competences of modern Western society, its commitment to rational procedures, its concerns with individual rights, and its anxieties about individual and social survival, and one had then to say what a modern religion might look like, would not Scientology appear as altogether congruous to the secularized world in which it operates and from which it draws so much of its organizational structure and therapeutic preoccupations?

Author Index

Subject Index